The Greatest of All Time

Americans love to talk about "greatness." In this book, Zev Eleff explores the phenomenon of "greatness" culture and what Americans really mean when they talk about greatness. Greatness discourse provides a uniquely American language for participants to discuss their "ideal" aspirational values and make meaning of their personal lives. The many incarnations and insinuations of "greatness" suggest more about those carrying on the conversation than they do about those being discussed. An argument for Abraham Lincoln or Franklin D. Roosevelt over George Washington as America's greatest statesman says as much about the speaker as it does about the legacies of former US presidents. Making a case for the Beatles, Michael Jordan, or Mickey Mouse involves the prioritization of politics and perspectives. The persistence of Henry Ford as a great American despite his toxic antisemitism offers another layer to this historical phenomenon. Using a variety of compelling examples, Eleff sheds new light on "greatness" and its place in American culture.

Zev Eleff is President and Professor of American Jewish History at Gratz College. He is the author, most recently, of *Dyed in Crimson: Football, Faith, and Remaking Harvard's America*.

The Greatest of All Time

A History of an American Obsession

ZEV ELEFF
Gratz College

Shaftesbury Road, Cambridge CB2 8EA, United Kingdom

One Liberty Plaza, 20th Floor, New York, NY 10006, USA

477 Williamstown Road, Port Melbourne, VIC 3207, Australia

314–321, 3rd Floor, Plot 3, Splendor Forum, Jasola District Centre,
New Delhi – 110025, India

103 Penang Road, #05–06/07, Visioncrest Commercial, Singapore 238467

Cambridge University Press is part of Cambridge University Press & Assessment,
a department of the University of Cambridge.

We share the University's mission to contribute to society through the pursuit of
education, learning and research at the highest international levels of excellence.

www.cambridge.org
Information on this title: www.cambridge.org/9781009572736
DOI: 10.1017/9781009572743

© Zev Eleff 2025

This publication is in copyright. Subject to statutory exception and to the provisions
of relevant collective licensing agreements, no reproduction of any part may take
place without the written permission of Cambridge University Press & Assessment.

When citing this work, please include a reference to the
DOI 10.1017/9781009572743

First published 2025

Printed in the United Kingdom by CPI Group Ltd, Croydon CR0 4YY

A catalogue record for this publication is available from the British Library

Library of Congress Cataloging-in-Publication Data
NAMES: Eleff, Zev, author.
TITLE: The greatest of all time : a history of an American obsession / Zev Eleff.
OTHER TITLES: G.O.A.T., a history of an American obsession
DESCRIPTION: Cambridge, United Kingdom ; New York, NY : Cambridge
University Press, 2025. | Includes bibliographical references and index.
IDENTIFIERS: LCCN 2024023592 | ISBN 9781009572736 (hardback) |
ISBN 9781009572743 (ebook)
SUBJECTS: LCSH: Heroes – United States. | Gifted persons – United States – Public
opinion. | Celebrities – United States. | Fame. | National characteristics, American. |
United States – Civilization. | Public opinion – United States.
CLASSIFICATION: LCC E169.1 E535 2025 | DDC 920.073–dc23/eng/20240819
LC record available at https://lccn.loc.gov/2024023592

ISBN 978-1-009-57273-6 Hardback

Cambridge University Press & Assessment has no responsibility for the persistence
or accuracy of URLs for external or third-party internet websites referred to in this
publication and does not guarantee that any content on such websites is, or will
remain, accurate or appropriate.

*For Melissa, Meital, Jack, Adir, and, most especially,
the little one on the way
– by any measure, the greatest*

Contents

List of Figures	*page* ix
Acknowledgments	xiii
Introduction	1
1 The Economics of American Greatness	10
2 The Problem of the Great All-Knowing Answer Man	47
3 The Rise and Fall of the Great Changemakers	81
4 How the Babe Became the Greatest (and the Roosevelts, Too)	122
5 The Great Counterculture Conundrum	160
Conclusion: Michael Jordan in the "Age of Lists"	197
Index	219

Figures

1.1 A political cartoon from the 1880s by J. A. Wales depicting Jay Gould's political corruption for his own financial gain was symbolic of the uphill climbs his supporters faced to refurbish his reputation as one of America's great men. *page* 13

1.2 The heiress Helen Gould financed the NYU Hall of Fame of Great Americans enterprise, admitting that it was her hope that her father, the polarizing robber baron Jay Gould, would be enshrined there (he wasn't). 17

1.3 The stately Hall of Fame of Great Americans was meant to be a testament to American greatness. 21

1.4 A profile image of Sir Francis Galton from 1886. Galton was the inspiration for the eugenics movement that flourished in Europe and, to a certain extent in the United States. American opposition to Galton's theories spurred deeper thinking about "changemakers" and "greatness." 28

1.5 Henry Mitchell MacCracken, chancellor of New York University and founder of NYU's Hall of Fame of Great Americans. 34

1.6 This daguerreotype rendering of Edgar Allan Poe by W. S. Hartshorn in 1848 is representative of the misanthropic depictions of Poe at the end of the poet's life and afterward. 39

2.1 On December 11, 1930, Albert Einstein looks out a window on S. S. *Belgenland* upon arrival at Pier 59 in New York. 50

2.2 Henry Ford and Thomas Edison admired each other and had much in common as all-knowing answer men. 56

x *List of Figures*

2.3 Albert Einstein's image (top, second from the right) caused a stir when it was added to Riverside Church's "Arch of Scientists."   78

3.1 Charlie Chaplin, dressed as "the Tramp" in the 1936 film *Modern Times*. Chaplin was viewed as the greatest filmmaker – not narrowly the greatest comedian – in the world.   88

3.2 Charles Lindbergh standing beside *The Spirit of the St. Louis* shortly after his transatlantic flight in May 1927.   94

3.3 Walt Disney and Mickey Mouse board a plane to headline the 1933 World's Fair in Chicago.   104

3.4 Certainly by 1951, Walt Disney had embraced the perception that Donald Duck had overtaken Mickey Mouse as America's "greatest" cartoon.   114

4.1 Ty Cobb and Babe Ruth examine a baseball bat during the 1927 season.   131

4.2 An estimated 75,000 mourners, young and old, lined New York's streets in the rain to watch the funeral motorcade in honor of Babe Ruth in August 1948.   137

4.3 Franklin and Eleanor Roosevelt at the former's presidential inauguration on March 4, 1933. Although it was a long process and had several iterations, the ceremony introduced America to two of its "greatest" individuals of the twentieth century.   155

5.1 Upon arrival in New York in February 1964, the Beatles pose in front of an American flag, symbolic of the so-called British Invasion and the music group's fascination with US culture.   162

5.2 With certain unease, the Beatles pose for a playful photoshoot in Miami with heavyweight contender Cassius Clay (later Muhammad Ali).   171

5.3 The Beatles were eager to conclude their photoshoot at heavyweight contender Cassius Clay's gym. Tellingly, Paul McCartney is compelled to hold a placard that declared Clay the "greatest."   172

5.4 The Ali Summit featured some of the greatest African American athletes, such as those seated (from left to right): Bill Russell, Cassius Clay, Jim Brown, and Lew Alcindor.   181

List of Figures xi

5.5 The Celtics' Bill Russell guards his rival Wilt Chamberlain
    (#13) of the Philadelphia 76ers in 1966.   183
5.6 In 1966, the Beach Boys examine *Hit Parade* magazine,
    one of many music tabloids that printed cover stories
    on the rivalry between the Beach Boys and the Beatles.   188
5.7 Muhammad Ali was so convinced he was the "greatest"
    that he made the phrase the title of his autobiography,
    published in 1975.   195
C.1 Michael Jordan "flying" past Larry Bird in a playoff
    game in 1987. Back then, though, more pundits preferred
    Bird's "greatness" over Jordan's.   209
C.2 The media had hoped Detroit's Grant Hill would emerge
    as the NBA's next great pitchman after Michael Jordan's
    1993 retirement. But in short order, Jordan returned to
    basketball and (literally) wrestled the mantle away from Hill.   213

Acknowledgments

In July 1816, Naphtali Phillips eulogized Gershom Mendes Seixas. The Phillipses were among the most prominent families that established Congregation Shearith Israel, the very first synagogue in North America. Seixas was the synagogue's longtime minister, the first native-born religious leader in American Jewish history. Phillips's tribute to Seixas was one of the earliest sources I found that grapple with the contours of American greatness, and how it might be applied to make meaning for Jews and other groups who wished to endow their own ranks – and by extension, themselves – with greatness. The source also explains, to some extent, how I, an American Jewish historian, got involved with a research subject far afield. In his eulogy, Phillips rattled off the recently deceased and still living "great and patriotic characters" – Franklin, Washington, and Jefferson – and then considered the addition of some others. "And while the history of our eminent political men are transmitted to posterity, there are also niches reserved for those who have been eminently good or great in another sphere of action."[1] Researching this book constantly led me to consider individuals in the other "spheres of action."

I had a lot of help in my journeys in and out of the spheres of literature, history of science, rock and roll, and all varieties of American sport. Accounting for the breadth and depth of myriad subjects requires more than a modicum of support. Foremost, I am grateful to the staff of the Gratz College Tuttleman Library: Director of Libraries Donna

---

[1] Naphtali Phillips, *An Eulogium to the Memory of the Rev. Gershom Mendes Seixas* (New York: H. H. Sherman, 1816), 10.

Guerin and Collections Assistant Sheila Stevens. Thanks, as well, to the Bala Cynwyd Library circulation and interlibrary loan offices for fielding my frequent requests for books. Many archivists scanned materials to make scores of primary sources available to me. These include the staffs at the Archives of the Archdiocese of Boston, Benson Ford Research Center, Bryn Mawr College Archives, Library and Research Center of the National Baseball Hall of Fame, New York Public Library, and Riverside Church. I hasten to single out my brother-in-law, Jonathan Stieglitz, whose patience and detective work at the Superior Court of California uncovered depositions and filings pertaining to Charlie Chaplin Jr.'s libel lawsuit after the Hollywood Chamber of Commerce refused to designate his famous father a star on the Walk of Fame. The same goes for my friend, Noam Friedman, who unearthed terrific material at Riverside Church concerning Albert Einstein's 1930 visit to the Manhattan cathedral.

Friends and scholars read various chapters or discussed numerous aspects with me that improved this book. Accordingly, I offer my thanks to Menachem Butler, Yitzy Ehrenberg, David Hackett Fischer, Christopher Gehrz, Seth Jacobs, Josh Katz, Andrea McDonnell, Lincoln Mullen, Dovi Safier, Jonathan Sarna, Matt Sienkiewicz, and John Turner. Most of all, I extend my gratitude to Cecelia Cancellaro and Victoria Phillips of Cambridge University Press for their excitement, encouragement, and constructive criticism. I am also indebted to Lisa Carter and Vigneswaran Gurumurthy for their expert supervision during the production stages of this book, as well as to Sheila Hill for furnishing the index.

The stories and histories included in these pages are new, even though many of the historical figures are well known. I was therefore aided by the books and essays produced by the biographers of Francis Galton, Edgar Allan Poe, Thomas Edison, Henry Ford, Albert Einstein, Charlie Chaplin, Charles Lindbergh, Walt Disney, Ty Cobb, Babe Ruth, the Roosevelts, Muhammad Ali, the Beatles, and Michael Jordan. My dutiful appreciation is evident throughout the notes and citations in this book.

"What are you working on?" is a fraught question when directed at me. For the past three years, my stock answer has been "Gratz College." Leading this historic institution together with its students, faculty, staff, board members, and growing number of stakeholders has been the honor of a lifetime. Many of these colleagues and friends have also experienced the second part of my typical response: "When I find some free time, I'm working on a history of the greatest of all time." Most friends in the Philadelphia area and elsewhere have indulged my excitement to overshare the contents of this book. In many instances, their comments have provoked further thought and refined my writing. To this incalculable roster of people, I am most grateful for your wisdom.

As always, I am indebted to my family more than I can ever repay. My parents, Susan and Scott Eleff, might trace the genesis of this research to my unflagging appreciation for Billy Joel and youthful downright refusal to acknowledge the achievements of other songwriters. Perhaps they might recall the mid 1990s when I never shied away from a chance to debate Emmitt Smith's greatness against the forces of Barry Sanders fandom. My grandparents, Annette and Morton Eleff, will remember my frequent requests for my grandmother's oatmeal chocolate chip cookies on the grounds that it was – and always will be – the greatest dessert. My apologies if I did not always wait fifteen minutes between snacking and swimming in their backyard pool. My brothers – David, Ben, and Joey – will likely claim that this book was seeded during trenchant arguments comparing the merits of superheroes situated in the DC and Marvel universes.

No doubt, my wife, Melissa, would tell them that they're all correct; that my research into the discourse around the greatest of all time is somehow autobiographical, a historical inquiry into a slice of American culture that has intrigued me since, well, baking cookies as a young boy with my grandma. Meital, Jack, and Adir will agree with their mother – always a wise position. Privately, they will wonder if this isn't just part of an elaborate attempt to obtain the scholarly credentials to once and for all dethrone Tom Brady or reject anyone with an allegiance to the Pittsburgh Steelers. Melissa and our children – our family – is the greatest thing I have ever been a part of. By the time anyone reads these lines, we will have welcomed Baby #4 to our Hall of Fame family; and, hopefully, we will have settled on her name. While I haven't met her yet, I have no doubt our daughter is bound for greatness. It is to her – as well as to her mother and siblings – that I dedicate this book.

Introduction

On May 8, 1973, Pelé visited the White House to meet with President Richard Nixon. The latter gushed at the chance to greet the Brazilian soccer legend. "You are the greatest in the world," exclaimed Nixon. Pelé knew a modicum of English at the time but didn't know how to respond. Pelé was a three-time World Cup winner and Santos FC's leading scorer. Yet, he was surprised by Nixon's appellation. Outside of the United States, people didn't talk that much about greatness or define symbolic exemplars as the very greatest. Pelé didn't reply. Instead, he handed Nixon an old newspaper from São Paulo that reported on an earlier meeting between the pair and hurried through that awkward second encounter.[1]

Pelé was right. Over the course of the twentieth century, Americans were overeager to engage in conversations that designated "great people." They were particularly poised to elevate individuals to the ranks of the "greatest of all time." They liked that greatness was indexical, that there was no absolute definition of greatness; that it changed with the ebbs and flows of American cultural sensibilities.

This book tells a history that reads in between the lines of "greatness" discourse. It's not an encyclopedia that selects areas of expertise and decides who is the greatest of all time. There are plenty of heavy tomes that set out to do this, from modern music to oratory excellence.[2] Some

---

[1] See Michael Beschloss, "A Quick and Awkward Meeting between a President and Pelé," *New York Times*, June 28, 2014, D5; and Pelé and Brian Winter, *Why Soccer Matters* (New York: Celebra, 2014), 225.

[2] See, for example, Fred Bronson, *The Billboard Book of Number One Hits* (New York: Billboard Publications, 1992); and Stephen E. Lucas and Martin J. Medhurst, *Words of a Century: The Top 100 American Speeches, 1900–1999* (New York: Oxford University Press, 2009).

rank the "greats" of a stated field using popular polls or by tabulating the results of a survey submitted to so-called experts. More recent iterations use math and machine learning to settle longstanding greatness debates.[3] Withal, the unsettled arguments about the greatest cartoon character, parish preacher, economist, statistician, and action hero of all time will not be decided in these pages.[4]

To borrow from the essayist Raymond Carver, this book explores what Americans talk about when they talk about greatness. These are coded conversations. The history of greatness discourse provides a uniquely American language for participants to discuss their "ideal" values and make meaning of their personal lives. The many incarnations and insinuations of "greatness" suggest more about those carrying on the conversation than it does about the famous people under discussion. An argument for Abraham Lincoln or, later on, Franklin Delano Roosevelt, over George Washington as America's greatest statesman says as much about the interlocuter as it does about the legacies of former US presidents. Making a case for the Beatles, Michael Jordan, or Mickey Mouse involves the prioritizations of politics and perspectives. The same goes for selecting between Jane Addams versus Eleanor Roosevelt or whether Thomas Edison, the so-called greatest inventor of all time, possessed a station or wisdom to pontificate about God or another nonscientific area. The persistence of Henry Ford as a great American despite his toxic antisemitism offers another layer to this historical phenomenon, one that Ford would, as was his wont, no doubt, describe as "bunk."

Why did Americans take to greatness? It helped that the term defied discrete definition. "Greatness," and therefore someone deemed "the greatest," is not measured by a uniform standard. To the contrary, the calculus of greatness varied by time and place. The only constant (excepting the 1950s) was that greatness, intuitive to Americans' collective understanding, was inextricably tied to change. Americans fawned over changemakers, social disrupters with designs to transform the status quo. This contrasted with more incorrigible forces in Europe

---

[3] See Steven Skiena and Charles B. Ward, *Who's Bigger: Where Historical Figures Really Rank* (New York: Cambridge University Press, 2014).

[4] Some useful citations on these matters include Bill Diamond, "Things Really Hopping at 'Roger Rabbit' Premiere," *Los Angeles Times*, June 23, 1988, 3; "The World's Greatest Orator to Speak," *Chicago Defender*, September 11, 1915, 3; A. K. McClure, "Tom Corwin, the Greatest Orator," *Nashville American*, November 17, 1901, 26A; "Lincoln Greatest Orator," *Washington Post*, November 7, 1913, 2; "Greatest Orator of United States," *Boston Globe*, April 3, 1912, 10; "Jesus, Greatest Orator, to be Rev. Sanders Subject," *Atlanta Daily World*, July 7, 1951, 2.

that discouraged change in favor of established traditions and status. Celebrating change was also important for a liberal American spirit to distance itself from a pernicious force that had just migrated to its shores from Europe. Eugenics was steeped in people's incapacity to change. Sir Francis Galton, the forefather of the movement, had singled out America's unexceptional state as proof that people cannot deviate all that far from their genetic code. Galton surmised that since the United States was formed by, according to his judgment, the lowest crust of European life, its current stock lacked the biological wherewithal to elevate to Europe's high cultural standards.

It took a very long time for Europe to consider the American standards of greatness, and even then, critics observed that celebrants of greatness on the Continent had missed the point. In 2002, the British Broadcasting Corporation (BBC) aired the TV show *100 Greatest Britons*, based on a poll of the British people. Such programs were commonplace in the United States but in the UK the BBC's two seasons of indigenous greatness rankings was unusual and fascinated viewers. The show also called for public comment. Critics quipped that the BBC's poll merely proved that the nation was still overly focused on royals and that the shadow of Galton's chauvinism had darkened any potential light to illuminate "poets, artists and women [who were] woefully under-represented."[5] Three years later, the TV channel France 2 debuted *Le plus grand Français de tous les temps* (*The Greatest Frenchmen of All Time*), a show that apparently "baffled" viewers.[6] The French press blasted their surveyed compatriots for a very poor sense of French history; lack of appreciation for women and feminists such as Simone de Beauvoir, who was left off the list; and generally resolved that "Nous voilà avec un sondage sympathique et idiot," that the public television venture had resulted in a "nice and idiotic survey."[7] Hence, my focus on the United States. Here, the History Channel's *Greatest of All-Time* series, hosted by football legend Payton Manning, debuted in 2023 to rave reviews.[8]

Once braided together and placed into historical context, the stories shared in these chapters suggest something, well, deeper. The historian David Hackett Fischer called the phenomenon "Deep Change."

---

[5] Matt Wells, "The 100 Greatest Britons," *Guardian*, August 22, 2002, 1. See also Nicola Methven, "The 100 Greatest Britons, but Why Are They All White?" *Daily Mirror*, August 22, 2002, 11.

[6] Jon Henley, "French Baffled by List of National Heroes," *Guardian*, March 16, 2005, 13.

[7] "Grands hommes et petits sondages," *Le Monde*, April 19, 2005, 15.

[8] See "Today's Picks," *Newsday*, February 27, 2023, 16.

In the language of political science, Fischer explained his phrase as a "change in the structure of change itself." In mathematical terms, "deep change is the second derivative. It may be calculated as a rate of change in rates of change."[9] In somewhat plainer parlance, I detect that there's something afoot, historically speaking, when Charles Lindbergh, Charlie Chaplin, and Mickey Mouse are all demoted from their high stations around the start of World War II. There's a change regime in motion as America suddenly takes unparalleled interest in the greatness of Babe Ruth and the Roosevelts, and perhaps that untold history suggests something even more important for how Americans think about change and greatness in the postwar 1950s. The same is the case for a historical coupling the Beatles with Muhammad Ali to throw new light on the countercultural 1960s.

The philosopher Ludwig Wittgenstein taught that words carry significant value.[10] Beginning at the start of the twentieth century, Americans found value in "greatness" because they intuited a corresponding devaluation in fame. The rise of new technologies enhanced media, permitting publishers to print images in their newspapers. Advances in radio science broadcasted music and speech to a widening public audience. Suddenly, a larger swath of people became better known and, therefore, more famous. In economic terms, Americans detected a fame inflation and required a new currency to transact meaning in their conversations about the influential people they held up on a pedestal. The reason they cared so much about that pedestal in the first place is the subject of this book. Their choice of a new coveted commodity, "greatness" and those deemed "the greatest," is the lens to see and, ultimately, to understand their thinking. The wide reach of this coded language extended to feelings about race and gender, as I will show through prejudices of Jimmy Cannon to accept the greatness of Muhammad Ali and the contentious deliberations at Bryn Mawr College to award the M. Carey Thomas Prize to a most "eminent woman."

---

[9] See David Hackett Fischer, *The Great Wave: Price Revolutions and the Rhythm of History* (Oxford: Oxford University Press, 1996), xv. See also, David Hackett Fischer, *Growing Old in America* (Oxford: Oxford University Press, 1878), 100–101; and David Hackett Fischer, *Washington's Crossing* (Oxford: Oxford University Press, 2004), 449; and in Fischer's student, Lincoln A. Mullen, *The Chance of Salvation: A History of Conversion in America* (Cambridge: Harvard University Press, 2017), 9.

[10] See, for example, Theodore Redpath, "Wittgenstein and Ethics," in *Philosophy and Language*, eds. Alice Ambrose and Morris Lazerowitz (London: George Allen and Unwin Ltd, 1972), 95–119.

Introduction 5

The erasure of women and people of color (and Jews, according to some bigoted critics who sought to eliminate Albert Einstein) from the ranks of greatness is an important subject taken up in these pages. In addition to my treatment of Muhammad Ali, I have selected the cases of Eleanor Roosevelt and Michael Jordan to highlight the American limitations of greatness discourse and its implications for how the public has narrowly imagined its great symbolic exemplars. Eleanor Roosevelt's climb to the high station of greatness in the 1950s required that she shed her association with feminism and restyle herself as a loyal wife (turned widow) and doting grandmother. In the case of Jordan, I examine how basketball aficionados worried that the famous men who flourished in the National Basketball Association (NBA) after Jordan's (first) retirement in 1993 were not fit to inherit Jordan's throne. The potential heirs to the clean-cut "Air Jordan" were raised in a generation of rap music and dreadlocks – and therefore deemed unbecoming of a sport league that had overcome an epoch of rampant drug use by elevating the likes of Magic Johnson, Larry Bird, and Jordan. Pundits seized on the light-skinned, piano-playing, Duke-educated Grant Hill as the worthiest successor to Jordan, despite an ample roster of more famous and, frankly, much more dominant basketball players.

Fame wasn't immediately and summarily discarded. Being famous was often a prerequisite for becoming the greatest. Some believed that the greatness (or lack thereof) of someone's personality could be approximated by fame. In 1932, for example, Mark May of Yale University published a paper that postulated that personality could be evaluated by the "responses made by others to the individual." Or, as May put it a sentence later, personality ought to be measured by someone's "popularity."[11]

May's take on personality stuck, at least for a short while. Four years after May first wrote on the subject, Henry Link, a psychologist and self-help philosopher, judged there was "general agreement" about May's assigned correlation between personality and popularity. An "unattractive boy" who impresses friends through masterful tennis skill or a "homely girl" who gains renown after an exemplary piano recital had, suggested Link, accrued more personality by "bringing friends."[12] It didn't take all that long for the Harvard psychologist Gordon Allport to

---

[11] Mark A. May, "The Foundations of Personality," in *Psychology at Work*, ed. Paul S. Achilles (New York: Whittlesey House, 1932), 83.
[12] Henry C. Link, *The Return to Religion* (New York: The Macmillan Company, 1936), 89–90.

point out the fallacy, that personality could not be mistaken for a popularity contest. "A queen of the movies seen by millions of people on the screen," wrote Allport, "would have incomparably 'more' personality than a complex and tortured poet dwelling in attic obscurity."[13] Yet, it betokened the odd predicament that reputable researchers clung to the challenge of parsing "greatness" from "fame." Beginning with the troubling posthumous "life" of Edgar Allan Poe, fame remains a part of this book, even as I do my very best to isolate one term from the other.

The scholarly literature on "fame" is significant. It helped develop this book's argument and framed its chapters – even as I allow the storytelling to control the tempo of this work. In American Studies, researchers – perhaps not so different from the public – are captivated by the circumstances that surround celebrities. To borrow from terms deployed by the noted film expert, Richard Dyer, the piles of books and journal articles on the subject tend to center on the "commodification" of the "idealized" icons manufactured by famous people and the attendant media and fans.[14] Fame, thus, has value and possesses measurable influence and power in daily life.

The increased attention paid to celebrity culture did much to revive interest in Leo Löwenthal, a member of the Frankfurt School. Löwenthal was part of a circle of scholars that included the likes of Theodor Adorno, Walter Benjamin, and Max Horkheimer. These intellectuals flourished during the interwar period and employed critical theory in a host of disciplines. Löwenthal's area was communication and social thought, with a rather middlebrow interest in popular culture and media technologies.[15]

Löwenthal aimed to pave inroads in New York, where he fled to escape Nazi Germany on the eve of World War II. In the United States, Löwenthal observed how his new neighbors idolized famous people. In step with the Frankfurt School that demanded consideration of historical and political context, Löwenthal had hoped to show his American colleagues how the biographies and magazines that their indigenous media machines used to depict "successful people" were deeply indebted to "historical processes."[16] He was rather nonplussed, therefore, that his readers – ensconced, in Löwenthal's view in a "empiricist-positivist"

---

[13] Gordon W. Allport, *Personality: A Psychological Interpretation* (New York: Henry Holt and Company, 1937), 41.
[14] See Richard Dyer, *Heavenly Bodies: Film Stars and Society* (London: British Film Institute, 1986), 2–11.
[15] Chris Rojek, *Celebrity* (London: Reaktion Books, 2001), 29–45.
[16] Leo Löwenthal, *Literature and Mass Culture* (New Brunswick, NJ: Transaction Books, 1984), 207.

point of view that discounted external forces – that did not seem to care all that much about context.[17] Löwenthal's work was not all that much consulted until scholars started to consider "celebrity."[18]

This book answers a question unanswered by Löwenthal, perhaps because it was not discernable when he conducted his research in the 1940s. Back then, Löwenthal tabulated and aggregated the biographical articles that had appeared in *Collier's* and the *Saturday Evening Post* since the turn of the century. He was astounded that the percentage of stories about famous people in the entertainment sector – and mostly women and men detached from what Löwenthal classified as "entertainers from serious arts" – had become the dominant proportion of biographical pieces in these magazines. How did this come to pass?

Löwenthal downplayed the fact that famous people associated with "Political life" and the area of "Business and Professional" no longer held the pole position in these journals. However, articles about them had increased, too. From 1901 to 1914, Löwenthal counted about sixteen articles per year about statesmen and politicians and ten that centered on businessmen and high-ranking professionals. These articles comprised three-quarters of all published biographies in these two important magazines. In 1941, the same journals published thirty-one articles about people in the political sector and twenty-five that concerned well-known figures in the business and professional ranks. Löwenthal focused his attention on the fifty-five pieces on entertainers, the so-called idols of consumption, leisure moguls, that made up more than half of all published biographical articles. Yet, it seems to me noteworthy that the total number of all human interest stories on famous people had increased, albeit at a disproportionate scale.[19]

In truth, Löwenthal's math suggests that America had become deeply invested in consuming information about celebrities, craving further access to these famous people far beyond what radio, cinemas, and, in time, television could provide to them. Yet, the influence of any one of these unprecedented number of celebrities had decreased. No longer could a Mary Pickford, Humphrey Bogart, or, for that matter, Henry Ford, hold, by themselves, a dominant market share of cultural

---

[17] See Leo Löwenthal, *Critical Theory and Frankfurt Theorists: Lectures, Correspondence, Conversations* (New Brunswick, NJ: Transaction Books, 1989), 234.
[18] See Hanno Hardt, "The Legacy of Leo Löwenthal: Culture and Communication," *Journal of Communication* 41 (September 1991): 60–85.
[19] Leo Löwenthal, "Biographies in Popular Magazines," in *Radio Research, 1942–1943*, eds. Paul F. Lazarsfeld and Frank N. Stanton (New York: Arno Press, 1979), 509–11.

currency in the United States. It was, then, a case of fame inflation. That Americans sought a new taxonomy to describe cultural powerbrokers is evident from a national survey conducted concurrent to Löwenthal's research. It reported that when asked to "name two or three living Americans you would really call great," those polled were far more likely to rate Franklin Roosevelt, Douglas MacArthur, or James Doolittle than Babe Ruth, Joe DiMaggio, or a Tinseltown movie star.[20] Amid the run on celebrity and fame, "greatness" emerged as a new commodity packed with Wittgensteinian value. Greatness was traded in a variety of denominations and the market for great men (and eventually women) fluctuated based on historical context, as taught to us by Leo Löwenthal's Frankfurt School.

Löwenthal's ideas inform these pages, even as I examine greatness as a commodified contrast to "fame." This book is the flipside of his pioneering work on fame. I draw from Löwenthal's well-known distinction between "idols of production" ("heroes" who led a "productive life") and the "idols of consumption" ("magazine heroes" famous for leisure activities) that emerged in the post-Depression period. In the chapters that follow, I analyze the shift and use it to explain how the metrics of American greatness had changed, quite drastically. Likewise, scholars such as David Marshall, Chris Rojek, Karen Sternheimer have published books in Media Studies which build on Löwenthal's arguments to examine how fame is negotiated by journalists in a way that detaches the image of celebrities from the personal lives of those well-known women and men. The idea of Taylor Swift is perhaps disconnected from the daily life of that famous music performer. By contrast, the arbiters (which is all of us) of American greatness are discombobulated by such dissonance. The perception of great people and their personal lives and decisions are rarely decoupled. Perceived authenticity and sincerity function as key attributes in the formulation of greatness; another critical differentiation between the present book and aligned work on Fame Studies.

This book is both lively and learned. The scholarly scaffolding is crucial for all that it helps with comparisons and contrasts. I am indebted to these scholars for providing frameworks that inform "achieved" versus "attributed" renown, as well as the rise and fall of the American "cult of veneration," even as I refocus my lens on "greatness" and take my cue from Leo Löwenthal's call to remain most mindful to the historical circumstances and forces that determined significant change in

---

[20] "The Fortune Survey," *Fortune* 26 (November 1942): 14.

American culture.[21] Scholars, I hope, will appreciate this useful framing as much as other curious readers will value the unusual tales of "great" people (and an animated rodent) that follow.

This book isn't exhaustive. Its goal is to spur thought, and perhaps add to the terrific literature on reception history that draws from the biographer Carl Van Doren's insight about Benjamin Franklin, that "the death of a great man begins another history, of his continuing influence, his changing renown, the legend which takes the place of fact."[22] Biographies of varying qualities directed me to primary sources and archival data to add new information to our collective understanding of so-described great individuals. In keeping with this book's big idea, and in concert with Michael Oriard's important book on media and historical reception, I often learned much more about the people who wrote about the greatests of all time.[23] My hope is that this book will shed light on the way Americans, perhaps without realizing it, have sanctified the mundane through their oft-tired debates about their favorite Hollywood actress or legendary football star. The reader will be the judge of whether the succeeding chapters provide historical antecedents to Donald Trump's "Make America Great Again" motto, and why his opponents took exception to Trump's use of the phrase as opposed to when Ronald Reagan and Bill Clinton had deployed a similar incarnation.[24] I will happily permit others to tackle that subject. I'll also defer to others whether there's attendant learning to be applied to current discussions on the appropriateness to maintain statues and monuments memorializing problematic American figures such as Thomas Jefferson and Woodrow Wilson whose "great" lives no longer measure up to contemporary expectations. These are the most recent examples of the contested contours of a most important word in the American cultural lexicon. It invites us to consider what Americans are truly talking about when they talk about greatness.

---

[21] Robert Michels, *Political Parties: A Sociological Study of the Oligarchical Tendencies of Modern Democracy*, trans. Eden and Cedar Paul (New York: Hearst's International Library Co., 1915), 63–68.

[22] Carl Van Doren, *Benjamin Franklin* (New York: Viking Press, 1938), 781. In addition to the many reception histories directly cited in the subsequent chapters, I learned much from John Rodden, *The Politics of Literary Reputation: The Making and Claiming of 'St. George' Orwell* (New York: Oxford University Press, 1989); and Robert E. Kapsis, *Hitchcock: The Making of a Reputation* (Chicago: University of Chicago Press, 1992).

[23] See Michael Oriard, *Reading Football: How the Popular Press Created an American Spectacle* (Chapel Hill: The University of North Carolina Press, 1993).

[24] See Karen Tumulty, "How Trump Came Up with 'Make America Great Again,'" *Washington Post*, January 20, 2017, H3.

I

The Economics of American Greatness

Chancellor Henry Mitchell MacCracken of New York University established the Hall of Fame of Great Americans in 1900. This was a peculiar name for the first Hall of Fame formed in the United States. MacCracken tended to conflate "greatness" with "fame." It had been more forgivable to confuse the terms in his youth since the United States had possessed an ample supply of great men, mostly famous patriots and statesmen, and there was nothing anyone else engaged in another profession could do to manufacture similar quantities of fame. MacCracken had come of age in Antebellum America, an epoch marked by an impulse to valorize the founders of the Republic who had died a generation earlier.[1] The very same spirit washed over men of letters. That "Great Man" fascination, for instance, occupied the writings of Henry Wadsworth Longfellow and Ralph Waldo Emerson. "Lives of great men all remind us," wrote Longfellow, "we can make our lives sublime." Emerson wrote a book on Representative Men on the presumption that it was "natural to believe in great men."[2]

As a young man in Oxford, Ohio, Henry MacCracken was raised in this creed of Great Men; Longfellow's prose made an indelible impression on MacCracken as a small child. His father, John Steele MacCracken,

---

[1] See Douglas Adair, *Fame and the Founding Fathers*, ed. Trevor Colbourn (New York: W. W. Norton, 1974), 3–26; Drew R. McCoy, *The Last of the Fathers: James Madison and the Republican Legacy* (Cambridge: Cambridge University Press, 1989), 171–216. See also Harlow Giles Unger, *The Last Founding Father: James Monroe and the Nation's Call to Greatness* (Cambridge, MA: Da Capo Press, 2010).

[2] Peter H. Gibbon, *A Call to Heroism: Renewing America's Vision of Greatness* (New York: Atlantic Monthly Press, 2022), 18–28.

was a proud Presbyterian minister blessed with the "spirit of the pioneer." Reverend MacCracken liked to tell his son about his namesake, Henry MacCracken of Sunbury, Pennsylvania. The elder MacCracken died defending his young nation in the Revolutionary War.[3] Henry appreciated his father's stories of his patriotic great-grandfather and other "great" martyrs who had furnished his United States. In his youth, young Henry liked to line up the chairs in his mother's modest kitchen, pretending each was another "great man of his time." The boy made a case for each candidate, explaining to no one in particular the merits of the nominee to warrant a sacred place in nascent American history.[4]

As an older man and in charge of a university, MacCracken evolved his boyhood fantasy into the NYU Hall of Fame of Great Americans. As the name of the august institution suggests, MacCracken wished to honor the famous and the greatest as if these were interchangeable terms to describe the very best stock of American life. But these notions were no longer all that aligned. By the close of the nineteenth century, the United States possessed, in sociologist Orrin Klapp's terms, an "oversupply" or "inflation" of fame.[5] The inflation of fame – another useful term, one preferred by the British, was "status" – had to do with visibility. By 1890, 35 percent of Americans lived in cities; that figure was 5 percent of the population one hundred years prior. Americans had increased access to dignitaries, politicians, and entertainers. If they did not see them in theaters or in other public spaces, the common folk could ogle at famous people in newspapers. This resulted in the acquisition of more fame by more people.

The initial fanfare around the Hall of Fame project seemed to confirm all this. Newspapers conducted popular polls to maintain the public's high interest in MacCracken's grand contest. America was apparently home to many famous people. A Brooklyn daily received 776 mock ballots and tallied 938 proposed candidates. One observer made much amusement, comparing the New York newspaper's results with a vote conducted in Minneapolis. He reasoned that the variances highlighted geographic biases and was encouraged that the newspapers' polls shared forty great men in common.[6]

---

[3] *Henry Mitchell MacCracken: In Memoriam* (New York: New York University Press, 1923), 3.
[4] Diana A. Farkas and Robert N. Farkas, "Henry Mitchell MacCracken and the Hall of Fame at New York University," *Bronx County Historical Society* 8 (July 1971): 51.
[5] Orrin E. Klapp, *Inflation of Symbols: Loss of Values in American Culture* (New Brunswick, NJ: Transaction Publishers, 1991), 84.
[6] Thomas Wentworth Higginson, "Guesses at Fame," *Independent*, August 16, 1900, 1964–66.

MacCracken intended for his Hall of Fame to combat this – to "deflate" fame – and developed a much more discerning process to limit fame to women and men who were irreproachably great people.[7] He assembled a slate of a hundred highly educated, geographically varied judges to gatekeep the NYU Hall of Fame. MacCracken anticipated that just a few individuals would pass the panel's scrutiny since, by rule, candidates needed to appear on more than half of the ballots for successful election.

Henry MacCracken's attempt to reset the market of American culture was an impossible task, however. He didn't stand much of a chance to control the run on fame. No one could repair the damage wrought by technology and new forms of media that had so irrevocably depreciated its value. Newspapers had by this time mastered new print technologies that permitted publishers to insert photographs directly into wordy columns.[8] The newspapermen recognized that all this had piqued a curious interest and became invested in helping famous people acquire more fame. Journalists indulged in filling the society columns with salacious rumors and fancy illustrations. Readers happily welcomed Albert Nelson Marquis's *Who's Who* biographical dictionaries, the first edition appearing in 1898 and containing 8,500 entries of "distinguished Americans."[9]

In time, MacCracken learned that fame and greatness were two separate commodities. What's worse, he learned that the voters for the NYU Hall of Fame of Great Americans privileged fame over greatness, insofar as they permitted the former to mediate the latter. No better examples were Robert E. Lee and Edgar Allan Poe, two individuals whose greatness was self-evident. Yet many discounted their personal virtue; that either man possessed requisite levels of fame to then be considered for greatness. MacCracken's institution served as an important forum, particularly in the case of Poe, to question whether infamy – the darker side of fame – could disqualify the otherwise unimpeachable cases of American greatness. The answer, to MacCracken's chagrin, was that fame and greatness often informed one another – but they were not the same thing.

***

[7] "Hall of Fame Eligibles," *New York Sun*, October 12, 1900, 2.
[8] Leo Braudy, *The Frenzy of Renown: Fame and Its History* (New York: Oxford University Press, 1986), 508.
[9] Susan J. Douglas and Andrea McDonnell, *Celebrity: A History of Fame* (New York: New York University Press, 2019), 28–29.

The Economics of American Greatness

The heiress Helen Gould financed MacCracken's Hall of Fame of Great Americans. She sponsored the project to recast America's image of her father, Jay Gould (Figure 1.1). The elder Gould had never paid attention to things like "fame." It did not matter to Gould whether others considered him a "great man." He did not have much use for these commodities. To the contrary, Gould cultivated wealth through a canny style that produced a rather infamous reputation. He was the most despised member of the robber barons: those tycoons who dominated America's marketplaces during the latter half of the nineteenth century. It was a somewhat unfair reputation of the shrewd businessman, but Wall Street never did forgive Gould for his failed attempt in 1869 to leverage his relationship with President Ulysses S. Grant to control the nation's gold supply. The newspapers reviled Gould, once designating him the "worst man on earth since the beginning of the Christian era."[10]

FIGURE 1.1 A political cartoon from the 1880s by J. A. Wales depicting Jay Gould's political corruption for his own financial gain was symbolic of the uphill climbs his supporters faced to refurbish his reputation as one of America's great men. Courtesy of Bettmann/Getty Images.

[10] Richard O'Conner, *Gould's Millions* (New York: Doubleday, 1962), 191.

Gould was a short man, and the diminution projected a Napoleonic spirit that increased the fierce and unyielding characterizations. In most situations, Gould embraced his ignominy, believing that the darkened reputation afforded him a competitive advantage in boardrooms and on trading floors. He made significant efforts to maintain that reputation. He gave reporters quotes that betokened his hardened humanity. There was a kindness inside Gould, but the wealthy man could not afford to let it show. Much of his philanthropic efforts were handled anonymously to perpetuate the tough persona. No one was permitted to share the stories of Gould strolling beside the railroads to inquire about the wellbeing of the station agents and repairmen under his employ. The omissions meant that Jay Gould suffered a status far below the charitable ranks of the magnanimous Rockefellers and Carnegies.

But Helen Gould cared, and she was determined to campaign on behalf of her father's legacy. No one was more sympathetic to this mission than NYU's MacCracken. MacCracken had been a member of Jay Gould's inner circle, one of the few who was neither a business associate nor a family member. Gould held an affinity for MacCracken's school. His support of higher education was personal. As a young man, Gould had been too busy bookkeeping for his father to enroll in a university. "I intended as soon as my finances would permit to take a course through college," Gould once confessed, "but as my father requires a share of my time here it seems wrong to do otherwise."[11] His friendship with MacCracken made amends for that missing experience and was further sparked by Gould's fascination with Samuel Morse's telegraph. Gould owned controlling interest in the Western Union Telegraph Company. The magnate liked that Morse had served as an art professor at NYU, back when it was known as the University of the City of New York. Gould knew that NYU played an even more pivotal role in the creation of his favorite invention. Another scholar there, Leonard Gale, was most useful in correcting a circuitry problem that led to Morse's great breakthrough. Both MacCracken and Gould believed that there was more good fortune in store for the university.

They were on the surface an odd pair. MacCracken looked like Gould's physical opposite. The former was tall and sported white hair that flowed behind his ears to the top of his neck. In middle age,

---

[11] Robert Irving Warshow, *Jay Gould: The Story of a Fortune* (New York: Greenberg, 1928), 34.

MacCracken allowed his beard to sprawl so much that parts of his unkempt mane covered the shoulder pads of his suit. Upon assuming the helm of NYU, MacCracken took better care of his appearance. He combed and tucked his beard to provide a significant buffer for his chin. Jay Gould's hair never fully greyed and, like everything else in his life, he was very intentional about how he used his presence to his advantage. He wore his substantial beard around his entire face and trimmed it where it reached his throat. The color and intensity of Gould's facial hair correctly suggested that he was a person of significant power.

In 1892, MacCracken was one of the few "close advisors" permitted to visit with the aged and unwell Gould at his summer estate in Irvington, New York.[12] There, MacCracken convinced Gould that NYU's future resided uptown in University Heights because downtown Washington Square had become far too congested with shops and general loudness. MacCracken theorized that his students required something much more serene to succeed in their studies. The idea resonated with Gould, who had spent his childhood in the rural environs of upstate New York and, fondly recalling his youth, retreated to his bucolic estate in Irvington for holidays. Gould assented and wrote a very large check, rendering him the most substantive supporter of MacCracken's "up-town movement." Gould died several months later. MacCracken participated in the funeral, reading before Gould's grieving family members the committal service of the Episcopal Church.[13]

Helen Gould maintained her father's connection to Henry MacCracken. NYU's head man saw much of Jay Gould within Helen and became her partner in preserving his memory. Her physical qualities served as a metaphor for what few others could see that linked the daughter with her late father. Jay Gould's imposing black beard hid the resemblance he shared with Helen. Both had dark brown hair. Their common rounded noses were framed by puffy cheeks. On Helen, the fullish sides to her face ingratiated her with other socialites and complemented the smile she adorned in public appearances. That disposition did not do much for her father and might explain why he hid his face under a stern beard.

All told, Helen Gould donated more than $2 million to NYU, "speaking always of her father's intentions, of his strongly expressed confidence

---

[12] Edward J. Renehan Jr., *Dark Genius of Wall Street: The Misunderstood Life of Jay Gould, King of the Robber Barons* (New York: Basic Books, 2005), 294.
[13] Murat Halstead, *Life of Jay Gould: How He Made His Millions* (Philadelphia: Edgewood Publishing Co., 1892), 154.

in Chancellor MacCracken."[14] In 1897, Helen sponsored the construction of the Gould Memorial Library. Her relative once relayed that the idea was Helen's. "I am thinking of donating a library to New York University," she remarked to a cousin. "My thought is to have it as a memorial to father. You know about his gift to the Heights moving fund, and how he had been looking forward to assisting the university in a large way. I have written to Chancellor MacCracken already on the subject."[15] Made in the likeness of the Roman Pantheon, the edifice was in its time the most prominent building on NYU's Bronx campus.

Three years later, MacCracken pitched another idea to the heiress. He conjured a vision of a Hall of Fame of Great Americans (Figure 1.2). No shrine of this kind had ever existed in the United States, although hundreds more, dedicated to narrower fields such as sports, music, and recreational vehicles, would later pattern themselves after MacCracken's concoction. He described it to Gould as a "Westminster Abbey of the United States," comparable to the Ruhmeshalle in Munich containing busts of important Bavarian dignitaries. Their earlier efforts to reconstruct an American Pantheon on NYU's campus, the Gould Memorial Library, that is, had an implicit goal to celebrate indigenous greatness but had been far too understated. Marcus Agrippa had constructed the Pantheon with statues honoring the Roman gods. The replica that doubled as NYU's uptown library required space for bookcases and tables, so no room remained for busts of American statesmen and heroes. MacCracken persuaded Gould that a 500-foot-long colonnade could house a museum dedicated to American greatness and feature exhibits of the women and men most responsible for founding and developing their beloved nation. She was "quick to perceive the enormous patriotic and educational value inherent in the idea" and "promptly made available something over $100,000 to start the work."[16]

An unfounded rumor circulated that Helen Gould's gift bought her father a mantle among America's greatest, that his "candidacy for fame is prescribed in advance by the founder."[17] However, Helen Gould had conducted her social affairs with altruism and was above fixing the contest to suit her self-interests. Still, she did confess her hope that the small fortune she had donated to the Hall of Fame would ingratiate

---

[14] Alice Northrop Snow, *The Story of Helen Gould: Daughter of Jay Gould, Great American* (New York: Fleming H. Revell Company, 1943), 238.
[15] Ibid., 237.
[16] Ibid., 264.
[17] Higginson, "Guesses at Fame," 1964.

FIGURE 1.2 The heiress Helen Gould financed the NYU Hall of Fame of Great Americans enterprise, admitting that it was her hope that her father, the polarizing robber baron Jay Gould, would be enshrined there (he wasn't). Courtesy of Library of Congress Prints and Photographs.

her father's nomination to the judges. "I do not deny that the name of my father, the late Jay Gould," she confirmed to reporters, "is to be among the distinguished dead inscribed in the walls of this Hall of Fame."[18] But Helen Gould underestimated the degree to which businessmen in general gave Americans pause when it came to determining greatness among its ranks. No one denied a correlation between skill and wealth. They usually used this as the basic formula to rank semi-tangible notions such as "success," "achievement," and, most importantly, "fame."[19] But a growing number of critics had raised the possibility that America's increased focus on material wealth had rerouted many young people's professional trajectories from literature

[18] "Helen Gould Gave $100,000," *Evening World*, March 7, 1900, 2.
[19] Richard Weiss, *The American Myth of Success: From Horatio Alger to Norman Vincent Peale* (New York: Basic Books, 1969), 48–63.

and the arts to the stock market. The result, they argued, was a pipeline shortage in fields that made more direct impact on American life. The robber barons countered that their largesse bankrolled concert halls, supported the publication of books, and endowed universities.

That line of argument was not persuasive. Jay Gould and the other robber barons were famous men, probably better known than many of the earliest inductees to MacCracken's Hall of Fame. Yet, none of these rich men had managed to accrue the commodities that redounded to greatness. During its seven decades of activity, the Hall of Fame of Great Americans inducted just two businessmen: George Peabody was included among the very first class (1900) and Andrew Carnegie was enshrined in the very last cohort (1976) selected. On the paucity of businessmen (or -women) from the Hall of Fame, its longtime director surmised that Americans "have considered achievement in material things, however useful, as inferior to intellectual and uncommercial success."[20] It was a referendum on fame. Famous men such as Jay Gould and John D. Rockefeller and Cornelius Vanderbilt were just as poor as the rank and file when audited for assets measured in greatness.

***

What is greatness and how is it measured? During the first half of the twentieth century, Americans by and large reserved applications of greatness to discussions that centered on change. George Washington was the nation's first changemaker, even though his reserved disposition did not always suit that moniker. The people looked to him as an aspirational figure. The descriptions of Washington blurred the boundaries between "fame" and "greatness." In his lifetime, Washington rose to a transcendent figure because he was the very model of change; his "greatness" was much more than the sum of his achievements. Americans, once they elevated Washington to the central symbol of the Revolution, liked to juxtapose him with England's King George III. "God save great Washington," sang Americans, "God damn the King!" they chorused, mocking the well-known British refrain. The jeers were not merely about overthrowing England. Americans recognized that with Washington they had a new model of leadership that contained within his growing reputation important virtues such as "liberty" and "honor." Everything about "great Washington" contrasted with

---

[20] Robert Underwood Johnson, *Your Hall of Fame* (New York: New York University Press, 1935), 65.

his European counterparts. He was envisaged as a self-made man and flourished because he had earned that station rather than claimed it by birthright. "I presume that no man in his sober senses," wrote Thomas Paine, "will compare the character of any of the kings of Europe with that of General Washington."[21]

Americans understood at this early period that their expectations of greatness were tied to "change," even if they didn't always use that word. Sometimes they wrote about it as the "spirit of innovation gone forth," lauded the "powers of invention," or described their situation as "favorable for great reformations."[22] These writers had in mind the change wrought by the Revolution that forced Americans to reconsider its forms of government, education, range of religious tolerance, and rights offered to those who were not "white, male, property owners." The Revolution did not resolve these matters, but it set in motion the debates and discussions that animated reconsideration of these critical issues. Change presented hope for an improved future rather than other measures of greatness that peered backward into a self-aggrandized past. Henceforth, Americans would measure the curve of greatness by an individual's ability to augur change whereas Europeans, much more invested in entrenched legacies and established traditions – or convinced that Karl Marx was correct that economic determinism and social forces render the great man less crucial – defined it based on a person's linear achievements and fame.

Helen Gould did not have this perspective in mind when she evaluated her father's legacy. "Change," that is, was not a factor in her calculations. Jay Gould, his daughter reckoned, was a great man because he had led a Bible-bound life and, without fanfare, distributed his wealth to other noble causes. She had assessed his worth based on a little-known legacy of doing good work rather than making aspirational change. This might have sold in Europe. But along American lines, this fine work could purchase fame, not greatness. The heiress might have come to understand the disconnect a little better after learning something about her own recognition as a public figure. One report in 1901 concluded that she and George Washington held the highest

---

[21] For a deeper discussion and these quotations, see Paul K. Longmore, *The Invention of George Washington* (Charlottesville, VA: University of Virginia Press, 1999), 184–211, esp. 201 and 207.

[22] See Pauline Maier, "Revolution and Change in America," in *The American Revolution: A Heritage of Change*, eds. John Parker and Carol Urness (Minneapolis, MN: Association of the James Ford Bell Library, 1965), 114.

status among American schoolgirls. This, however, was how the tabulations were presented: "The greatness of Washington and the wealth of Miss Gould come first."[23]

***

Henry MacCracken's Hall of Fame was meant to be distinctively American. He found the European models very "faulty." By this, MacCracken suggested that none was very democratic or broadminded about who ought to be enshrined as a "Great Man." England's Westminster Abbey dwelled too much in the past and "chiefly magnifies kings and a church that was king-ridden for many centuries." His research of the London site suggested that the British provided minimal space to saints and that a "Statesmen's Corner" and "Poets' Corner" in the north and south transepts were insufficient to honor nonregal English citizens.[24]

MacCracken held misgivings about the other European shrines. He determined that the French Panthéon was too unstable, usurped by various governments and uneven in its contents. In Germany, the Ruhmeshalle in Munich and the Walhalla in Regensburg were well-conceived ideas but ended up unfinished and "too monarchical and also too militaristic."[25] MacCracken also disapproved of an earlier American institution. In 1864, the Capitol in Washington, DC, repurposed a vacant space to serve as a Statuary Hall. No one was of one mind on how to go about this project. Politicians fought over who ought to be included. Snobbish observers marveled over the ensuing hodgepodge of variously sized and unrelated figures in the undignified shrine known to its critics as the "Chamber of Horrors."

The Hall of Fame of Great Americans (Figure 1.3) became an altogether grand spatial project. Seeing as it was her own philanthropic investment, Helen Gould desired an open granite structure supported by columns instead of walls so that visitors would keep the Gould Memorial Library in clear view. The original plan for the colonnade measured 500 feet. Owing to MacCracken's ambition and the potential slate of future inductees, the length was extended another 130 feet. The extra spacing was due to a recalculation, to ensure that a total of 150 bronze busts of great Americans could comfortably fit in the hall.

---

[23] Catherine L. Dodd, "The Ideals of the American School-Girl," *Living Age*, August 10, 1901, 340.
[24] Johnson, *Your Hall of Fame*, 1–2.
[25] Ibid., 2.

FIGURE 1.3 The stately Hall of Fame of Great Americans was meant to be a testament to American greatness. Courtesy of Library of Congress Prints and Photographs.

MacCracken established several other rules to help along his uniquely American experiment. He encouraged anyone to submit candidates for the first enshrinement class. MacCracken placed three qualifications on nominees. First, only the deceased were eligible, and had to have been dead for at least ten years since "no man should be counted surely great until his life is ended."[26] The decade-since-death statute was also a very helpful device to shield NYU from engaging with the precariousness of Jay Gould's candidacy on the pilot election. Second, each entrant had to be American born. Interested parties immediately understood that this disqualified the Caribbean-born Alexander Hamilton, an adopted son of New York. One frustrated Manhattanite described that rule as an unbecoming "littleness" of NYU's election system.[27] Third, a candidate needed to fall within one of the following broad categories, including a final catch-all type:

[26] MacCracken, *The Hall of Fame*, 21.
[27] Edward Saunders, "A Statue of Alexander Hamilton," *The Sun*, August 17, 1900, 6.

Authors and editors; businessmen; educators, inventors, missionaries and explorers; philanthropists and reformers; preachers and theologians; scientists; engineers and architects; lawyers and judges; musicians, painters and sculptors; physicians and surgeons; rulers and statemen; soldiers and sailors; distinguished men and women outside the above classes.

MacCracken stipulated no further parameters on how to measure "greatness" apart from "fame." His advisors encouraged the Hall of Fame's founder to establish a rubric to guide voters on how to decide on the merits of prospective candidates, but MacCracken eschewed that pressure to apply pseudo-quantitative metrics. He judged that the impulse to impose a set of standards on greatness had doomed the prior European incarnations. It's what rendered the British far too rigid, believed MacCracken, about casting all writers in a Shakespearean shadow. It narrowed much too much how the French rated their statesmen and generals based on their levels of anticlericalism. MacCracken savored an openmindedness that he liked to frame around America's founders and earliest writers. These were iconoclasts who had a knack for redefining the molds of greatness, whether established in the United States or abroad. Rather than dictate the terms of qualifications and reduce greatness into a rigid formula, MacCracken left the matter in the hands of his election system since he defined fame as the "opinion of the wise in regard to great men accepted and held by the multitude of the people."[28] Critics charged that MacCracken had missed an opportunity to define greatness on behalf of Americans. MacCracken countered that what he had done was in the spirit of American democracy and left it as an open-ended experiment. The people, then, would be the most helpful resource in both honoring and disrupting past conceptions of greatness in America's Hall of Fame. Today, the NYU Hall of Fame of Great Americans is a mostly abandoned shrine but MacCracken's decision to keep "greatness" malleable has informed American culture for more than a hundred years.

Those multitudes and their opinions required a scrupulous vetting process. In toto, NYU's governing senate received about a thousand unique submissions. A candidate advanced to the next round by virtue of a nomination and a second by a member of that body. Much ado was made over the nomination card submitted by Caroline Frye, the wife of a longtime senator from Maine. Frye furnished a roster of fifty respectable people to grace MacCracken's so-called "Temple of Fame." Her first

---

[28] MacCracken, *Hall of Fame*, 292.

choices were Martha and George Washington, the God-fearing, in her estimation, founders of the United States. She excluded – and urged others to follow her lead – anyone associated with Jefferson Davis, Robert E. Lee, or the other "heretics" of the Civil War. The outspoken Frye explained her rationale on this was also theological, again in her view: "I would say that no man or woman should be given a niche in this worthy temple whose work has tended to destroy faith and trust in the higher life held out by religion."[29]

However, Frye did not convince NYU's senate. It advanced 234 candidates for a final round, the Washingtons and General Lee among that esteemed group. The decisive decision was placed at the discretion of one hundred electors. Each of the then-forty-five states had a representative on the panel. Almost half were university presidents or historians.

The terms at this juncture of the election were straightforward: any nominee included on at least half of the ballots made it into the Hall of Fame. If there was too much agreement on the ballots, then priority for the inaugural list would be reserved for the top fifty vote-getters. Some complained that the system was a fix. A writer in North Carolina alleged that MacCracken's slate of judges was "strictly northern," even though twenty electors hailed from Southern states. Nonetheless, complained this journalist, most of the appointed judges have "never heard a word perhaps of the truly great men of southern birth."[30]

In October 1900, MacCracken announced that the discriminating electors had elevated just twenty-nine great men to the Hall of Fame. To those who might have been discouraged by the small number (the judges were permitted to elect fifty great people), MacCracken announced that "no harm has resulted from this, but rather great gain."[31] Withal, journalists attested that "public interest in the matter has been keen."[32] Most of this group predeceased the Civil War, owing to NYU's rule that candidates must have died ten years prior as well as the premium placed on the Revolution's heroes. George Washington was the only unanimous decision; Abraham Lincoln, Daniel Webster, and Benjamin Franklin trailed just behind. A Louisiana chief justice, Francis Nicholls, was the lone elector who withheld a vote from Lincoln and Webster.

[29] "Mrs. Frye Picks Immortals," *Chicago Tribune*, April 9, 1900, 8.
[30] "The New York Education Standard," *Wilmington Messenger*, August 19, 1900, 2.
[31] Henry Mitchell MacCracken, *The Hall of Fame* (New York: G. P. Putnam's Sons, 1901), 23.
[32] "The Hall of Fame," *Youth's Companion*, November 15, 1900, 74.

The class included other statesmen and generals like Jefferson and Grant. It was comprised of authors such as Emerson, Hawthorne, and Longfellow. It was graced by preachers including Jonathan Edwards and Henry Ward Beecher. The group made room for inventors such as Eli Whitney as well as Jay Gould's favorite, Samuel Morse. "It is doubtful if any period but ours," praised New York Senator Chauncy Depew, "the great statesman, writer or artist ranked with the soldier."[33] Depew sat on the dais alongside Henry MacCracken and Helen Gould at the Hall of Fame induction ceremony on Memorial Day of 1901.

On the whole, observers celebrated the inaugural cohort, believing that it kept to a high standard and rebuffed claims from Europe that "we are a vainglorious people, unduly puffed up by our achievements."[34] Some were not fully satisfied. Women's organizations were disappointed that Martha Washington, appearing on just 14 percent of ballots, underperformed in the vote, and she led all other worthy women candidates.

Many more were indignant that the electors had chosen Robert E. Lee. The Confederate hero owed the victory to the fact that eighteen of twenty Southern judges selected him, as did two-thirds of electors based in the so-called "middle" and "western" states. That tally compensated for a poor showing for Lee among the twenty-two judges settled throughout New England. Many pundits above the Mason–Dixon Line were "disgusted." In line with columns of letters to the *New York Times*, one writer posited that Lee's election upended the whole attempt to identify "great Americans" since the Confederate general "did his utmost to destroy American nationality."[35]

The inclusion of General Lee brought to bear MacCracken's fraught equating of fame and greatness. Northerners might admit that Lee was a great military tactician; Lee, however, possessed no fame; he was infamous. The North's outcry against Lee was more than just about lingering hostilities concerning the Civil War. What was at stake in his candidacy to the Hall of Fame was central to the American conception of greatness. No one disputed that Lee was a decorated soldier and a standout tactician during the Mexican–American War. Lee also enjoyed familial status, hailing from the Lees who were at one point the largest landholders in Virginia. Lee, then, held an outstanding pedigree

---

[33] "Hall of Fame Dedicated," *New York Times*, May 31, 1901, 3.
[34] "Names for the Hall of Fame," *Brooklyn Eagle*, October 11, 1900, 4.
[35] R. J. H., "That Hall of Fame," *New York Times*, October 21, 1900, 21.

and a noble profession. In Europe, they sculpted statues of Lee's type and arranged for them to stand beside many others just like him in Westminster Abbey. To Northerners who measured greatness by way of "change," however, Robert E. Lee was the antithesis of a great change-maker. He was a champion of the status quo.

Americans also disagreed whether Lee could be construed as a symbolic exemplar. "No man," warned the detractors, "should be held up as a pattern or model for the young to follow who was not true to his country in her direst distress."[36] His supporters, some among the Unionists, pleaded that Lee had "acted on his honest conviction" and then dutifully abided by the terms of the Confederate's surrender.[37] He was a sincere and honorable man. In Baltimore, the *Sun*'s editorial board evaluated Lee's life and compared him to the nation's most aspirational and "Ideal American":

In some of his personal characteristics, in his unselfish patriotism and self-sacrificing devotion to his cause, in his qualities as a military commander, Lee perhaps approaches more nearly to the august character of Washington than any other American. As a military commander he was Washington's superior. Whether he would have measured up to him as a statesman can never be known, because in this he was never tested. But these two great and good men seem always associated together.[38]

No one seceded.[39] Most Americans reportedly "settled down" and "adjusted" to the "list adopted," even if they found it preposterous to compare Lee with Washington.[40] The brief text that accompanied Lee's enshrinement did not hide his generalship of the South in Civil War, but focused on his scholarly contributions as a "superintendent of the West Point Military Academy" and later as "president of Washington College, now called Washington and Lee University."[41] Surely, these biographical points, implicitly linking the legacies of Lee and Washington, were more forward-thinking and aspirational; items that Americans at a university-sponsored Hall of Fame could get behind. Despite a late appeal by the Association of Survivors of the Sixth Army Corps to change its decision, the NYU Senate ruled on merit, that Lee advanced soldiering and battle strategies. Those who suggested that it

---

[36] Henry S. Allen, "Lee and the Hall of Fame," *New York Times*, October 21, 1900, 21.
[37] G. M., "Lee's Claim to Fame," *New York Times*, October 28, 1900, 19.
[38] "An Ideal American," *Baltimore Sun*, January 19, 1901, 4.
[39] "The Thrusting of Greatness," *Life*, November 15, 1900, 383.
[40] "Precedence in the Hall of Fame," *New York Times*, November 17, 1900, 787.
[41] Johnson, *Your Hall of Fame*, 175.

was treason rather than conviction and independent thinking that motivated Lee's decision to resign from the Union had missed the point, implied NYU, of American greatness.[42] Journalists detected a "gradual change of feeling" among "those whose attitude toward it was more or less scornful."[43] The catalog of the men enshrined embossed a renewed self-confidence in American greatness, even if the commentary around the Hall of Fame had failed, albeit intentionally, to pinpoint exactly how to define that greatness, its compatibility with fame, or how it compared with the attributes of Europe's leading wise men.

***

The results of the Hall of Fame vote alerted some to the currency of greatness. Americans had anticipated that their statesmen – Washington, Franklin, and Jefferson – could rival the legacies of England's and France's ruling classes. They were unsure whether their New England writers could rise, as well. The snobbiest Europeans regarded the work of the so-called Fireside Poets as too simple, relying on ordinary conventions of meter and rhyme. This style made it easier for young children to memorize. The Fireside Poets were America's most well-known Transcendentalists, part of a movement that sought out the goodness in people and the world around them. Boston was the hub of it all. New England had raised Ralph Waldo Emerson, Nathaniel Hawthorne, and Henry Wadsworth Longfellow.

Europeans were not the only critics of the Fireside Poets. A new generation of American writers detached from New England wondered whether this group merited so much attention. These women and men lived in cities and witnessed squalid conditions and unfair treatment of immigrant people who could not trace their heritage back to the Boston Brahmins. They questioned their forebears' grasp of the realities of American life. Yet, the novelist Ellen Glasgow recalled how she and other young writers understood the Fireside Poets' formative place in America at the close of the nineteenth century. The new age of women and men of letters no longer wrote in the same style, nor did the up-and-comers share the "ever-green optimism" of Emerson or Hawthorne. Yet, there was no denying the Fireside Poets' contributions: "They were important, and they knew it, but they were also as affable as royalty; and no one who valued manners could help liking them. Life had been easy for them,

---

[42] "Robert E. Lee's Name to Remain," *Washington Post*, December 14, 1900, 1.
[43] "The Hall of Fame," *Home Journal*, October 18, 1900, 3.

and literature had been easier. They had created both the literature of America and the literary renown that embalmed it."[44]

It was not just reverence that furnished these men into Hall of Famers. The Fireside Poets emerged just after the Founding Fathers had departed and transformed that patriotic heritage into memorable verse. Hence, Longfellow's famous poem opens: "Listen my children, and you shall hear,/Of the midnight ride of Paul Revere."[45] Walt Whitman, who rarely agreed with the Fireside Poets, neither in form nor perspective, was still very grateful for their efforts to transition "greatness" from statesmen to writers: "Of all nations the United States with veins full of poetical stuff most needs poets and will doubtless have the greatest and use them the greatest. Their Presidents shall not be their common referee so much as their poets shall."[46]

The Hall of Fame's addition of the Manhattan-native Washington Irving, of *Rip Van Winkle* renown, to this group convinced Americans that their kind fared much better than Europe's ranks, so much so that "its members do not seem natural products of an American environment."[47] To the contrary, even as American poets departed from the earlier stylings, they recognized that the Fireside Poets had created a new genre of verse that had come to represent an era of patriotism. It was through a simpler form that their writings conveyed a passionate spirit of American domestic life, romanticized the tranquility of the indigenous landscape, unencumbered by the messiness of layers of past civilizations. The type is captured in Longfellow's ode, "To The River Charles." He wrote: "Thou hast taught me, Silent River!/Many a lesson, deep and long;/Thou hast been a generous giver;/I can give thee but a song."

This was Henry MacCracken's goal. His Hall of Fame of Great Americans was meant to "represent the wisdom of the American people."[48] What that wisdom taught MacCracken, through trial and error, was that fame was not the same as greatness. The Hall of Fame's judges elevated individuals who made something of themselves due to

---

[44] Ellen Glasgow, *The Woman Within: An Autobiography*, ed. Pamela R. Matthews (Charlottesville, VA: University Press of Virginia, 1954), 139.
[45] On the reception of Longfellow's "Paul Revere's Ride," see David Hackett Fischer, *Paul Revere's Ride* (New York: Oxford University Press, 1994), 331–33.
[46] Leo Marx, *The Americanness of Walt Whitman* (Boston: D. C. Heath and Company, 1960), 51.
[47] "Precedence in the Hall of Fame," 787.
[48] Henry Mitchell MacCracken, "The Hall of Fame," *American Monthly Review of Reviews* 22 (November 1900): 563.

an acquired and learned genius that was not inherently bequeathed to them by their parents or grandparents. They parlayed their talents to make change, not merely to accrue fame. Helen Gould figured that it was enough that her father had obtained status and fame – his rivals called it infamy – rather than inherit it. Yet, Jay Gould never received the requisite number of votes to enter the Hall of Fame. Few aspired to be like Gould because he wasn't enough of a changemaker.

***

Sir Francis Galton (Figure 1.4) held the opposite view of American greatness. He doubted whether there was any sort of greatness, a term he associated with "genius," residing in the United States. Galton much preferred to seek out greatness in the more formalized and stable arena of status, a term that the British favored over the Americans' "fame." The English-born Galton was Charles Darwin's distant cousin and, as the pioneering proponent of eugenics, took his relative's ideas about evolution to a rather pernicious extreme. Galton's research on heredity did much to advance statistics as a formal academic discipline. In time, his

FIGURE 1.4 A profile image of Sir Francis Galton from 1886. Galton was the inspiration for the eugenics movement that flourished in Europe and, to a certain extent in the United States. American opposition to Galton's theories spurred deeper thinking about "changemakers" and "greatness." Courtesy of Bettmann/Getty Images.

efforts on behalf of eugenics informed Nazism. Galton wrote about a "utopian" world – at least, in his view – in which world leaders prevented people with undesirable features (Galton called them "idiots and imbeciles") from procreating.

Many of Galton's theories were packed into his book, *Hereditary Genius*. In it, Galton shared his research of hundreds of biographies and family histories of "illustrious men," judges and statesmen who had flourished from 1660 to 1868. These were individuals of an esteemed pedigree and status who Galton deemed had achieved significant "eminence." The author showed that most of these men held lineal connection to other eminent men – "men of Literature and of Science, Poets, Painters, and Musicians" – and were therefore predisposed to acquire most of Europe's greatness. Or in Galton's words, a "high reputation," that is social class, "is a pretty accurate test of high ability."[49]

Galton's tome received mixed reviews when it first appeared, but it earned high praise from Galton's most famous relation. "I do not think I ever in all my life read anything more original," wrote Darwin to Galton. "And how well and clearly you put every point!"[50] By the 1880s, Galton's research had become mainstream. In 1886, the Royal Society awarded him a gold medal for his work on biological statistics. Upon accepting the prize, Galton, ever consistent in his thinking, told the audience that his personal contribution to the field was predictable from a scientific vantage point. "On my father's side I know of many most striking, some truly comic, instances of statistical proclivity." On his maternal side of the genetic ledger, Galton opined that "there is a similarity between the form of the bent of my mind and that of my mother's father, Dr. Erasmus Darwin."[51]

More adoration from his British climes followed. Toward the end of Galton's life, into the first decade of the twentieth century, George Bernard Shaw resolved that "nothing but a eugenic religion can save our civilisation." The chemist Alice Vickery also took Galton at full depth, although the women's rights activist prayed that "in the future the question of population will, I hope, be considered very much from the feminine point of view."[52]

---

[49] See Francis Galton, *Hereditary Genius: An Inquiry into Its Laws and Consequences* (London: Macmillan and Co., 1869), 2–3.
[50] Karl Pearson, *The Life, Letters and Labours of Francis Galton*, vol. 1 (Cambridge: Cambridge University Press, 1914), 6.
[51] See Martin Brookes, *Extreme Measures: The Dark Visions and Bright Ideas of Francis Galton* (New York: Bloomsbury, 2004), 236.
[52] Ibid., 272–73.

Galton, then, was a very influential person and his dim view of American greatness on a scientific basis was an indicator of larger trends of thinking. In his research of hereditary genius, Galton had ruled out including Americans in his sample. The prospects of their achievements were limited by biology. "The North American people has been bred from the most restless and combative class of Europe," determined Galton. "Whenever, during the last ten or twelve generations, a political or religious party has suffered defeat, its prominent members, whether they were the best, or only the noisiest, have been apt to emigrate to America, as a refuge from persecution."[53] The American stock were a genetically restless group of iconoclasts who had, in Galton's view, happily removed themselves from the possibility of crossbreeding with the upper classes of Europe. The departure of these women and men had helped preserve the most eminent strands of European genetics. This also explained the American Revolution as a byproduct of this high concentration of rabble-rousers rather than any noble cause for change set in motion by wise or creative people:

Every head of an emigrant family brought with him a restless character, and a spirit apt to rebel. If we estimate the moral nature of Americans from their present social state, we shall find it to be just what we might have expected from such a parentage. They are enterprising, defiant, and touchy; impatient of authority; furious politicians; very tolerant of fraud and violence; possessing much high and generous spirit, and some true religious feeling, but strongly addicted to cant.[54]

Galton repeated this theory in *Hereditary Genius*. Compared with his evolutionarily enhanced Britain, averred Galton, "America most certainly does not beat us in first-class works of literature, philosophy, or art." Galton could never take Longfellow and the Fireside Poets, the artistic exemplars of MacCracken's first Hall of Fame class, very seriously. Galton was predisposed to think less of these American men of letters because they were made of lesser stuff. Without genetic material to advance the life of the mind, the American people could not, no matter how hard they worked at it, produce men of eminence. This meant that Americans were surprisingly wise to import art and literature from Europe. Galton, who never did travel to the United States, suggested that America was a cultural backwater, still very much an intellectual vassal state of England. He therefore offered a supportive

---

[53] Francis Galton, "Hereditary Talent and Character," *Macmillan's Magazine* 12 (August 1865): 325.
[54] Ibid.

half-truth: "The higher kind of books, even of the most modern date, read in America, are principally the work of Englishmen."[55]

Some historians write about a cross-continental "Eugenic Atlantic."[56] However, Galton was initially far better received in England and Germany: these were nations that boasted deep traditions and fixed elite classes. Perhaps the very best example of this synergy was Galton's best student and the longtime holder of the Galton Chair of Eugenics at University College London, Carl Pearson. Pearson, who had studied math at the University of Heidelberg, so embraced German culture that he changed the spelling of his first name to "Karl." He had followers in the United States, but Americans by and large rejected Galton's deep belief in the lineal transmission of greatness. Instead, Americans preferred the "Great Man Theory" put forward by so-called liberals such as the British-born James Froude and Scot Thomas Carlyle. Both men wrote histories that, in Froude's words, appealed to those who tended to "an extravagant worship of great men."[57] Both historians allowed for the contingencies of history to shape their heroes – "the outward shape of whom," wrote Carlyle, "will depend on the time and the environment he finds himself in."[58]

The "Great Man" fascination found deep roots among American writers, inspiring a spate of consideration on how their indigenous environment, rather than a prodigious bloodline, begot eminence. This idea occupied, for instance, the writings of Ralph Waldo Emerson and Walt Whitman.[59] William James was perhaps the last in that generation of nineteenth-century American commentators who took up a pen to argue in favor of the acquisition of greatness over an innate disposition for it. In 1880, James – a Harvard man who laid significant groundwork in the fields on philosophy, religion, and psychology – defended American ingenuity against Herbert Spencer and other British Darwinists who had refused to believe that greatness might "spring from the soil, like a Mahomet or Franklin." Spencer had coined the phrase "survival of

---

[55] Ibid., 40.
[56] See David Mitchell and Sharon Snyder, "The Eugenic Atlantic: Race, Disability, and the Making of an International Eugenic Science, 1800–1945," *Disability and Society* 18 (December 2003): 843–64.
[57] J. A. Froude, "Introduction," in *The Hundred Greatest Men*, vol. 7 (London: Sampson Low, Marston, Searle, and Rivington, 1880), v.
[58] Thomas Carlyle, *On Heroes, Hero-Worship, and the Heroic in History* (London: Chapman and Hall, 1840), 137.
[59] See, for example, Gay Wilson Allen, *A Reader's Guide to Walt Whitman* (Syracuse, NY: Syracuse University Press, 1970), 120.

the fittest" and whose writings convinced Charles Darwin to accept the tenets of Social Darwinism.[60] James could not accept that certain classes of people were fated for fame and greatness while most others were marked for mere mediocrity:

> The mutations of societies, then, from generation to generation, are in the main due directly or indirectly to the acts or the example of individuals whose genius was so adapted to the receptivities of the moment, or whose accidental position of authority was so critical, that they became ferments, initiators of movement, setters of precedent or fashion, centres of corruption, or destroyers of other persons ... Societies of men are just like individuals, in that both at any given moment offer ambiguous potentialities of development. Whether a young man enters business or the ministry may depend on a decision which has to be made before a certain day.[61]

James was right to fear the migration of Galton's and Spencer's ideas to the United States. In 1882, Spencer, unwell at the time, traveled to America to vacation on the advice of physicians. He salubriously tried to keep a low profile, but the press and others hounded him. To mollify his public, Spencer shared a thought, a backhanded compliment of sorts, with them: that because of America's "heterogeneity" – that is, the mixing of classes – it would likely be a "long time in evolving its ultimate form." Still, Spencer had full confidence that society would stratify to help form an "Aryan race" and that "America may reasonably look forward to a time when they will have produced a civilization grander than any the world has known."[62]

That view was far more positive than anything Galton had previously advised. That warmed Spencer to America's social upper crust – men desirous of "status." Andrew Carnegie "became his intimate friend." Fellow robber barons, John D. Rockefeller and James J. Hill, routinely justified their wealth and power on the grounds that they were proof of Spencer's logic, namely, "survival of the fittest."[63] None of these men, each of whom was raised in humble means, recognized that according to Spencer (himself, ironically, derived from an unremarkable stock) cast significant doubt that people born into their non-elite predicaments

---

[60] Carl N. Degler, *In Search of Human Nature: The Decline and Revival of Darwinism in American Social Thought* (New York: Oxford University Press, 1991), 11.
[61] William James, "Great Men, Great Thoughts, and the Environment," *Atlantic Monthly* 46 (October 1880): 446.
[62] Herbert Spencer, "The Americans," *Contemporary Review* 43 (January 1883): 7.
[63] See Richard Hofstadter, *Social Darwinism in American Thought* (Philadelphia: University of Pennsylvania Press, 1944), 44–45.

could rise up to a very high social station. This, however, was not lost on William Graham Sumner of Yale who, according to historian Richard Hofstadter, spent a career in the social sciences writing and teaching that the "principles of social evolution negated the traditional American ideology of equality and natural rights."[64] Sumner chose Galton over American Whiggism. Others did, as well. By 1915, reported Hofstadter, eugenics in the US had "reached the dimensions of a fad."[65]

Sumner had likeminded colleagues at America's other leading universities. In 1913 at Columbia, President Nicholas Murray Butler dispatched Edward Thorndike to tell a large audience in Morningside Heights that "there are hereditary bonds by which one kind of intellect or character rather than another is produced. Selective breeding can alter a man's capacity to learn to keep sane, to cherish justice or to be happy."[66] A psychologist at Harvard, unmoved by his colleague, William James's warnings, allowed that "we have good evidence that different races possess it in widely different degrees; that races differ in intellectual stature, just as they differ in physical stature."[67] Nearby, an MIT professor, Frederick Adams Woods, declared that "History is really but a branch of biology" – and hoped aloud that mathematics and the "other sciences" could soon make similar important contributions to the study of eugenics.[68] That banter had severe consequences. It tended to fuel talk and political action toward immigration restrictions and, what was the world's first sterilization legislation, served as the intellectual scaffolding behind a law passed by the governor of Indiana in 1907 that banned procreation for the "confirmed criminals, idiots, imbeciles and rapists."[69]

Probably most of America's leading minds were not in accord and preferred a competing school that Brown University's Lester Ward described as "Intellectual Egalitarianism." Ward had Francis Galton and Herbert Spencer in mind when he defended the "lower classes

---

[64] Ibid., 59.
[65] Ibid., 161.
[66] Edward L. Thorndike, "Eugenics: With Special Refence to Intellect and Character," *Popular Science Monthly* 83 (August 1913): 130.
[67] See Degler, *In Search of Human Nature*, 50.
[68] Frederick Adams Woods, *Mental and Moral Hereditary in Royalty: A Statistical Study in History and Psychology* (New York: Henry Holt and Company, 1906), iv.
[69] See Mark H. Haller, *Eugenics: Hereditarian Attitudes in American Thought* (New Brunswick, NJ: Rutgers University Press, 1963), 40–57. See also Wendy Klein, "Eugenics in the United States," in *The Oxford Handbook of the History of Eugenics*, eds. Alison Bashford and Philippa Levine (Oxford: Oxford University Press, 2010), 511–22.

of society" who were the "intellectual equals of the upper classes."[70] A goodly number called William Graham Sumner's circle to task, for a lifelong attempt to "fit the facts" of their elitist theories.[71] Perhaps the most outspoken was William James, that nemesis of Herbert Spencer, who regretted that a stream of Social Darwinism had gained a foothold in the New World, as well as the "entire modern deification of survival *per se.*" James surmised that the language recycled so much by the Wall Street elites was "surely the strangest intellectual stopping-place ever proposed by one man to another."[72]

Henry MacCracken's Hall of Fame of Great Americans (Figure 1.5) positioned itself in James's camp. In a souvenir volume that honored the Hall of Fame's founding, MacCracken republished a remark by journalist Talcott Williams that expressed awe that among the first class "only six or seven had any advantages of life." Williams happily

FIGURE 1.5 Henry Mitchell MacCracken, chancellor of New York University and founder of NYU's Hall of Fame of Great Americans. Courtesy of Library of Congress Prints and Photographs Division.

[70] Lester F. Ward, *Applied Sociology: A Treatise on the Conscious Improvement of Society by Society* (Boston: Ginn and Company, 1906), 95.
[71] See Haller, *Eugenics*, 70.
[72] William James, "Clifford's Lectures and Essays," *The Nation*, November 6, 1879, 313.

explained that MacCracken's shrine countered Francis Galton's theories and suggested that, based on the early voting results, in the United States "average ability finds its path more open, its opportunity easier, and its career more visible from the start."[73]

MacCracken and his circle celebrated the contingencies of history and the opportunities afforded to free people to do great things. In essence, MacCracken's novel institution was proof that America provided freedom to make change. In all probability, MacCracken was either amused or bemused if he had read a paper published by Frederick Adams Woods that studied the lineage of members of NYU's Hall of Fame (as of 1910) to show that a "careful analysis of our own history speaks no less strongly for the inherited nature of exceptional ability."[74] Woods documented familial networks of elites in the United States that involved members of the Hall of Fame of Great Americans. Encouraged by Spencer's hope for American-style Aryanism, Wood's research was meant to correct Galton's dismissiveness of homegrown greatness in the United States. It was frankly shoddy research that stretched the limits of biology to make a case for eugenics. The findings would have horrified William James. To most observers, the Hall of Fame of Great Americans had demonstrated just the opposite.

**

The litmus test for MacCracken's Hall of Fame experiment was Edgar Allan Poe. Poe operated in a literary arena dominated by the Fireside Poets. Through the output of this New England group, the canon of American poetry centered on the freedoms and liberties offered to the common man. Poe challenged that presentation with shades of darkness and experiences with death – themes later associated with a "Gothic" tone. He anticipated literary figures such as Walt Whitman and later Robert Frost, who adopted a much more sober – far "lonelier" – stance to the American experience. In challenging the status quo, Poe emerged as a renegade and, to some people's estimation, an un-American writer. His detractors used his muddled biography to deepen the argument against Poe, assigning to him all the wrong kinds of fame – infamy, that is – rather than singling him out for signaling a new epoch of literary originality.

---

[73] MacCracken, *The Hall of Fame*, 287–88.
[74] Frederick Adams Woods, "Heredity and the Hall of Fame," *Popular Science Monthly* 82 (May 1913): 446.

The result was an understandable tension. Poe stood out as a genius and bona fide changemaker. His best work was full of pessimism. His rhythm was both hypnotic and uneven. Poe offered America a very different sound. Later writers, eager to pull away from the conventional and patriotic prose of the Fireside Poets, looked to Poe as a lodestar counterexample. The sea change started ten years before MacCracken's Hall of Fame invention. Much aware of the state of affairs, a sufficient number of Hall of Fame judges blocked Poe, believing that his complicated personal life – or what was said about it – was far too pernicious and unwholesome for entry into the sacred place of "Great Americans." Unlike Robert E. Lee, Poe lacked the European-type lineal pedigree and Washington-like generalship to instantly overcome his other "failings."

The ban on Poe suggested an interesting relationship between fame and greatness. Henry MacCracken had instructed his judges to stingily pluck the great people from the larger pool of famous individuals. The decision to block Edgar Allan Poe indicated that fame, no matter its depreciated value at the dawn of the modern era, was a discrete nonnegotiable prerequisite for greatness. Fame wasn't the same as greatness, though, as MacCracken had hoped his Hall of Fame would prove. Poe could be otherwise great. Yet, his candidacy for NYU's Hall of Fame was just a nonstarter due to the infamy that had supposedly surrounded his personal life. A historical figure required at least a modicum of fame to prove themselves admirable, if not aspirational. Men such as Poe who could not manufacture fame had no business vying for a more precious commodity like greatness.

The ballots were a referendum on this point. Poe accumulated just thirty-eight votes in the inaugural Hall of Fame election. He collected affirmative nods from thirteen of twenty electors based in the South and seven of thirteen among those settled in the western sections of the United States. The regionalism seemed to confirm a "sectional" prejudice that had haunted MacCracken's Hall of Fame project. Skeptics wondered aloud whether Poe had been a casualty of bias that strongly favored the New England school of writers who had preferred a conventional meter and rhyming scheme that tended to solidly nurture American ideas. Of course, the Fireside Poets – Henry Wadsworth Longfellow, William Cullen Bryant, John Greenleaf Whittier, and James Russell Lowell – held strong ties to New England and wrote in a very accessible manner, often to mythologize America's founding, glorify its scenery, and rail against the wickedness of Southern slavery.

Poe was none of that. While he was Boston-born, Poe was a nonconformist and eschewed the indigenous impulse to romanticize the

American experience. Stately men such as Longfellow and Lowell adorned their faces with sagacious beards. Poe's portraits evoked a more troubled person, displaying the "ravage made by a vexed spirit within."[75] His choice of a mustache rather than a beard betokened his rejection of conventions. The supposed experts swept up with the reasonings of phrenology – that is, the association of the cranium with mental abilities – pointed out the "pronounced irregular" halves of Poe's face and the "inordinate expansion above the regions of the temple."[76]

Neither form nor style united Poe with the New Englanders. In 1827, Poe published his first collection of poems under the pseudonymous authorship of "a Bostonian." No one believed that the work read anything like someone from that New England tradition. Poe centered his work too much on death and a "broken heart" rather than love. He was an iconoclast, much preferring the company of scientists and free-thinking heretics than the typical American scholar that abided by the wholesome transcendentalist order of Unitarianism.[77] His comportment and social calendar placed him outside of the Puritan-bred elites. For all these reasons, Poe was better identified as a Baltimore-native, and therefore a Southerner.

Hence the assumptions that undergirded his failed first candidacy for MacCracken's Hall of Fame. Poe's most ardent defenders couldn't understand it. By 1900, more than a third of Americans lived in urban areas and had little use for Emerson's (eighty-seven votes) or Hawthorne's (seventy-three votes) idyllic descriptions of America's green landscapes.[78] The popular writers at the turn of the century pointed their interest to the wonders of technology and the social challenges of city dwelling. Poe was a forerunner to their work. But just eighteen of forty-six Yankee electors backed him. Still, the exclusion of Poe in the vote for the first NYU Hall of Fame class was deemed less egregious than other snubs. Most angry pundits reserved their rancor to protest the ineligibility of Alexander Hamilton or the dearth of female representation.[79] Some still spoke out. For instance, Poe's rejection

---

[75] E. C. Stedman, "Edgar Allan Poe," *Scribner's Monthly* 2 (May 1880): 108.
[76] Oliver Leigh, *Edgar Allan Poe: The Man, the Master, the Martyr* (Chicago: The Frank M. Morris Co., 1906), 4, 14.
[77] See John Tresch, *The Reason for the Darkness of the Night: Edgar Allan Poe and the Forging of American Science* (New York: Farrar, Straus and Giroux, 2021).
[78] See Larzer Ziff, *The American 1890s: Life and Times of a Lost Generation* (Lincoln, NE: University of Nebraska Press, 1966), 3–23.
[79] "The First Thirty," *The Sun*, October 14, 1900, 6.

infuriated a woman in San Francisco who decried America's "failure to appreciate him extraordinary, sinister, and disastrous."[80]

That he merited consideration should have been beyond question. Five and a half decades prior, Poe had published "The Raven," setting off a wave of interest in the poet and his verse. "The Raven" was a narrative poem, telling of a talking bird and a rhythmic adventure into the decline of a distraught lover's fragile psyche. The appearance of "The Raven" prompted publications of collections of Poe's works, earning him a very high station among America's literary class. It was perhaps an even greater smash among the British, likely to the chagrin of eugenicists such as Francis Galton. "Your 'Raven' has produced a sensation, a 'fit of horror,' here in England," reported the English poet Elizabeth Barrett to Poe. "Some of my friends are taken by the fear of it and some by the music. I hear of persons haunted by the 'Nevermore.'"[81] His raised reputation in England earned Poe significant European-style status but it did not translate into an American type of fame.

Edgar Allan Poe's fallout from American fame has a significant backstory. Poe's life was tragic. He was born in 1809 to a pair of middling actors. His father abandoned his mother when Edgar was an infant. Poe's mother died shortly thereafter, and the child was taken in by a wealthy foster family that sometimes indulged their charge and at other times abused him. Poe remained markedly unstable. First, he dropped out of the University of Virginia. Then, he abandoned his studies at West Point. Poe had little prospects. He was estranged from his foster family. He was a submediocre and indebted gambler. He was driven to alcohol, an addiction that made Poe an unreliable magazine writer and undependable romantic suitor. By twenty-two, Edgar Allan Poe moved to Baltimore to live with his aunt, Maria Clemm, his cousin, and brother Henry. Some six months later, Henry died – the result of ill health due to alcoholism. Some likely thought Henry Poe's troubles foretold a similar fate in store for his beleaguered brother.

Poe's personal life languished but he gained a following as a poet and prose writer. Never successful with romance, Poe married his cousin, Virginia Eliza Clemm, in 1836, when she was just thirteen years old. Poe's reputation rose but was again derailed by personal anguish (Figure 1.6). Virginia contracted tuberculosis and suffered through a

---

[80] Kate W. Beaver, "Poe and the Hall of Fame," *Dial*, January 1, 1901, 8.
[81] See Dale H. West, "Poe's Early Reception in England" (MA Thesis, University of Southern California, 1955), 17–18.

FIGURE 1.6 This daguerreotype rendering of Edgar Allan Poe by W. S. Hartshorn in 1848 is representative of the misanthropic depictions of Poe at the end of the poet's life and afterward. Courtesy of Library of Congress Prints and Photographs Division.

protracted period of illness during the couple's eleven years of marriage. Their ordeal inspired well-received work, including "The Raven," published in 1845. "No single poem," wrote one British literary figure, "ever had greater success in America."[82] Poe recognized that he had struck on something with that poem, and that it was "generally [the] most known" in his portfolio.[83] Poe also distinguished himself as an incisive critic.[84] No less a figure than James Russell Lowell envied Poe's "analytic power." Lowell, who admitted that he often found Poe's reviews of New England's Fireside Poets far too acerbic, still had to admit that "Mr. Poe is at once the most discriminating, philosophical, and fearless critic upon imaginative works who has written in America."[85]

That should have made Poe into a Hall of Famer. He was a recognized great writer and challenged America's men of letters to change. Yet, he never acquired the prerequisite levels of fame. To the contrary, infamy

[82] James Hannay, *The Poetical Works of Edgar Allan Poe, of America* (London: Addey & Co., 1856), 48.
[83] Edgar A. Poe, "The Philosophy of Composition," *Graham's Magazine* 28 (April 1846): 163.
[84] See Killis Campbell, "Contemporary Opinion of Poe," *Publications of Modern Language Association* 36 (June 1921): 142–66.
[85] James Russell Lowell, "Edgar Allan Poe," *Graham's Magazine* 27 (February 1845): 49.

buried him as an insincere misanthrope. This had much to do with his first biographer: the poet and anthologist, Rufus Griswold. Griswold had first entangled himself with Poe's American legacy in 1841. He had solicited Poe to submit several poems for a volume that desired to canonize a "national literature." Poe had happily submitted "The Coliseum," "The Haunted Palace," and "The Sleeper" for inclusion into Griswold's *Poets and Poetry of America*. In print, Poe had feted Griswold's book, expressing full agreement that the publication refuted accusations that Americans had "been forced to make rail-roads" and that the distraction with that busyness "deemed [it] impossible that we should make verse."[86] Privately, however, Poe had told women and men in his circle that he had despised Griswold's project and took umbrage with a number of the anthologist's selections that Poe believed misrepresented the very best of American literature.

Griswold learned of Poe's sharp criticism and wrongly assumed that Poe was the author of an unsigned review printed in a Philadelphia journal that prayed the anthology would become "forgotten" and that its editor might "sink into oblivion." Poe no doubt influenced the opinion of the true author, an acquaintance of his. Enraged and emboldened to mangle America's memory of Poe, Griswold took vengeance, a mission made possible because Griswold was appointed Poe's literary executor. "Poe was not my friend—I was not his—and he had no right to devolve upon me this duty of editing his works," complained Griswold about this odd responsibility.[87] Griswold nonetheless accepted the role. He recognized that control of Poe's estate provided him with a stranglehold on Poe's posthumous chances to accrue fame.[88]

Poe's mysterious death on October 7, 1849, enabled his foe to go to work. Griswold committed his first assault on Poe's reputation under the protection of an alias. Writing pseudonymously as "Ludwig," Griswold announced Poe's demise in the pages of a well-circulated New York newspaper. He heartlessly predicted that, regarding Poe's death, the "announcement will startle many, but few will be grieved by it." Poe, alleged Griswold, "had few or no friends," and was far better received abroad ("had readers in England, and in several of the

---

[86] Edgar A. Poe, "Griswold's American Poetry," *Boston Miscellany of Literature and Fashion* 2 (November 1842): 218.

[87] See Jeffrey A. Savoye, "The Works of the Late Edgar Allan Poe: Poe's Legacy and Griswold's Authority," *Edgar Allan Poe Review* 20 (Spring 2019): 5.

[88] See Burton R. Pollin, "A Posthumous Assessment: The 1849–1850 Periodical Press Response to Edgar Allan Poe," *American Periodicals* 2 (Fall 1992): 6–50.

states in Continental Europe").[89] In his lifetime, rumors had circulated about Poe's penchant for drinking and erratic courtship of leading ladies of letters such as Sarah Helen Whitman and Frances Sargent Osgood. Griswold had also pursued a romantic relationship with Osgood and this likely contributed to his antipathy for Poe. Griswold made no mention or substantiations of Poe's bad behavior but also refrained from suggesting anything very positive about his personal traits. This contrasted with the reports from Poe's native Baltimore. There, newspapermen wrote that "Mr. Poe is said to have been a man of polished manners, fine colloquial powers, warm and amiable impulses, and of a high and sometimes haughty spirit."[90]

Rufus Griswold did much more damage in the "Memoir of the Author" chapter he included in a collection of Poe's literary criticisms, a chance afforded to him by the rather unwise decision to make him the executor of Poe's oeuvre. He seized his chance to embellish the rumors that had for a while surrounded Poe and elevate them to "facts." In this and a series of other biographical entries, Griswold "tampered with the correspondence entrusted to him" and committed "forgeries" to annihilate Poe's status among American readers.[91] He maliciously altered letters from Poe's friends and published the doctored versions to suggest that Poe liked to "drink till [his] senses are lost."[92] Griswold attested to personal conversations with the dead poet that purported confessions that Poe had plagiarized from Henry Wadsworth Longfellow and forged quotations from Poe that let on a fervent desire to "be successful with the mob," "create a monthly sensation," and "play havoc."[93]

Griswold's influence was immediate. Poe's meager fame was transformed into a surfeit of infamy. Northerners compared him to General Lee, a pair that no school children should aspire to become. Those closest to Poe were unsure how to respond. His mother-in-law was "nearly sunk" by Griswold's portrayal. Griswold, after all, purportedly provided documentary evidence to support the character assassination. She and others spent their lives "bewildered" and silent on the scandal.[94]

---

[89] Ludwig, "Death of Edgar A. Poe," *New York Tribune*, October 9, 1849, 2.
[90] "Death of Edgar A. Poe," *Baltimore Patriot*, October 9, 1849, 2.
[91] Arthur Hobson Quinn, *Edgar Allan Poe: A Critical Biography* (New York: D. Appleton-Century Company, 1942), viii.
[92] Ibid., 229, n.14.
[93] Ibid., 282.
[94] See James M. Hutchisson, *Poe* (Jackson, MS: University Press of Mississippi, 2005), 252–53.

It became hard to detach Poe from his work. Griswold had linked Poe's tragic personal circumstances with the dreariness of his writings that stood out against the backdrop of other American writers such as, say, Nathaniel Hawthorne, whose works supplied ample measures of happiness and hopefulness.[95]

The few literary men who remained Poe's champions sought to decouple his sad life from his impassioned writing: "And we would wish to shut him up in the tomb, as he is, and think alone of his books."[96] Another supporter offered much of the same, explaining that a division between Poe's life and letters would make it plain that the man had "evinced far more originality than any of his contemporaries."[97] Theirs was an attempt to argue for great men, regardless of their attainment of fame or fitness of their personal dealings. Yet, the dissonance between Poe's work and his image appeared inauthentic to most observers involved in weighing the dead poet's greatness.

Just a sparse number sought to outright defend Poe from the harshness of Griswold's biographical descriptions. These people understood that redeeming Poe's personal life was key to remediating his aspirational form of greatness. The most important was Sarah Helen Whitman, who published a tract to vindicate Poe against Griswold and refuted some of the more sensational accusations that involved her own relationship with the deceased. Whitman resented that so many histories of Poe had been "based on the narrative of Dr. Griswold, a narrative notoriously deficient in the great essentials of candor and authenticity."[98] Yet, Whitman's defense of Poe and work to restore the personal notoriety he had achieved with "The Raven" did not stymie the opposition.

The dominant position on Poe in the 1850s was that his was a "melancholy history, but it is not without its lessons, which rightfully regarded, may prove salutary to the young, the impulsive, and the gifted."[99] In other words, Poe held something to impart to future generations. The pessimism and reminders of Poe's critiques of Fireside Poets such as Longfellow and other "acknowledged chiefs of poetry and fiction," revised the impression of Poe's impact, leaving some to misremember the facts and state that "in the Eastern States, his personal qualities,

---

[95] Eugene Benson, "Poe and Hawthorne," *Galaxy* 6 (December 1868): 742.
[96] "Edgar Allan Poe," *United States Magazine and Democrat Review* 28 (February 1851): 162.
[97] "The Life and Poetry of Edgar Poe," *Littell's Living Age* 37 (April 16, 1853): 157.
[98] Sarah Helen Whitman, *Edgar Poe and His Critics* (New York: Rudd & Carleton, 1860), 14.
[99] "Literary Notices," *Knickerbocker* 36 (October 1850): 372.

carried into his literary productions, have hitherto limited the number both of his friends and admirers."[100] Others piled on further, supposing, based on Griswold's uncharitable characterizations, that Poe might have desired to send his young wife to a "premature grave" to gain inspiration and write his poems about a forlorn widower.[101]

Poe's American infamy dropped him even deeper from the ranks of greatness. Some suggested the very worst in Poe, claiming that Griswold had done Poe a favor by excising some of his worst traits. "A truthful delineation of his career," wrote another biographer without supporting facts or details, "would give a darker hue to his character than it has received from any of his biographers."[102] Others dubbed him a "Mad Man of Letters."[103] Another dared to describe "The Raven" as the "weird fancies of a brain distempered by wild fits of drinking."[104] This was the lowest point in the American reception of Poe. His biography had overtaken his oeuvre, demoting his most well-known writing to a rant of scribbles. Griswold and his caustic descendants had dropped Poe to the ranks of a madman.

Overseas was different. The spokesman for the British publisher Routledge revealed that his company sold 29,000 copies of Poe's volumes in 1887, at least threefold more than any other American writer on its book roster.[105] Europeans lamented "poor Edgar" when asked about the sorry state of appreciation he had garnered among Americans.[106] That he was valued in Europe only helped prove Poe's utter unworthiness in the United States.

* * *

Two more members of the Fireside Poets entered the Hall of Fame in 1905. The electors cast fifty-nine votes for James Russell Lowell and fifty-three for John Greenleaf Whittier. Edgar Allan Poe received forty-two votes in that second election. He was still rated more infamous

---

[100] "Edgar Allan Poe," *North American Review* 83 (October 1856): 427, 442.
[101] See Alice L. Cooke, "The Popular Conception of Edgar Allan Poe from 1850 to 1890," *Studies in English* 22 (1942): 147–48.
[102] "Memoir of Edgar Allan Poe," in *The Poetical Works of Edgar Allan Poe* (New York: W. J. Widdleton, 1866), xiii.
[103] "A Mad Man of Letters," *Scribner's Monthly* 10 (October 1875): 690–99.
[104] William Minto, "Edgar Allan Poe," *Fortnightly Review*, July 1, 1880, 69.
[105] Thomas Nelson Page, "Authorship in the South before the War," *Lippincott's Monthly Magazine* 44 (July 1889): 113.
[106] James Hannay, "Life and Genius of Edgar Allan Poe," in *The Poetical Works of Edgar Allan Poe, of America*, xxv.

than famous among a sizable portion of the judges. George Washburn of Robert College admitted that he could not countenance Poe and his "madness."[107] Arthur Hadley of Yale canvassed his colleagues and found that those who had rejected Poe were among the cluster of "practical" men who placed reputation above an appreciation for literature.[108] Hadley's survey revealed that fame was still a prerequisite to greatness. Current events did not help Poe find new sources of fame. The Temperance Movement was on the rise and therefore an inopportune moment for Poe, owing to his work's inextricable association with his personal proclivities.[109] The literary-minded judges such as the poet, Edmund Clarence Stedman, were "quite taken aback" that his fellow electors had once again rejected Poe.[110]

Henry MacCracken interpreted the Poe affair as a blemish on his Hall of Fame experiment. The discussion around Poe's nomination invested too much capital in a depreciated commodity like fame and, in effect, separated it from that scarce commodity known as greatness. MacCracken sought to fix that. His aim was to show that fame and greatness were still one and the same. Poe had failed to gain admission into the Hall of Fame because he was deficient as a great man. He told the newspapers that the majority decision to withhold Poe "should not be ascribed to the defects of the poet's moral nature, but to the lack of sincerity in his poetry."[111] As MacCracken had pitched it, Poe's unworthiness for entry into the Hall of Fame of Great Americans was due to a dearth of greatness, not fame. MacCracken did not elaborate on what he meant by "sincere," but it no doubt had something to do with Poe's lack of devotion to the presentation of America that was so evidently punctuated in the Fireside Poets' letters.

The Baltimore-area press took umbrage at MacCracken's assessment. The *Baltimore Sun* called it "colossal stupidity" and, to let the writing speak for itself, pledged to published instances of Poe's poetry for a full week.[112] "In saying this," offered the editor of the *Washington Post*

---

[107] "Electors of the Hall of Fame Give their Estimates of Poe," *New York Times*, January 17, 1909, SM1.
[108] Ibid.
[109] See W. G. "Five Years More May See Edgar Allan Poe Elected," *New York Times*, October 22, 1905, SM5; and "The Holy Willies," *Nashville American*, September 19, 1907, 6.
[110] Edmund Clarence Stedman, "Poe, Copper and the Hall of Fame," *North American Review*, August 16, 1907, 804.
[111] "'Nevermore' for Poe," *Boston Globe*, October 10, 1905, 2.
[112] See "Gems from Edgar Allan Poe," *Baltimore Sun*, October 16, 1905, 4; and "Poe's Rejection Scored," *Baltimore Sun*, October 11, 1905, 7.

about MacCracken's screed, "the Chancellor has, it is to be feared, written himself down an ass, as well as a malicious and biased critic unacquainted with the first principles of literary criticism."[113] MacCracken doubled down on his evaluation, believing that a fuller explanation for his criticism of Poe would mollify the opposition:

> The American people has not yet come to the stage when it prefers form to substance, and many are inclined to believe that Poe is attitudinizing in regard to "Annabel Lee." Judged by Milton's criterion, that poetry should be simple, sensuous and passionate, Poe's poetry has the first two qualities, but it is lacking in the third. Poe's poetry possesses the necessary simplicity of form to be easily understood, and the rhythm and picture-making qualities meant by Milton's "sensuous," but it does not suggest the wide range of feelings, nor does it give one the impression that Poe felt any very deeply. This is my idea why he has not been elected.[114]

That backfired. Poe's defenders read MacCracken's reasoning as a rehearsal of the "stock criticism of the poet's New England detractors."[115] MacCracken had conflated "greatness" and "fame" and made a mess of the deliberations. Others agreed that MacCracken gave voice to the Hall of Fame's supposed regionalism, paying no mind to the other side who liked to point out Robert E. Lee's membership to the pantheon of "Great Americans." Poe supporters described the ordeal as the "venom of sectional prejudice" and denounced the culprits as "stuck-up New England pettifoggers."[116] They described this group as fully out of touch with Poe's reputation abroad, which therefore tended to tarnish the Hall of Fame, they surmised, much more than Poe's reputation. "He is our only world-writer," cried one pundit, "and everybody outside of America knows it."[117] The message was clear: fame could no longer be a prerequisite for greatness if America wished to avoid becoming a cultural laughing stock.

Poe was finally inducted in 1910. His better fortune was due principally to the significant turnover among the judges. NYU replaced sixteen electors, including Grover Cleveland and other Poe detractors. A journalist polled the new voters and found that "several of them are great admirers of Poe."[118] He had now acquired the intangible amount of

---

[113] "Excluded from the Hall of Fame," *Washington Post*, October 11, 1905, 6.
[114] "Edgar Allan Poe and the Hall of Fame," *Current Literature* 39 (December 1905): 613.
[115] "Poe's Critic," *Baltimore Sun*, October 11, 1905, 4.
[116] See "Edgar Allan Poe and the Hall of Fame," *Current Literature* 39 (December 1905): 613; and Douglas Anderson, "Information Wanted," *New York Sun*, October 22, 1905, 8.
[117] Sydney C. Haley, "Poe Again," *New York Sun*, January 20, 1906, 6.
[118] "Poe Favorite Now for Hall of Fame," *New York Times*, February 12, 1910, 8.

fame to move forward. Poe dominated the press coverage, a situation that accrued him even higher levels of fame. A letter-writer in the pages of the *New York Times* lobbied for Poe based on European status: France and England admire Poe, so should America.[119] Another newspaper conducted a popular vote for the "purpose of aiding the electors of the Hall of Fame." Among the rank and file, Poe received more votes than the next two candidates – William Cullen Bryant and Patrick Henry – combined.[120] It was by now the general feeling that MacCracken's testament to American greatness would be a "vulgarian Hall of Fame" without Edgar Allan Poe.[121]

The Hall of Fame elected Poe, but not with a fervor that equaled the popular vote. The newly eligible Harriet Beecher Stowe topped all candidates with seventy-four votes. Poe came in second, tied at 69 votes with Oliver Wendell Holmes.[122] What is more, Poe scored lowest among the judges sorted as "publicists, editors and authors."

The episode proved to Poe's supporters that MacCracken's Hall of Fame had overvalued "fame" at the expense of "greatness." The men who had blocked Poe desired a great individual to have lived an aspirational fame-fit life. His defenders flouted that formulation. The *Washington Post* greeted the Hall of Fame's decision with a headline: "Poe Is Now Famous."[123] The *Baltimore Sun* took the jest a step farther: "Poe Is Famous at Last."[124] The fallout of the Poe affair sharpened Americans' attention to the relationship between "fame" and "greatness." It was apparent that these were not interchangeable terms, nor did these cultural commodities need correlation. At times, as with Edgar Allan Poe, the two qualities had nothing to do with one another. It was possible to be a great person but possess meager traces of fame. Likewise, an individual could have accumulated much fame but possessed no claim whatsoever to greatness. In its early history, the Hall of Fame of Great Americans of New York University reinforced the need to invest much more in the changemakers whose achievements were most often measured in something described as "greatness."

---

[119] Malcolm French, "Poe for the Hall of Fame," *New York Times*, August 6, 1910, BR9.
[120] See coverage of the *New York World* poll in "The Hall of Fame," *Washington Post*, May 23, 1910, 6.
[121] "Books and Men: Some Reminiscences of Richard Watson Gilder," *The Forum* 43 (January 1910): 73.
[122] "Poe Gets a Place in Hall of Fame," *New York Times*, October 22, 1910, 1.
[123] "Poe Is Now Famous," *Washington Post*, October 22, 1910, 1.
[124] "Poe Is Famous at Last," *Baltimore Sun*, October 22, 1910, 2.

2

The Problem of the Great All-Knowing Answer Man

In November 1930, the English author G. K. Chesterton told a crowd at Canisius College in Buffalo about "one of the most surprising idiosyncrasies of American life." The students and faculty of the Catholic college assembled to award Chesterton an honorary doctorate. The local bishop, Father William Turner, was on hand to confer the degree. The pious people of Buffalo were eager to receive the noted writer's impressions of their climes, and how they differed from Britain. Chesterton seized on a particular form of American hubris. "Men and women who have achieved eminence in one field feel themselves fully qualified to be leaders in other unrelated ones."[1] He called out three men who had, in Chesterton's estimation, overstepped the boundaries of their expertise: "Henry Ford, Albert Einstein and Thomas Edison should not go about the country giving their opinions and setting themselves as experts on subjects with which they are entirely unfamiliar."[2]

Edison and Ford ranked among the most popular men in America. The social thinker Max Weber would have called them charismatic man, possessed of a "certain quality" that "by virtue of which [they are] set apart from ordinary men and treated as endowed with supernatural, superhuman, or at least specifically exceptional powers or qualities."[3] Edison and Ford leveraged that high perch to opine, whether solicited or not, like "little tin gods on pretty much every question."[4] Just as

---

[1] "Chesterton Assails Ford and Edison," *Boston Globe*, November 20, 1930, 6.
[2] Ibid.
[3] Max Weber, *The Theory of Social and Economic Organization*, ed. Talcott Parsons (Glencoe, IL: The Free Press, 1947), 358–59.
[4] "Thoughts of an About-to-Be-Convert," *Catholic World*, April 1927, 745.

today, America looked toward its most well-known people for guidance. This was especially so for the famously great. It's been a tradition in the United States that achievement of greatness in one field translates, however supernaturally, to a rare sort of intuition to provide solutions to complex problems in unrelated areas. Men such as Edison and Ford certainly subscribed to this inscrutable skill.

Einstein was different, and it was probably unfair to include him in the same rebuke of Edison and Ford. First, he was German, not American. In contemporary times, if it happens that European-born individuals exhibit this uncanny trait, it's because, most assuredly, they were endowed by or learned about these psychic powers from friends in the United States. A hundred years ago, most of Europe's elites didn't yet believe in such things.

Second, Einstein, in truth, agreed with Chesterton. He, too, considered it a rather unbecoming trait for great men who had excelled in one area of learning and achievement to trespass into other arenas of expertise. "There actually exists a grotesque contrast," wrote Einstein about the "exaggerated respect" accorded to him in the United States, "between what of capability and accomplishment people accredit to me, and what I really am."[5]

Third, Einstein's overreach was a matter of opinion. Chesterton placed the scientist in his crosshairs because of a well-disseminated column that had originated in America's foremost newspaper. Einstein's article about "cosmic religion" in the *New York Times* sought to reconcile the predictable rhythm of science with a God and a Bible full of miracles that, purportedly, from time to time, destabilized that scientific order of things.[6] Chesterton and other religious traditionalists charged that Einstein had overstepped, that he was unprepared to speak about theology, even as the issues at hand related to the scientific realm. Rev. Fulton Sheen, for instance, told 1,200 listeners at the Catholics Teachers Association that Einstein's religion was full of "stupidity and nonsense." Rev. Sheen went on to explain, "because Einstein knows a great deal about mathematical physics it doesn't follow that he knows about religion."[7] Einstein's defenders claimed that a great scientist had just as much a right to consider the chasms of science and religion as a master theologian. Einstein was

---

[5] Albert Einstein, "Prof. Einstein Divulges What He Thinks about Us," *Los Angeles Times*, March 29, 1931, B13.
[6] Albert Einstein, "Religion and Science," *New York Times*, November 9, 1930, SM1.
[7] "Assails Einstein's Views on Religion," *New York Times*, November 16, 1930, N1.

certainly more expert than, say, the politician William Jennings Bryan or the lawyer Clarence Darrow, the two major dueling figures who argued about the merits of teaching scientific evolution versus religion-aligned creationism in the relatively recent Scopes Trial.

None of this mattered to rank-and-file Americans. To them, Einstein was an all-knowing answer man. Take, for example, an irritating encounter that took place en route to California Institute of Technology (Cal Tech). On December 11, 1930, Albert Einstein, accompanied by his wife, Elsa, arrived in New York (Figure 2.1). It had been just three weeks since Chesterton had blasted Einstein for, to paraphrase, "giving opinions on subjects with which he was entirely unfamiliar." That wasn't his intention. After his ship docked, Einstein reluctantly allowed a fifteen-minute interview to a fleet of a hundred reporters and photographers. The newsmen asked Einstein to summarize his scientific theories in a single sentence, to which the Noble Laureate demurred. He had no crisp way to pithily express his research on time, gravity, and the warping of space. Instead, Einstein, evincing more than a modicum of impatience, told the press that "it would take me three days to give a short definition of relativity." Then the reporters peppered him with questions about religion, prohibition, and his opinion about an upstart political figure in Germany named Adolf Hitler. To these lesser complex queries, Einstein responded, and with a lightheartedness that, he hoped, would mask his unease about fielding questions on topics far afield from his specialization.

The quarter-hour session elapsed, and Einstein called an end to the "nightmare." Yet several reporters would not halt. The annoyed Einstein upbraided them, castigating them for volleying questions that went far beyond his expertise, veering into the "eccentric."[8] In his private diary, Einstein declared that the experience was altogether "asinine."[9] To the public, however, Einstein had surrendered to the Americans' wide-ranging expectations of greatness, exposing him to the harsh accusations hurled at him from agitators such as G. K. Chesterton. To more forgiving Americans, Einstein had provided them what they had wanted from great men.

The German-Jewish physicist was among a small elite group of men whose solutions to scientific problems had raised them to all-knowing

---

[8] "Einstein on Arrival Braves Limelight for only 15 Minutes," *New York Times*, December 12, 1930, 1.
[9] Walter Isaacson, *Einstein: His Life and Universe* (New York: Simon & Schuster, 2007), 369.

FIGURE 2.1 On December 11, 1930, Albert Einstein looks out a window on S. S. *Belgenland* upon arrival at Pier 59 in New York. Courtesy of Bettmann/Getty Images.

answer men. Americans looked up to these individuals – Thomas Edison and Henry Ford, most notably – to solve political and social issues. The public cared deeply about their opinions. But what happened when their great men did not possess all the answers posed to them? What about the times in which their opinions in areas truly beyond their learned expertise were perceived as faulty or ignobly unpopular? How invulnerable were these rare all-knowing answer men, far more redeemable (save, perhaps for Ford) than, say, Edgar Allan Poe or Robert E. Lee, and to what lengths did Americans go to preserve their greatness?

***

On April 10, 1878, a New York newspaper designated Thomas Edison the "Wizard of Menlo Park."[10] The appellation and its wide reception certified Edison's place among a small circle of scientists. Some scientists had dismissed Edison as a hack.[11] They were unimpressed that the self-educated and self-made inventor had by that time registered about 120 patents. Their insults vanished with the approval of Patent No. 200,521. With that, the US Patent Office provided Edison with sole ownership of the "phonograph" or "speaking machine," an invention that "recorded in permanent characters the human voice and other sounds." The scientific community had to close ranks. They marveled over Edison's application of a diaphragm device to create vibrating waves that could reproduce a "human voice or other sounds." Edison's rival, the Scottish-born Alexander Graham Bell, improved upon the phonograph but it was Edison who was credited for the invention that in essence created the music industry.

The phonograph transformed Thomas Edison into a great man. In assessing the invention and its inventor, Joseph Henry of the Smithsonian Institute dubbed Edison the "greatest genius not only of this age, but of any age."[12] In 1892, Edison's first biographers recalled Henry's adulation and recast it as the final sentence in their "first complete and authentic story of [Edison's] life."[13] By then, Edison had created the incandescent lamp, a feat that convinced the balance of the scientific

---

[10] Edmund Morris, *Edison* (New York: Random House, 2019), 551.
[11] Jonathan Hughes, *The Vital Few: The Entrepreneur and American Economic Progress* (New York: Oxford University Press, 1986), 177.
[12] "A Visit to Edison," *Boston Globe*, May 24, 1878, 2.
[13] W. K. L. Dickson and Antonia Dickson, *The Life and Inventions of Thomas Alva Edison* (New York: Thomas Y. Crowell & Co., 1892), 362.

community that Henry and his other admirers had not oversold Edison's greatness. Many of these men lived in cities illuminated by "light plants" that made their own work brighter and Edison much wealthier.

Thomas Edison was the "famous American magician."[14] His genius was "many-sidedness," an improvement, perhaps on the original American renaissance man, Benjamin Franklin.[15] Just about everyone in the United States believed that Edison could solve anything, much to the surprise of Europeans. Part of the resistance in Europe was that Edison was also a businessman. Scientists, so it was believed on the Continent, were not supposed to profit from their work. In 1865, Napoleon III asked Louis Pasteur why he hadn't sought financial gains for his discoveries. Pasteur answered that an embrace of the commercialization of science would have "lowered himself by doing so."[16] In the United States, that Edison had amassed wealth was a testament to the broadness of his work. George Bernard Shaw, who had briefly worked for the Edison Telephone Company in London, recollected that the Americans who traveled to England to install the city's first telephone lines "adored Mr. Edison as the greatest man of all time in every possible department of science, art and philosophy."[17] What Shaw observed could also be gleaned from the pages of *Scientific American*. After his invention of the phonograph, the editors feted Edison, "one of the wonders of the world." The magazine ranked him above his European counterparts because Edison, in very American terms, deigned to effect change: "While Huxley, Tyndall, Spencer and other theorists talk and speculate, [Edison] produces accomplished facts, and with his marvelous inventions is pushing the whole world ahead in its march to the highest civilization."[18]

In the United States, newspapers ran columns and interviews seeking "advice from the greatest inventor in the world."[19] The mathematician Charles Steinmetz "consider[ed] Edison today as the man best informed in all fields of human knowledge."[20] Human knowledge covered quite a lot. Edison was "invited to comment for the public on

---

[14] "The Greatest Inventor in the World," *Man's Magazine*, April 1, 1908, 112.
[15] See Nian-Sheng Huang, *Benjamin Franklin in American Thought and Culture, 1790–1990* (Philadelphia: American Philosophical Society, 1994), 154.
[16] Matthew Josephson, *Edison: A Biography* (New York: McGraw-Hill, 1959), 336.
[17] George Bernard Shaw, *The Irrational Knot* (London: Constable, 1905), ix–xi.
[18] Quoted in Hughes, *The Vital Few*, 174.
[19] "Edison Talks about Patents," *Courier-Journal*, December 26, 1897, B2.
[20] "To Thomas Alva Edison," *Saturday Evening Post*, October 17, 1914, 1.

almost every topic of current interest, and without hesitation," surmised Edison's biographer, Matthew Josephson. Edison was not at all reticent about weighing in on a variety of subjects: Josephson's list included "family, modern woman, clothing, diet, medicine, on the vice of cigarette smoking, on education, war, religion, progress, and the future of science."[21]

No one minded Edison's near-limitless range of self-designated expertise until a journalist, Edward Marshall, asked the great inventor to talk about God. Marshall was at that moment a young and unseasoned reporter in Rochester under a good deal of pressure to write stories that could hold public interest. On a whim he wrote to Edison. Marshall filled a single page with seventeen questions about the implications of electricity. "We take the liberty of burdening you with these questions," concluded the precocious Marshall to Edison, "because you are one of the great authorities on electricity."[22] Above Marshall's typed letter, Edison scribbled instructions for his secretary to turn away the journalist on the grounds that "I do not like to go into future possibilities just at present."[23]

Edison eventually warmed to Marshall. The change had to do with Marshall's personal misfortune, a run of bad luck that, counterintuitively, increased his professional success. In 1898, the newspaper publisher William Randolph Hearst dispatched Marshall to cover Theodore Roosevelt's Rough Riders regiment in Cuba. There, a bullet struck Marshall's spine. The injury paralyzed him. Marshall wrote about the ordeal for the press, and upon his return to New York, published the first book-length account of Roosevelt's famed corps. Marshall had a knack for near-death experiences. He later survived three train wrecks, a boating disaster, and a torpedo attack from a German U-boat during World War I. All these escapes bolstered Marshall's acclaim and the genuineness of his reporting.[24] During a calmer portion of his career, Marshall authored books and penned columns at his home in New Brunswick, not all that far from Edison's residence. In New Jersey, Marshall, now one of the more well-known elites in the neighborhood, befriended Edison. Marshall was, in Mina Edison's words, "one of the few men to whom

---

[21] Matthew Josephson, *Edison: A Biography* (New York: McGraw-Hill, 1959), 434–35.
[22] Edward Marshall to Thomas A. Edison, February 26, 1896, Letter D9604-AAS, The Thomas A. Edison Papers Digital Collection [hereafter, TAEP Digital Collection], Rutgers University, New Brunswick, NJ.
[23] Ibid.
[24] "Edward Marshall Dies; Noted Writer," *New York Times*, February 26, 1933, F26.

the laboratory door was always open."[25] The now famous journalist routinely reported on the inventor's patents and ventures.

In October 1910, Edward Marshall asked Thomas Edison to discuss the eternality of the soul. It was a most unusual conversation, inspired by curious circumstances. Marshall drew the idea from rumors circling that William James of Harvard, who had died earlier that year, had communicated from beyond the grave with his friend Rev. Fredric Wiggin in Brookline, Massachusetts.[26] Marshall raised the issue while the pair sat in Edison's laboratory. "I cannot believe in the immortality of the soul," Edison told Marshall.

Edison closed his eyes to ponder Marshall's next question about the afterlife.

"Heaven?" asked Edison. "Shall I, if I am good and earn reward, go to heaven when I do? No—no. I am not—I am not an individual—I am an aggregate of cells, as for instance, New York City is an aggregate of individuals. Will New York City go to heaven?"[27]

Marshall was stunned. That Edison did not believe in a "merciful and loving Creator" placed him in a tiny minority of Americans. It was not until 1944 that George Gallup or anyone else started to poll people in their views of God. Gallup asked American respondents "Do you believe in God?" Just 1 percent of those polled answered "no."[28] Before then, it was a virtually uncontested opinion that "Americans believe in God."[29] But Edison was an iconoclast.

Edison sensed that Marshall was waiting for him to proceed with the discussion. He raised his head from his desk. Edison pitched his vision above Marshall, to look at nothing in particular. "I do not think we are individuals at all," said Edison with a slowness that suggested a deep meditation. "The illustration I have used is good. We are not individuals any more than a great city is an individual." Edison blamed people's desire to "go on living," even beyond death. "Personally I cannot see any use of a future life," he concluded.[30]

---

[25] "Edward Marshall, Writer, Is Eulogized," *New York Times*, February 28, 1933, 19.
[26] "His 'Spirit' Talks," *Washington Post*, September 5, 1910, 1.
[27] Edward Marshall, "'No Immortality of the Soul,' Says Thomas A. Edison," *New York Times*, October 2, 1910, SM1.
[28] Frank Newport, *God Is Alive and Well: The Future of Religion in America* (New York: Gallup Press, 2012), 9.
[29] J. L. Spalding, *Religion, Agnosticism and Education* (Chicago: A.C. McClurg & Co., 1903), 134.
[30] The descriptions and quotations of the interview are all derived from Marshall, "No Immortality of the Soul," SM1.

"But the soul!" Marshall protested.

"Soul? Soul? What do you mean by a soul? The brain?" countered Edison. For the sake of argument, Marshall acquiesced. "Call it the brain, or what is in the brain. Is there not something immortal of or in the human brain—the human mind?"

"Absolutely no!" thundered Edison. "There is no more reason to believe that any human brain will be immortal than there is to think that one of my phonographic cylinders will be immortal."

The discussion moved circularly. Marshall asked about the afterlife in terms of God and procreation. Each time, Edison analogized Marshall's question to the atoms that composed Manhattan or one of his 700 inventions. The common denominator was that Edison refused to endow humankind with religious meaning unknown to science.

"Shall we, in the course of time, discover life's actual source?" asked an exasperated Marshall.

Edison digressed with another imperfect analogy. Marshall, still trying hard to be differential, halted Edison's response. "Shall we ever really solve the problems of our What and Why?"

"I'll be darned if I know," replied Edison.

Marshall published the interview in the *New York Times*. It appeared on the front page of the newspaper's prominent Sunday magazine and immediately tested the limits of the all-knowing answer man. Some described it as "the most interesting article I've ever read."[31] Marshall surmised that "during the last ten years no newspaper interview has, I think, created so far reaching a sensation among thinkers."[32]

The bulk of the reaction was outrage. Some reevaluated the terms of the all-knowing answer man and decided to deny a great American that limitless range of expertise. Rev. Charles Aked ascended his pulpit at Fifth Avenue Baptist Church to tell his parishioners that Edison was an "intellectual anarchist." Anarchist, as we'll see with Henry Ford, was a useful term to dislodge the accused individual from the American mainstream (Figure 2.2). The cleric's goal was to narrow the scope of Edison's greatness. There was no denying the inventor's contributions to technological advancement. He was, in this respect, a very great man. Father Aked, like so many others, had to admit to Henry Ford's confession that "wherever

---

[31] Adele Malette, "Soul Is the Brain," *New York Times*, October 9, 1910, SM6.
[32] Edward Marshall, "Wizard with Amazing Powers Astounds Scientist," *New York Times*, November 13, 1910, SM1.

FIGURE 2.2 Henry Ford and Thomas Edison admired each other and had much in common as all-knowing answer men. Courtesy of Library of Congress Prints and Photographs Division.

civilization exists, there also is Edison."[33] Aked acknowledged Edison's significant contributions. "He has given the world the phonograph and other very useful things," admitted Aked.

Father Aked stopped far short of Ford's assessment that Edison's inventions rendered him "our greatest American."[34] His accomplishments, the clergyman argued, certainly did not provide Edison the standing to speak on areas beyond his scientific expertise, no matter how frequently he had encroached on these matters in the past. "What has he ever done to entitle him to be heard as an authority on the human spirit and its relation to God? Because a man has achieved some great thing in one branch of endeavor it does not entitle him to be heard as an authority in an entirely different one."[35] This, though, was precisely the assumption that Americans made about their great men. Until his assault on organized religion, Edison was held as an authority on all kinds of subjects for which he did not claim a patent. The key

---

[33] See Albert Lee, *Henry Ford and the Jews* (New York: Stein and Day, 1980), 152.
[34] Ibid.
[35] "Dr. Aked Derides Edison's Theory," *New York Times*, October 17, 1910, 7.

difference was that now Edison's position on God was decidedly at odds with most everyone else in the United States.

His detractors took different stances on why Edison was forbidden to trespass on theological terrain. One approach was that Edison was insufficiently learned in the areas of religion or in the nascent field of psychology, the area of science that, purportedly, had the most to say about the supernatural and the human psyche. They all agreed that Edison's expertise needed to be curbed.

In Chicago, the Bible scholar George Robinson of McCormick Theological Seminary agreed with Aked, describing Edison's "inability to appreciate immortal life" as "most pathetic." His rationale matched Rev. Aked's: "Mr. Edison may be a great specialist in electricity, but he certainly is not up to date in religion or even in psychology."[36] The pious psychologist William Thomson, whose book Edison offhandedly cited in his discussion with Edward Marshall, denied that his scholarship on the "Brain and Personality" supported Edison's conclusions about the soul. "Mr. Edison's view is unscientific," asserted Thomson. He therefore had no standing to opine. "The fact that he is prominent in one branch of science," said Thomson of Edison, "does not entitle him to pass on other branches of science. He is very unscientific when he speaks of the human brain." That Edison deigned to weigh in on the subject, concluded Thomson, suggested, in his own expert opinion, that the inventor was "abnormal, if not pathological."[37]

Others were more forgiving of Edison's encroachment. One theologian supposed that Edison was embarrassed by his comments and that he must have uttered them because "somebody worked him into a frenzy."[38] The Archbishop of Baltimore blamed it all on Edison's inventiveness. Cardinal James Gibbons figured that Edison's thinking had become too mechanical to effectively ponder metaphysical matters. "He has maimed his own mind," commiserated the pontiff, "just as Darwin did, by a too one-sided exercise of its powers."[39]

Some replied directly to Edison. Concerned Americans sent him reading lists and composed poetry meant to reorient Edison to a godlier track and reinstate his multidiscipline expertise. Edison's response to his

---

[36] "Clergy to Edison: Future Life Sure," *Chicago Tribune*, December 1, 1910, 1.
[37] "Author of 'Brain and Personality' Replies to Edison," *New York Times*, October 9, 1910, SM6.
[38] "Clergy to Edison," *Chicago Tribune*, December 1, 1910, 1.
[39] "Mr. Edison's Views, from a Symposium in the Columbia Magazine," *Bible Student and Teacher* 14 (April 1911): 216.

interlocuters was uneven. To some, he wrote that "I have not time just now to go into it."[40] To others, he argued that he had not rejected God, just heaven. This was inferred by the interviewer, Edward Marshall. "There is no such denial," claimed Edison, "what you call God I call Nature, the Supreme Intelligence that rules matter."[41] "They say I am an atheist," defended Edison in newspaper interviews. "Well, I am not, never have been, never said I was. Those people who have called me one, have not read what I said." Edison was just as confident about his superior understanding of God, compared to "unscientific" clergymen. "They tell me I am heading straight for Hades. Maybe I am, but I'll take my chances with the fashionable ministers, and if there is such a spot as heaven, I'll bet I get there first."[42] To another reporter, Edison was even more condemning. "When I die, I shan't be playing a harp or boiling in oil or haunting any one. I shall be dead. Ministers of fashionable churches don't say what they think. Often, they don't even think."[43] But to fellow freethinkers, the famous inventor confessed that "nearly all great men of science are Agnostics. We are just emerging from the mental dark ages as far as religion is concerned."[44]

The Marshall interview did not disqualify Edison's all-knowingness. Marshall published subsequent columns in which Edison weighed in on overpopulation, nutrition, city planning, and political science; all strong indications that Americans were still very invested in what Thomas Edison had to say beyond his natural expertise in electrical physics.[45] Still, that he had to live with the lingering question about God and the afterlife haunted Edison and others who believed that great men were great in all things.

The solution was to backpedal. America could not countenance his heresy so Thomas Edison would have to restore his all-knowingness through repentance. In 1923, when asked about it by reporters that joined

---

[40] Thomas A. Edison to Samuel Fine, October 4, 1910, Letter LB084195, TAEP Digital Collection.
[41] Thomas A. Edison to H. Toyer, October 15, 1910, Letter LB084261, TAEP Digital Collection.
[42] "Edison Invents His Own Aeroplane," *New York Times*, December 1, 1910, 1.
[43] "Golden Rule," *Cincinnati Enquirer*, December 1, 1910, 4.
[44] Thomas A. Edison to J. A. Hennesy, December 20, 1910, Letter LB085034, TAEP Digital Collection.
[45] See Edward Marshall, "Where Europe Can Give America Valuable Points," *New York Times*, October 29, 1911, SM4; Edward Marshall, "The Future Man Will Spend Less Time in Bed," *New York Times*, October 11, 1914, SM1; and "Edison Predicts End of Skyscraper Era," *New York Times*, November 15, 1926, 1.

him at President Warren Harding's funeral, Edison posited that "the soul after death takes flight but in what form and manner is unknown."[46] Four years later, Edison conceded his belief in the afterlife based on simple arithmetic. He told Edward Marshall that "there exist more known evidences favoring than against the immortality of the individual human intelligence."[47] This was a more positive response than what Edison had told Marshall a few months earlier, that "we really haven't any very great amount of data on this subject."[48] Perhaps for this reason, Henry Ford was thrilled and described Edison's admission as a watershed moment for religion and science.[49] The question resurfaced when Edison died in 1931. The Edison family vigorously defended their father's belief in heaven, and his personal physician testified that the great inventor had come around to the spiritual notion of the afterlife in his final years.[50] Their campaign to restore Edison's clout was also a crusade on behalf of the all-knowing answer men, the most prominent example of whom was, of course, the great Thomas Edison.

***

It was much harder to defend Henry Ford's all-knowingness. All that Ford knew was self-taught. The autodidact did not attend high school, let alone college. He had studied basic engineering by tinkering with his father's pocket watch and learned to read budget tables from a bookkeeping class offered at a local trade school. Ford never felt lacking for knowledge. Instead, he flouted what he didn't care to learn more about. The most well-known instance was his declaration that "history is more or less bunk." The long-term impact of that pronouncement was the inspiration to coin a term to describe all later "debunkers" and contrarian interpreters of historical inquiry.[51] But the much more immediate response was a concerted effort by Ford's opponents to discredit the industrialist, at least in all things unrelated to automobiles and mass production.

---

[46] "Edison Convinced the Soul Lives On," *New York Times*, August 11, 1923, 6. See also, Edward W. Townsend, "Edison Talks of Immortality and the Basis of Life," *New York Times*, October 7, 1923, 31.
[47] Edward Marshall, "Edison at 80 Views the World He Changed," *New York Times*, February 6, 1927, SM4.
[48] Edward Marshall, "Has Man an Immortal Soul?" *Forum* 76 (November 1926): 642.
[49] "Henry Ford on Reincarnation," *Messenger* 15 (October 1927): 103.
[50] "Inventor Thought Soul Might Live On," *New York Times*, October 18, 1931, 35.
[51] See Fischer, *Washington's Crossing*, 442–44.

Henry Ford was "great." However, the attributes of his greatness were a matter of interpretation. To some, he was the "greatest man of his time."[52] His peers regarded him as the "greatest industrialist alive."[53] The Ford Motor Company more modestly marketed him in advertisements as the "greatest automobile manufacturer."[54] Critics regarded Ford as the "world's greatest opportunist."[55] Those imperiled by him designated Ford the "greatest antisemite in American history" or the "greatest anarchist on earth."[56] For some reason or another, Henry Ford was indisputably great.

The consensus around Ford was odd. Wealth was usually not useful for those in search of greatness. To be sure, money provided quantitative evidence of the utility of Thomas Edison's inventions, but did not, by itself, make him great. Recall that Jay Gould and most of the other deep-pocketed men of the prior generation were shut out of NYU's Hall of Fame of Great Americans and ignored in most other discussions of American greatness. Affluence also purchased limited amounts of fame, compared to those whose prominence pivoted on political power or sporting achievement. In the 1920s, President Calvin Coolidge and Babe Ruth outslugged nearly any other celebrity in the newspaper columns, save for Henry Ford. The *New York Times* claimed Ford had a "real genius" for "grabbing attention."[57] To contrast, industrialists such as Charles Schwab and John Rockefeller received about a fifth of the media coverage that Ford had accumulated.[58]

Book publishers also caught onto this trick of the Ford trade. In the 1920s, fifteen different writers authored biographies on Ford; "no other American of the period received so much attention in book form."[59] Ford's fame matched his measure in greatness. In "great men" polls published in the first decades of the century, most rich men rarely ranked. Ford, however, routinely rated at the top, beside Theodore Roosevelt in American surveys and, among Europeans, with Benito Mussolini.[60]

---

[52] "Henry Ford – Ship Owner," *American Exporter* 98 (April 1926): 14.
[53] "Henry Ford Fights Unionism within His Empire," *Life*, May 31, 1937, 28.
[54] See "Henry Ford and Thos. A. Edison Buy," *Saturday Evening Post*, March 28, 1914, 44.
[55] Charles W. Wood, "A Modern Business Leader Discovers Real Success," *Forbes*, June 1, 1927, 14.
[56] Frank Bonville, *What Henry Ford Is Doing* (Seattle, WA: Bureau of Information, 1920), 94.
[57] "Well Devised, But Ill Timed," *New York Times*, August 1, 1914, 8.
[58] David L. Lewis, *The Public Image of Henry Ford: An American Folk Hero and His Company* (Detroit, MI: Wayne State University Press, 1976), 213.
[59] Lewis, *The Public Image of Henry Ford*, 216.
[60] Ibid., 232.

The Problem of the Great All-Knowing Answer Man 61

Why was Henry Ford so different? First, his genius was not restricted to money making, as was the case with the erstwhile robber barons – at least by reputation. Like Thomas Edison, Ford was a changemaker, a principled component of American greatness. Ford had overcome several false starts to produce an affordable automobile, the Model T, in 1908. There was another feature to Ford's greatness: he was a forward-thinking manager. Ford lowered the cost of his cars, and therefore made them more accessible to the American public, with the development of the assembly line. Mass production revolutionized industry by encouraging specialization and generating efficiency. "It's the man," said Ford, "who is the ablest specialist in his line who wins the biggest success."[61]

In Ford's industrial world, everyone had a purpose, a part in producing something grand. "Specialization," commented a writer about Ford's management revolution, "has been the keynote of the life of Henry Ford and the keynote of the company of which he is president."[62] The economist Adam Smith introduced subdivision of labor but warned that too much of it could make a man "as stupid and ignorant as it is possible for a human creature to become." Ford disregarded Adams' caution and turned his disavowal of the status quo into a social ethic. "Each man has a particular job—a particular operation to perform in the construction of the car—and by doing this particular job over and over again each becomes a specialist in his line."[63] Ford encouraged his employees to become experts in their very focused chore to help build a very specific type of automobile. These men came to better value their work and earned more because of the efficiency of their combined production. One worker could not perform his colleague's mechanical task as well as that person. No single person could build a car on his own. There was great pride and comfort in specialization: knowing what you know and feeling at ease with what you don't. All this elevated Ford above the ruthlessness associated with the robber barons of the prior epoch in American capitalism.

Second, Ford's greatness was connected to how he *used* his largesse. To some, but certainly not all, Ford was a philanthropic exemplar, someone who leveraged his wealth to, in decent Christian terms, help others.[64] The car market made Ford one of the richest men in the world,

---

[61] "Ford, the Exponent of Specialization," *Engineering and Contracting*, May 30, 1917, 487.
[62] "Ford Method of Handling Men," *Factory* 12 (June 1914): 482.
[63] Ibid.
[64] A. T. Simonds, "Mr. Ford's Philanthropy," *Christian Century*, January 6, 1927, 22.

but he became one of the most well-known individuals for pioneering the five-day working week and the relative high wages paid to his employees. "The average citizen," figured a writer about Ford's reputation, "was far less likely to think of the Ford Company as a huge manufacturing concern than he was to think of its efficient mass production techniques, enlightened labor policies, and price reductions which had become the firm's hallmarks."[65] Ford's human resource protocols became a social gospel for labor reform, and he an enlightened apostle fit to speak on a myriad of issues facing the American public.

Did his wealth, mechanical ingenuity, and enlightened labor policies provide Ford carte blanche authority to speak on all other matters? Most believed it did. Robert Rutherford McCormick, however, disagreed. In 1914, together with Joseph Medill Patterson, McCormick purchased the *Chicago Tribune*, the self-styled "World's Greatest Newspaper." McCormick, a vigorous advocate of America's entry into World War I, figured that he could help his cause if he could "make a jest of Ford."[66] The latter was a spokesman for nonaggression. Ford even chartered a so-called Peace Ship, an ocean liner that carried a delegation of pacifists to Europe to broker an end to the war. McCormick published stories about Ford's business and printed advertising paid by him – sometimes in support of pacifism – all the while declaiming the "ignorance and shallow sophistry of men like Mr. Ford."[67]

McCormick's newspaper put Ford's competence to a test in a series of interviews that was "part smear, part debate, and part good public relations for Ford."[68] In one installment, the interviewer, Charles Wheeler, challenged Ford's pacifist position during World War I on historical grounds. Ford didn't refute his interlocutor's facts. Instead, he called into question the importance of history. "I don't care," Ford said in total dismissiveness of an entire academic discipline. "It means nothing to me. History is more or less bunk." According to the self-immolating Ford, "the only history that is worth a tinker's damn is the history we make today."[69]

---

[65] Lewis, *The Public Image of Henry Ford*, 211.
[66] "Proper Treatment of Ford," *Chicago Tribune*, December 20, 1915, 8.
[67] "The Fallacies of Henry Ford," *Chicago Tribune*, April 11, 1916, 8. For Ford's pacifist-aligned advertising in the Chicago newspaper, see "Humanity – And Sanity," *Chicago Tribune*, April 11, 1916, 13.
[68] Roger Butterfield, "Henry Ford, the Wayside Inn, and the Problem of 'History is Bunk,'" *Proceedings of the Massachusetts Historical Society* 77 (1965): 54.
[69] Charles N. Wheeler, "Fight to Disarm His Life's Work, Henry Ford Vows," *Chicago Tribune*, May 25, 1916, 10.

Ford's uncharitable view of history received "little attention," at least initially.[70] Most people apparently figured that Ford, as a reputed great man, was entitled to his point of view. Just a small number of conventional men such as Chauncey Depew, a former US Senator, read Ford's comments and recoiled. "I differ entirely from Mr. Ford," argued Depew. "It is the history of the past," listing the American Revolution and Civil War, "that makes possible the history we make to-day."[71]

Determined to make something much more of it, the *Chicago Tribune* doubled down on "Fordism." Woodrow Wilson, worried about Germany's connections to Mexico and Pancho Villa, had just ordered the National Guard to the southern border. To show his personal support, McCormick enlisted in the Illinois National Guard. Concomitantly, McCormick's newspaper stirred more controversy. Upon request, a Ford Motor Company executive reported to the newspaper that Ford's factories would not hold workers' jobs if they volunteered to join "Wilson's army."[72] The Ford employee had actually misspoken. Nearly ninety Ford workers would serve along the Mexican border, and all returned to their jobs without penalty. Armed with these incorrect facts, the *Tribune*'s editorial board believed this rendered Ford an "anarchist," a daring allegation to level. Most understood that anarchists made for bad Americans, not great ones. Just to be sure, the editors sought approval from McCormick who, upon learning about the (faulty) evidence, reportedly responded: "Well, call him one then."[73]

It wasn't personal. Insiders attested that there was never "any personal animosity between McCormick and Ford."[74] Yet, McCormick could not hold back against Ford's pacifism. He resented, according to one account, that while there were other wealthy men who agreed with Ford, "they have the gift of silence and a correspondingly low visibility."[75]

---

[70] Butterfield, "Henry Ford," 54.
[71] Chauncey M. Depew, *Speeches and Literary Contributions at Fourscore and Four* (New York: [no publisher], 1918), 69.
[72] "Flivver Patriotism," *Chicago Tribune*, June 22, 1916, 3.
[73] Gregory R. Piché, *The Four Trials of Henry Ford* (Cambridge, UK: Open Books, 2019), 164.
[74] "The Reminiscences of Mr. E. G. Liebold" (Detroit: Ford Motor Company Archives, 1953), 313.
[75] Samuel S. Marquis, *Henry Ford: An Interpretation* (Boston: Little, Brown, and Company, 1923), 57.

The editorial decried Ford as an "anarchist" as well as an "ignorant idealist."[76] Ford's lawyers complained that McCormick's men had gotten it wrong, that no one would lose a position at Ford Motor Company for enlisting. However, the *Tribune* refused to retract the claim that Ford was an ignorant anarchist since it had other, to their minds indisputable, facts to back up the harsh accusation. Before long, Ford's advisors resolved that the condemnation had reached a "limit" and lobbied him to respond. "Well," said Ford, "you better start a suit against them for libel."[77]

In July 1917, Ford's attorneys filed paperwork in Detroit to sue the *Chicago Tribune* for libeling him, claiming damages of a million dollars. Lawyers wrangled for the better part of two years. Neither side would agree to a hearing in Chicago nor Detroit. They settled to bring the case to the quaint resort town, Mount Clemens, Michigan. Eleven farmers and a road paver made up the jury. Throngs of reporters and expert witnesses packed into the local hotels. In anticipation of the massive media coverage, Western Union installed batteries of telegraph instruments to "maintain touch with leading cities Union by direct wire."[78] There was little to be done to improve the small courthouse, to have it match in aesthetics what it was bound to receive in attention. Its lone courtroom had a high ceiling but was hardly capacious enough to accommodate all its visitors. The room was encased by plain white walls decorated with a few canvas portraits of deceased judges.

The assessment of Ford's worldly knowledge became key to determine whether the *Chicago Tribune* was correct to call him an "ignorant idealist." The newspaper's attorney, Elliott Stevenson, who had litigated against Ford in an earlier suit, announced to the car manufacturer that "I shall inquire whether you are a well-informed man, competent to educate people."[79] Ford's counsel protested that an interrogation of Ford's cultural literacy was "outrageous, cruel, a shame to subject that man to such an examination."[80] However, Judge James Tucker denied the objection because the defense had "to get all of the man's trend of thought, his educational condition and the whole business." Tucker allowed, in his own words, "an inquiry as to all things that

---

[76] "Ford is an Anarchist," *Chicago Tribune*, June 23, 1916, 6.
[77] "The Reminiscences of Mr. E. G. Liebold," 295.
[78] Allan Nevins and Frank Ernest Hill, *Ford: Expansion and Challenge, 1915–1933* (New York: Charles Scribner's Sons, 1957), 131.
[79] Vincent Curcio, *Henry Ford* (Oxford: Oxford University Press, 2013), 109.
[80] Nevins and Hill, *Ford*, 138.

would go to make an ignorant idealist."[81] In truth, Ford's team had anticipated Stevenson's tactic and Judge Tucker's stance on the matter. For three days, Ford's lawyers "crammed him with facts about the life of Washington, the annexation of Florida, the battle of Bull Run, and the Dingley tariff."[82]

Stevenson's first question was rather reasonable: "What histories have you read?" he asked. "I admit that I am ignorant about most things," confessed Ford. He elaborated that he was just beginning to appreciate art and music. Ford listed his fondness for the banjo, a comment that elicited laughter from the courtroom.

Ford hoped the levity would conceal his discomfort. He was usually unflappable under pressure. But on this occasion, Ford was skittish. His tall body fidgeted in the witness chair. He couldn't arrange sentences in the fluid patterns that he had intended to pronounce them. Ford regained some composure as he and Stevenson traded philosophical ideas about the notion of government. Then the *Tribune*'s lawyer inquired about Ford's understanding of some basic facts of history. "Do you know whether there have been any revolutions in this country or not?" asked the lawyer.

"There was, I understand," responded Ford.
"When?"
"In 1812," answered a confused Ford.
"Don't you know there wasn't any revolution in 1812?" questioned Stevenson.
"I don't know that; I didn't pay much attention to that."
"Now can you tell us anything about the revolution in 1812."
"About aggression, I guess," responded Ford, vaguely.
"You don't know what the War of 1812 was about?" volleyed Stevenson.
"No," he conceded.

Ford proved equally unknowledgeable about the Spanish–American War, an event that had transpired in Ford's lifetime. Stevenson wrapped up his questions and vowed to return to the scope of Ford's historical knowledge when the trial reconvened. The next day, Ford surrendered. "If it will do any good, I will admit that I am an ignorant idealist," he told Stevenson and the rest of the courtroom. Stevenson clarified, asking

---

[81] Ibid., 137.
[82] Niven Busch Jr., *Twenty-One Americans* (Garden City, NY: Doubleday, Doran & Company, 1930), 5.

whether Ford's confession was meant to wipe out that part of his libel claim. "That is for the jury," answered Ford.

Stevenson continued to probe Ford's historical knowledge. "Did you ever hear of Benedict Arnold?"

"I have heard the name."

"Who was he?" Stevenson was confident that Ford was unaware of America's most infamous traitor. Like Arnold, Stevenson implied, Ford was a turncoat. If he was unaware of Benedict Arnold's double-crossing during the American Revolution, how could Ford understand the difference between a patriot and an anarchist?[83]

"I have forgotten just who he is," responded Ford. Sensing that was insufficient, he guessed. "He is a writer, I think."

"A writer?" repeated Stevenson, feigning surprise.

"I think so."

"What subjects do you recall he wrote on?"

"I don't remember."

"Did you ever read anything he wrote?"

"Possibly I have but I don't know – I don't know much about him."

Ford's lawyers interjected, pleading to the judge and jury that Ford's was a simple error, that he must have mistaken Benedict Arnold for Arnold Bennett, a popular British novelist. Ford's friend, the newspaper publisher William Randolph Hearst, instructed his reporters to explain in their columns that it was a mistake wrought by a very hot summer day in Detroit, and that Ford was, so it was claimed, unusually well-read, and knowledgeable.[84] No one bought these arguments. Most of the press's headlines read "Ford Wanders in Testimony;"[85] "Flunks on History;"[86] "Odd Definitions Given By Ford in Libel Suit;" and "Ford Admits He's Ignorant."[87] One syndicate commissioned a cartoon of Ford becrowned by a dunce cap, an illustration that reportedly "offended him."[88]

Ford, it turned out, was ignorant of both Benedict Arnold and Arnold Bennett. He professed to a close friend that in the throes of Stevenson's inquisition Ford had in mind Horace Arnold, a technical

---

[83] "Draw Out More Ford Notions in Libel Trial," *Chicago Tribune*, July 17, 1919, 1.
[84] Norman Beasley, "What Henry Ford Reads," *Hearst's International* 45 (June 1924): 59.
[85] "Ford Wanders in Testimony," *Boston Globe*, July 18, 1919, 11.
[86] "Flunks on History," *Washington Post*, July 17, 1919, 1.
[87] "Ford Admits He's Ignorant," *Los Angeles Times*, July 17, 1919, 11.
[88] Busch Jr., *Twenty-One Americans*, 6.

writer, author of *Ford Methods and The Ford Shops*. This Arnold was recalled as a strange man. He always wore a cap and an overcoat, no matter the weather.[89] His appearance must have made quite the impression on Henry Ford, and further beclouded his foggy historical memory.

The ordeal concluded several weeks later. Reports estimated that the *Chicago Tribune* must have spent a half million dollars on legal fees. "It is worth that," opined a member of the defense, "to show Ford up."[90] After closing arguments, the jury deliberated for ten hours and ultimately found McCormick and his newspaper guilty of just six cents' worth of libeling Ford's unredeemable reputation.

How did America react to the very public shortcomings of one of its greatest men? The responses broke down into three types: one group, the purists, determined that the embarrassing episode exposed Ford and forfeited his station – à la Lee's generalship of the Confederate forces and Poe's supposed drunkenness – among other great men; another preserved Ford's greatness but surrendered his all-knowingness; and the Ford loyalists found ways to excuse his ignorance.

The most unforgiving lot read about Ford's illiteracy of the elementary facts of American history and disqualified him from the realm of American greatness. "Now the mystery is finally dispelled," declared one pundit. "Henry Ford is a Yankee mechanic, pure and simple; quite uneducated, with a mind unable to 'bite' into any proposition outside of his automobile and tractor business, but with naturally good instincts and some sagacity."[91] His sense for cars and sales made him a very rich mechanic. Ford was, then, no different from that earlier generation of robber barons whose accomplishments could not register along the high station of great men. "He has achieved wealth," the editorial concluded, "but not greatness."[92]

There was one group above all the others who sought to void Ford's high station. American Jews desired to downgrade Ford, a well-known antisemite. Ford accused Jews of inciting Wilson's entry into World War I, and then blamed them for most everything else he found rotten in American life.[93] The feeling was mutual. Thinking aloud about Ford's

---

[89] "The Reminiscences of Mr. E. G. Liebold," 308.
[90] Richard Snow, *I Invented the Modern Age: The Rise of Henry Ford* (New York: Scribner, 2013), 266.
[91] "The Unveiling of Henry Ford," *The Nation*, July 26, 1919, 102.
[92] Ibid.
[93] Neil Baldwin, *Henry Ford and the Jew: The Mass Production of Hate* (New York: Public Affairs, 2001), 59.

testimony, Rabbi David Philipson called him "so stupid an ignoramus" and suggested that "such an individual is most dangerous, for he is obsessed with the idea that his vast wealth gives him the authority to rush in," explained Rabbi Philipson, borrowing from the British poet Alexander Pope, "where angels fear to tread."[94] Rabbi Stephen Wise added that "Mr. Henry Ford is the ignorant and unconscious tool and dupe of a dangerous and menacing intrigue in international politics."[95]

Perhaps the most poignant position was proffered by the Jewish writer, Montague Glass, who wrote in *Life* magazine to censure University of Michigan president, M. L. Burton for ranking Ford among his personal list of greatest living Americans.[96] "What on earth prompted a college president to vote for Henry Ford as one of the world's four greatest?" berated Glass. The writer called out Ford's antics in Mount Clemens, his ineffective responses to Stevenson's basic questions on American history. "I for one see this college president conscious of his own intellectual and educational equipment, comparing his attainments with those of Henry Ford, a man signally lacking in both intellect and education."[97] The common denominator was a shared feeling that Henry Ford was a charlatan changemaker. He did much more to pull America backward than push it forward.

The second contingent was unwilling to strip Ford of his greatness as a social reforming industrialist but relegated his genius to just that. The approach mirrored the many Americans who could not square Thomas Edison's greatness with his unprovoked streak of atheism. The journalist Norman Hapgood, for instance, was adamant that the automobile manufacturer's lack of knowledge rendered him ineligible to pontificate on all things. "Ford cannot," pleaded Hapgood, "be excused on the ground that he has not the slightest idea what he is talking about."[98] Others testified that this was the prevailing sentiment among Ford's employees and other modest workers: "In all Detroit there was no workman so humble that he could not laugh at the great man who

---

[94] David Philipson, "Henry Ford's Campaign of Hatred," *American Israelite*, November 25, 1920, 4.

[95] Stephen S. Wise, *Free Synagogue Pulpit*, vol. 6 (New York: Bloch Publishing Company, 1921), 81. Catholics took a similar stand against Ford's antisemitism. See "Editorial Comment," *Catholic World* 125 (September 1927): 833.

[96] "Ranks Ford, Edison, Wright and Roosevelt as Four Greatest Men of Twentieth Century," *New York Times*, February 17, 1924, 1.

[97] Montague Glass, "Broadcastings," *Life*, April 3, 1924, 30.

[98] Norman Hapgood, "To Henry Ford from Norman Hapgood," *Detroit Times*, November 7, 1921, 8.

did not know how to read, who thought Benedict Arnold was Arnold Bennett, and who thought the Revolution occurred in 1812."[99]

The *New York Times* reported that "Mr. Ford has been submitted to a severe examination of his intellectual qualities" and "has not received a pass degree." He was therefore a limited "genius in his own business" but, supposed the newspaper, "his qualifications as an instructor of the people are not too manifest, and he must feel that his appearances in that role are at an end."[100] (The report was wrong. Just two years later, Ford commissioned a series of articles in his antisemitic *Dearborn Independent* to demonstrate, spuriously, the connection between Benedict Arnold, the "most conspicuous traitor in American history," and his Jewish aide-de-camp, David Franks.[101] Franks was exonerated by George Washington and later entrusted with top secret documents to transport to Benjamin Franklin in Paris. The very ironic use of Benedict Arnold, by this time much better known to Ford, in the latter's antisemitic propaganda was not lost on Ford's opponents.[102])

But great men did not possess such narrow expertise. How could this group circumscribe Ford's? The answer was that it was Ford's own doing. Ford, after all, was the most prominent proponent of "specialization" of each employee along the assembly line. Noting this, the *New York Times* described the "Ford phenomenon," the trend among well-known people to possess uneven genius. Recalling Washington, a master statesman and general, and the other Founding Fathers, the newspaper waxed nostalgic about the "great men of those times, when they were ambitious, thought first of education."[103]

Ford, however, sought to change the expectations around greatness. He convinced his generation of leaders to focus narrowly on a single craft and forgo mastery of other disciplines that resided too far afield. "With division of labor as the very foundation of our present economic system, the specialist no doubt has his place," reflected a journalist after the Stevenson-Ford exchange. "Many of the wonders of this commercial world could not be accomplished without him. And Mr. Ford has done his share."[104] Others expressed more despair, that Ford's ways

---

[99] Jonathan Norton Leonard, *The Tragedy of Henry Ford* (New York: G. P. Putnam's Sons, 1932), 170.
[100] "A Derisory Verdict," *New York Times*, August 16, 1919, 6.
[101] "The Jewish Associates of Benedict Arnold," *Dearborn Independent*, October 8, 1921, 8.
[102] See E. G. Pipp, *The Real Henry Ford* (Detroit, MI: Pipp's Weekly, 1922), 50–51.
[103] "Dictated by Not Read," *New York Times*, July 20, 1919, 31.
[104] "The Grilling of Henry Ford," *Literary Digest*, August 9, 1919, 46.

betokened a national "calamity."[105] Another believed that the example Ford set for uneven expertise foretold, sarcastically, a new "Race of Giants in America," a breed that he hoped American universities would do their very best to impede.[106]

Then there was the third swath of the American public that chose to give up on history rather than Ford. Ford remained all-knowing. History, on the other hand, wasn't worth knowing. This was the group that numbered the 40,000 initial subscribers to Ford's *Dearborn Independent*, his weekly newspaper conceived (although not yet birthed) just as the Chicago press turned on him. Ford's weekly pledged to "chronicle the neglected truth," a shorthand for his conspiracies about Jews and other groups Ford hated but hadn't the facts to support his scorn.[107] His ignorance resonated with them. "The masses," wrote one Ford biographer, "liked Ford all the better for his slips. They preferred him without the varnish."[108] Another quipped that "by admitting on the witness stand he thought Benedict Arnold a 'writer,' Henry Ford probably made more real friends than by any other single small act."[109] A journalist in Ford's hometown described the phenomenon as a cureless disease. "Ford-osis" was both neurological and hematological:

> It's on the brain and in the blood of the American people. They gobble the Ford stuff, and never stop to reason whether they like it, or whether it has any real merit in it ... You may hear him confess that he doesn't know who this fellow Benedict Arnold was, and still you would like to get his personal viewpoints on facts of American history ... Some of his words and acts, if spoken and done by any other man, would strike you as being more or less silly. Yet, under the spell of Ford-osis, you would hail them as matters of boundless consequence, and you would be the first to snatch from the fingers of a screaming newsboy the edition that breaks this news to the world.[110]

What were the causes of this syndrome? Ford validated the intellectual weaknesses of others. One sociological diagnostician summed up that Ford's "performance did him no damage whatever in public esteem." Instead, "his simplicity, his earthiness, the weariness of his contempt for

---

[105] Walter Hurt, *Truth About the Jews, Told by a Gentile* (Chicago: Horton, 1922), 152.
[106] John Jay Chapman, "Henry Ford's Place in History," *Vanity Fair* 11 (December 1919): 51.
[107] Baldwin, *Henry Ford and the Jew*, 67–91.
[108] Keith Sward, *The Legend of Henry Ford* (New York: Rinehart & Company, 1948), 106.
[109] Kenneth M. Goode and Harford Powel Jr., *What about Advertising?* (New York: Harper & Row, 1928), 211.
[110] Ralph Z. Thatcher, "Have You a Case of Ford-osis, Too?" *Detroit Saturday Night*, January 28, 1928, 2.

the magniloquent word, his un-self-saving candor about what he had never had time to learn from books, endeared him to millions, all more or less like that themselves, only ashamed to confess it."[111]

All three groups shared a belief that it was atypical of great men to possess limited wisdom. In a very public venue, Ford had proven that his knowledge was inadequate in history and likely in any number of academic disciplines. The revelation compelled most Americans to either demote Ford or devalue history. The middle group, the one that wished to preserve Henry Ford's greatness and the importance of history, had to explain why this great man, unlike most great men who had preceded him, was not all-knowing. Their answer: it had to do with a revolution in expertise, a new era of radically narrow specialization that Henry Ford, in his greatness, introduced in the first place.

**

There might have been something more prejudicial about G. K. Chesterton's rebuke of Albert Einstein. On an earlier trip to the United States, when Chesterton was on better terms with Henry Ford, he visited Detroit and concluded that "if a man of that sort has discovered that there is a Jewish problem, it is because there is a Jewish problem."[112] Ford hadn't poisoned Chesterton. The English writer was already of the opinion that Jews were a "barbarous people, entirely primitive, and very like the simple savages who cannot count beyond five on their fingers."[113] Perhaps Chesterton grouped Einstein with Ford and Edison to censure the all-knowing answer man because he recognized something that others had, as well: Einstein posed a problem for the whole of Christian America.

In 1921, Einstein won the Nobel Prize "for his services to Theoretical Physics, and especially for his discovery of the law of the photoelectric effect." He was the third Jew to win the Nobel Prize, and the only one whose birthday each March 14 was a notable occasion in the international press. Einstein had gained even greater renown for formulating "the world's most famous equation," $E = mc^2$. The mass–energy equivalence formula was part of Einstein's breakthrough, his theories of relativity that, it will suffice here to write in brief, introduced the notion of spacetime and how movement and gravity are all interrelated. That

---

[111] Garet Garrett, *The Wild Wheel* (New York: Pantheon Books, 1952), 185.
[112] G. K. Chesterton, *What I Saw in America* (New York: Dodd, Mead and Company, 1922), 136.
[113] Ibid., 49.

scientists claimed Einstein had disrupted long-held theories established by Isaac Newton was sufficient to impress most people who did not fully comprehend Einstein's complex math. It was apparent, to most anyway, that Einstein had changed the study of the physical world and inspired a growing number to think that, perhaps, just maybe, we ought to reevaluate our understanding of the spiritual world, too. This concerned some of the most devout men of that time.

There was a precedent. It had occurred two hundred years earlier. Upon his death, Isaac Newton's friends went to significant lengths to suppress Newton's unorthodox views of church doctrine and rites, fearing that his private "heretical writings" might compromise his landmark contributions to science.[114] But there was no protecting Einstein and his theories from the great man's Jewishness, that he was a nonbeliever in Christ. For all those who saw in Einstein's work irrevocable theistic implications, there were two choices: either deny so-called Einsteinism, a term that quite deliberately carried with it scientific and religious connotations, on any grounds necessary or somehow universalize Einstein and find a place for him within Christian faith.

Einstein and Einsteinism were not the same. The scientist, up until that point, did not speak about religion. His discomfort standing at the New York port with scores of reporters betokened his usual reticence about discussing all things beyond his expertise. Einstein's Jewish identity was well-known, but it was equally understood that Einstein did not punctiliously observe Jewish rituals and practices. He did not promote or campaign against any form of religion. Einsteinism, unlike its namesake, was not bashful. It was a spirit, some sensed, that had overhauled long-held postulates in mathematics and science and had designs on doing the same to religion.

Opponents attacked Einstein to counter Einsteinism. Their strategy was to accuse him of blathering nonsense. On April 7, 1929, for example, Cardinal William Henry O'Connell addressed 300 members of the College Catholic Clubs of America with an intent to discredit. The audience was composed of young women and men enrolled in non-Catholic colleges, and probably most had not yet advanced to higher level coursework in theoretical physics.[115] The Archbishop of Boston did not mince words. He accused the world's most well-known

---

[114] Rob Iliffe, *Priest of Nature: The Religious Worlds of Isaac Newton* (New York: Oxford University Press, 2017), 4–10.

[115] "Cardinal Talks to Catholic Clubs," *Boston Globe*, April 8, 1929, 6.

scientist of charlatanism. Einstein, according to O'Connell's charges, had hoodwinked the scientific community and millions beyond that guild of intellectuals, about a belief in the anti-Newtonian warping of space and time. O'Connell shared his fear that Einstein's goal was to discombobulate the academy. "I have never met a man who understood in the least what Einstein is driving at," said Cardinal O'Connell about Dr. Einstein's complicated theories. "I very seriously doubt that Einstein himself knows really what he means."[116]

What was Einstein's earnest goal? Atheism. "It seems nothing short," explained O'Connell, "of an attempt at muddying the waters so that without perceiving the drift of innocent students may be led away into a realm of speculative thought, the sole basis of which, so far as I can see, is to produce a universal doubt about God and His creation." O'Connell admitted to his young listeners that Einstein had not yet confessed his desires to "destroy the Christian Faith and the Christian basis of life." Yet, he prophesied, "I half suspect that if we wait a little longer we shall find that he will ultimately reveal himself in his true colors."[117]

That Einstein posed a threat to Christian faith, as O'Connell had put it, was a curious formulation. After all, Einstein was Jewish, according to the Cambridge scientist, J. B. S. Haldane, the "greatest Jew since Jesus."[118] Interpreting Einstein's scientific work as an affront, perpetuated by an outsider, to Christian teachings was no small thing. The bishop was not "immune," wrote his biographer, "to the anti-Jewish bias that thrived among his people."[119] Besides Einstein, O'Connell's anti-intellectualism seized on Sigmund Freud, identified by the archdiocese's newspaper as a "Jewish physician" who created a "debasing cult that has claimed so many converts among the so called intelligentsia."[120]

O'Connell was not alone. In Germany, Paul Weyland and Phillipp Lenard, among others, led vociferous and hateful campaigns against Einstein. Einstein's rivals were motivated by different forces: jealousy, ignorance, racism, and fear, a kind of neophobia, of the implications

---

[116] William O'Connell, *Sermons and Addresses of His Eminence William, Cardinal O'Connell, Archbishop of Boston*, vol. 10 (Boston: Pilot, 1931), 26–27.

[117] Ibid., 27.

[118] Many others parroted Haldane's famous quip first said aloud at a Cambridge University group called the "Heretics." For the original citation, see J. B. S. Haldane, *Daedalus or Science and the Future* (New York: E. P. Dutton and Company, 1924), 11.

[119] James M. O'Toole, *Militant and Triumphant: William Henry O'Connell and the Catholic Church in Boston, 1859–1944* (Notre Dame, IN: University of Notre Dame Press, 1992), 247.

[120] Ibid., 246–47.

for traditional Newtonian physics in light of new scientific ideas.[121] That last point was particularly powerful in Europe where traditional notions reigned much more sturdily than ideas that augured change.

Bishop O'Connell's tirade, then, was not new to the famous physicist. Einstein was "left cold" by the bishop's criticisms but did not take the bait. Instead, Elsa Einstein told reporters that her husband was "disinclined" to respond to O'Connell.[122] Mrs. Einstein's nonreply grated at the bishop. He doubled down on his earlier claim, announcing that Einstein was not a "true scientist" and that the pontiff was in the process of gathering the many facts that would dispute the physicist's theories of relativity.[123]

American Jews detected antisemitism in Bishop O'Connell's attack and responded with unequivocal support for Einstein. They bristled upon learning that the Vatican's unofficial newspaper sided with O'Connell.[124] "We Jews will never excommunicate Einstein," said a Jewish leader in Boston, a neighbor of O'Connell's. "We are proud of him."[125] Louis Marshall, founder of the American Jewish Committee, penned an open letter to O'Connell to refute, what he had inferred from the pontiff, that only Christians could speak to the relationship between religion and science. "We glory in Einstein," wrote Marshall with an intention to raise Albert Einstein above sectarian lines, "as a true and faithful child of God."[126]

To set the record straight about Einstein and O'Connell's charges of atheism, Rabbi Herbert Goldstein of West Side Institutional Synagogue in New York telegrammed the Nobel laureate in Germany: "Do you believe in God?" Einstein cabled back a pithy response: "I believe in Spinoza's God who reveals Himself in the orderly harmony of what exists, not in a God who concerns Himself with fates and actions of human beings."[127] Rabbi Goldstein submitted Einstein's response to the press as evidence to rebut O'Connell's claims about Einstein's godlessness, that "quite the reverse is true."[128] That the Orthodox rabbi

---

[121] Milena Wazeck, *Einstein's Opponents: The Public Controversy about the Theory of Relativity in the 1920s*, trans. Geoffrey S. Koby (New York: Cambridge University Press, 2014), 2–9.
[122] "Einstein Ignores Cardinal," *New York Times*, April 9, 1929, 10.
[123] "Cardinal Says Einstein Theory Destructive," *Jewish Advocate*, April 18, 1929, 1.
[124] "Papal Newspaper Lauds Einstein Rap," *Washington Post*, May 24, 1929, 4.
[125] "Dr. Sokolow Says Jews are Proud of Einstein," *Boston Globe*, April 23, 1929, 16.
[126] Louis Marshall, "An Answer to Cardinal O'Connell," *Jewish Advocate*, May 2, 1929, C5.
[127] "Einstein Believes in 'Spinoza's God,'" *New York Times*, April 25, 1929, 30.
[128] Ibid.

was satisfied with Einstein's allegiance to Benedict Spinoza, who, some 250 years earlier, had been excommunicated by Amsterdam's Jews for heresy, betwixt some better-informed American Jews and suggested the dire need to accept any form of faith from Einstein to repudiate the bishop.[129] It helped the Jewish cause that most American scientists took Einstein's side, urging that "science was no threat to religion."[130]

Yet, the letters stored in the Archdiocese's archives reveal a troubling current. Very few of the letters – at least the ones still preserved – sent to Bishop O'Connell intended, as one rare kind had done, to tell the pontiff that "you are wrong."[131] Rather, most of the correspondence wrote in support of O'Connell's condemnation of Einsteinism. For example, a physician wrote to the bishop to reassure him that the "Jewish race is quite clever in advertising things that we do not need." Among the Jewish inventions, this doctor confirmed to O'Connell that "Bolshevism, a Jewish creation, Socialism the same, most labor troubles also, the perverted form of capitalism is also their creation." He added that the "perverted sex hygiene under Freud is theirs. The corruption of the press and books of the modern type are their hobby."[132]

The most important encouragement received by O'Connell came from the Swedish-born engineer, Arvid Reuterdahl. Based at the time in St. Paul, Minnesota, Reuterdahl was the "driving force behind the creation of an international network of Einstein's opponents in the early 1920s."[133] Reuterdahl convinced O'Connell and some others that Einstein had plagiarized him. To cover up his tracks and to deploy his godless intentions, Einstein had allegedly removed all the theistic portions of Reuterdahl's ideas included in the latter's pious tome, *The God of Science*.[134] Like other anti-Jewish bigots, Reuterdahl linked "Einsteinism" with "Freudianism" and "Humanism." He viewed himself as America's trailblazing defender against Einstein:

---

[129] "A Faith Answer," *American Israelite*, May 24, 1929, 4. Later on, Rabbi Goldstein changed his gentler stance on Einstein and repudiated his views on God and religion. See "Einstein's Views on God Criticized," *New York Times*, September 15, 1940, 47.
[130] See, for example, "Declares Science Can't Plumb Faith," *New York Times*, May 23, 1929, 1.
[131] Reinold Vernon Smith to Cardinal O'Connell, April 10, 1929, Box 20, Folder M1022, Office of the Chancellor Files, Archives of the Archdiocese of Boston, Boston, MA [hereafter, AAB]. See also W. C. Lamb to Cardinal O'Connell, April 22, 1929, Box 20, Folder M1022, AAB.
[132] William Meyer to Rev. Cardinal O'Connell, April 26, 1929, Box 20, Folder M1022, AAB.
[133] Wazeck, *Einstein's Opponents*, 12.
[134] Ibid., 282–84.

The American scientists were overwhelmed by the Einsteinian propaganda which was launched in December 1919. I was the first in the United States to oppose this fallacy and I spent much time and energy in placing the facts before the unbiased scientists of our country. The great majority are fanatical in their support of Einsteinism. Scientific journals, until recently, suppressed everything inimical to this doctrine. Even now the censorship is astoundingly rigorous. This fallacy thrives in our State and other universities. The seeds of Atheism and Behaviorism, etc., come into rapid fruition in such soil.[135]

What motivated Reuterdahl? He attested in a long letter to the bishop that "I am not an anti-Semite" but several sentences later wrote that "I cannot ignore the fact that the Jewish people, by the strength of their financial ramifications, either directly or indirectly, control the scientific journals of our country."[136] These were the same "facts," so to speak, that prejudiced Jews, and overexaggerated their influence, in Hollywood's film industry.[137] The premise of Reuterdahl's bigoted claims was that Einstein was the product of a Jewish public relations machine. Einstein wasn't much of a genius and certainly not all that great. Reuterdahl argued that the Jews had inserted their man at the top of the Nobel sweepstakes, part of a broader effort to first take over the sciences, and then stake out a bigger claim to the rest of the international establishment. No wonder, then, that Reuterdahl printed many of his ideas in Henry Ford's *Dearborn Independent*. Reuterdahl's propaganda aligned with the other morsels of "neglected truths," as the newspaper put it, not unlike Ford's summaries and reproduced sections from the dubious Protocols of the Elders of Zion, a tract that alleged similar conspiracies about Jews and international power.[138]

It's impossible to know how many readers Reuterdahl saved from Einsteinism. To Cardinal O'Connell, though, Reuterdahl was preaching to a fervently committed contrarian. A week after O'Connell's rebuke volleyed at the College Catholic Clubs of America, the bishop's office released a statement that Einstein had "filched" his scientific discoveries from Reuterdahl, a "man of international fame as a scientist." The only difference being, continued O'Connell, that Reuterdahl "states his theory

---

[135] Arvid Reuterdahl to Cardinal William Henry O'Connell, April 8, 1929, Box 20, Folder M1022, AAB.
[136] Arvid Reuterdahl to Cardinal William Henry O'Connell, April 17, 1929, Box 20, Folder M1022, AAB.
[137] Felicia Herman, "'The Most Dangerous Anti-Semitic Photoplay in Filmdom': American Jews and *The King of Kings* (DeMille, 1927)," *Velvet Light Trap* 46 (Fall 2000): 12–25.
[138] See Steven J. Zipperstein, *Pogrom: Kishinev and the Tilt of History* (New York: W. W. Norton, 2018), 145–83.

in such a way as to make it clear that there is, and must be, a first cause, a 'movens immobile,' and 'Absolute Being,' controlling and ruling the relative." Einstein's alleged plagiarism, on the other hand, "deliberately leaves out God and, therefore, it becomes now perfectly clear that behind the Einstein cloak lurks in very truth the ghastly spectre of atheism."[139] Bishop O'Connell concluded that Einstein's heralded research was simply "shoddy" and blatantly "borrowed" stuff mixed with bad religion. O'Connell's solution to the dangers of Einstein's all-knowing abilities was that, well, Einstein didn't really know that much at all.

Rev. Henry Emerson Fosdick took the opposite approach to square Einsteinism and Christianity. Rather than demote or demean the scientist, Fosdick idolized him – literally. Fosdick was a liberal theologian and did not fit neatly into classical Christian types. In 1925, he resigned his post at First Presbyterian Church (and risked arraignment at a heresy trial) in Manhattan because he would not assent to his congregation's demands to renounce his Baptist denomination and convert to Presbyterianism. John D. Rockefeller Jr. invited Fosdick to lead his congregation, Fifth Avenue Baptist Church. Rockefeller liked Fosdick's orations and his spirit, although he did not care all that much for the minister's labor politics.[140] Fosdick turned him down because he did not want to be known, or to reduce his legacy, as the "pastor of the richest man in the country."[141] Determined to figure something out, Rockefeller offered to pay $4 million to construct a new, huge edifice that could attract a broad collection of New Yorkers. Fosdick agreed.

Riverside Church in Morningside Heights, near Columbia University, opened its doors in 1930, in the liberal stylings of its founding minister, "to all Christians regardless of theological opinion or sectarian preference."[142] The neo-Gothic cathedral was an architectural wonder, a mix of tradition and modern sensibilities. The building was modeled, in theory, after Chartres Cathedral in northern France.

---

[139] "Cardinal O'Connell's Full Statement Against Professor Einstein's Theories," Jewish Telegraphic Agency, April 18, 1929.

[140] Peter Collier and David Horowitz, *The Rockefellers: An American Dynasty* (New York: Holt, Rinehart and Winston, 1976), 153–54.

[141] James Hudnut-Beumler, "The Riverside Church and the Development of Twentieth-Century American Protestantism," in *The History of the Riverside Church in the City of New York*, eds. Peter J. Paris, John Wesley Cook, James Hudnut-Beumler, Lawrence H. Mamiya, Leonora Tubbs Tisdale, and Judith Weisenfeld (New York: New York University Press, 2004), 19.

[142] *The Riverside Church in the City of New York: A Handbook of the Institution and Its Building* (New York: The Riverside Church, 1931), 9.

78 *The Greatest of All Time*

Riverside Church's 400-foot-high spire towered above the Hudson River. Passersby marveled at the symbolic statues and chiseled reliefs carved into the building's exterior.

Back in Europe, Einstein had learned about Fosdick's church chiefly because Fosdick's Committee on Iconography decided to include a sculpture of the great scientist among a set of fourteen statues above the church's west portal (Figure 2.3). Einstein's likeness sat beside other great scientists such as Hippocrates, Euclid, Newton, and Pasteur. The committee also chose controversial figures like Galileo and Darwin. Einstein was the only living member of the group, and he was the only Jewish representative. Only Einstein's inclusion "occasioned much comment."[143] More traditional Protestants did not agree with Fosdick's message: that Einstein, a nonbeliever, could make meaning on a religious level for Christians. Critics charged that Fosdick

FIGURE 2.3 Albert Einstein's image (top, second from the right) caused a stir when it was added to Riverside Church's "Arch of Scientists." Courtesy of Riverside Church.

[143] John Wesley Cook, "A Christian Vision of Unity: An Architectural History of the Riverside Church," in *The History of the Riverside Church in the City of New York*, 154.

had propagated a "bold" and "churchless religion" that was "open to many embarrassments."[144] Some complained that in the midst of negotiating his Baptist and Presbyterian backgrounds, Fosdick had "forgotten" his general Christian "creed" and flagrantly substituted it with a "denial of Jesus."[145]

Fosdick defended the decision to carve out space for Einstein on the side of the cathedral during the second Sunday service ever held at Riverside Church. Standing before 4,000 parishioners, Fosdick admitted that "some public interest has been aroused by the fact that in the exterior structure of this building we have included statues of men who were not believers in the Christian God." It is unclear who else Fosdick had in mind since the balance of his sermon focused solely on Einstein. "I am glad that Einstein is over the church's portal," explained the unrepentant minister, "because I hope that minds like his, facing the same great questions about God that he faces, will come through that portal and sit in these pews and profit by our ministry."[146] In other words, Einstein was a revelation to humankind far beyond theoretical physics. His research invited introspection and charted a course toward progress and change. American Jews hailed Fosdick's "rare evidence of liberalism."[147] Rabbi Solomon Freehof, then of Chicago, interpreted Fosdick's message to mean that "Einstein is so great a world figure that his opinion in any field carries immense weight."[148] Rabbi David Philipson gained a similar impression, celebrating, on behalf of many more American Jews, that one of theirs had transcended their tiny faith community to become a universal figure, capable of all-knowing implications.[149]

The only one who seemed to take a "middle ground" approach to his expertise was Albert Einstein. Upon touchdown in New York, before journeying to Cal Tech, Einstein remained in Manhattan for a few days to meet with important people and deliver a couple of speeches. He also arranged an appointment to visit Rev. Fosdick's newly constructed Riverside Church. As he put it, Einstein "wanted to see that oddity."[150] Fosdick greeted Einstein in Morningside Heights and immediately led

---

[144] "Churchless Religion," *Brooklyn Eagle*, October 13, 1930, 18.
[145] Livingston T. Mays, "Creeds and New Testament Forgotten," *Baptist and Reflector*, December 11, 1930, 6.
[146] "Dr. Fosdick Defends Statue of Einstein," *New York Times*, October 13, 1930, 23.
[147] David Schwarz, "Saint Albert Einstein," *Modern View*, October 17, 1930, 8.
[148] Solomon B. Freehof, "Einstein's Confession of Faith," *American Israelite*, October 23, 1930, 4.
[149] "No Conflict Exists," *Cincinnati Enquirer*, November 22, 1930, 15.
[150] "Einstein Saw His Statue in Church Here," *New York Times*, December 28, 1930, 1.

him to the Arch of Scientists. "I might have imagined that they could make a Jewish saint of me," Einstein quipped upon leaving Fosdick. "But I'd never thought I'd become a Protestant one."[151]

Einstein's humor hid a revelation about just how far Americans were willing to take his greatness, achieved by demonstrating genius in a very specific field of knowledge. As he strolled through Riverside Church, Einstein recognized that Fosdick and others thought his expertise went far beyond science. He was European and his arithmetic on stature did not add up to his hosts'. At the end of his tour, Einstein turned to Fosdick to react to the church's decision to engrave his likeness beside prophets and other holy men. "I will have to be very careful for the rest of my life," reflected Einstein, "as to what I do and what I say."[152] After all, Einstein wasn't an American. He was, therefore, a very reluctant all-knowing answer man.

---

[151] E. C. C., "A Distinguished Visitor," *Church Monthly* 5 (December 1930): 38.
[152] Ibid.

3

The Rise and Fall of the Great Changemakers

In 1928, Walt Disney debuted Mickey Mouse. The main inspiration for the renowned rodent was comedian Charlie Chaplin. By then, Chaplin's vagrant "Tramp" persona was Hollywood's most recognizable film character. Chaplin created the Tramp for a short film that appeared in February 1914. To prepare for the part, Chaplin "put on funny make-up" and found a derby and a pair of baggy pants. He added a tight-fitting jacket, a cane, and a pair of oversized shoes to complete the haphazard ensemble. The outfit was an overall effort to dress in a "mass of contradictions," an appearance that complemented the Tramp's raison d'être, a "brave but ineffectual" character of lowly social rank and grandiose ambitions.[1] The whole motif matched the paradoxes of the Modern Age in the early twentieth century: automobiles, telegraphs, and other machines promised peace and prosperity while the wealthy became far richer than their workers and nations threatened to use their technologies to wage war rather than suppress it.

Chaplin played the Tramp in films during a stretch of twenty-two years, for which he was routinely heralded by many as the "greatest comedian." Some expanded that to the "greatest actor," others widened it further to the "greatest entertainer." Leo Löwenthal made special mention of Chaplin as a rare exception among entertainers who "represent a serious attitude toward their art," and are therefore exempt from the contemptuous lot Löwenthal referred to as "idols of consumption."[2] Still, it was not easy to pin down exactly what made Chaplin great. He was

---

[1] See David Robinson, *Chaplin: His Life and Art* (London: Penguin Books, 2001), 118–19.
[2] Löwenthal, "Biographies in Popular Magazines," 512.

unlike the scientists explored in the Chapter 2 who had, in Chris Rojek's helpful phrasing, "achieved" celebrity. In Löwenthal's terms, Edison and Ford had invented something new, rendering them "idols of production." Chaplin's greatness was rather an "attributed" form.[3]

The scope of Chaplin's greatness therefore suggested less about him than it did about the commentators who described him in superlatives. But it was important to them to assign greatness to Chaplin because he represented something bigger. It was a hard thing to articulate the myriad changes in everyday life. These social shifts are complicated and freighted with cultural baggage. Pinning "greatness" onto symbolic exemplars was a shorthand method to discuss the prospect of new social, political, and technological realities. Great people became usable talking points. But the tale of Chaplin's rise to greatness must also tell about his precipitous fall. This speaks to the conditional aspect, the pragmatism of greatness to the American public. Once they weren't usable, the greatest women and men were not, it turned out, all that great.

Walt Disney, very much taken by Chaplin, envisaged Mickey Mouse to play a similar misfit role, and to become great at it. Disney's first animated shorts portrayed Mickey as a slight figure, made even smaller by dint of exaggerated circumstances and burlier foils. The template for Mickey Mouse was apparent. Chaplin, Disney had claimed, was "the greatest of them all." The public adored Chaplin's feistiness and courage to topple a stronger opponent. Disney desired that same acclaim for Mickey. The Progressive era suggested to the lower classes that they too could rise and "make it." This was the latest incarnation of the so-called American Dream.[4] Chaplin's brilliant cinematic routines simultaneously glorified and satirized it. Disney wanted Mickey Mouse to fit just as seamlessly into the rhythm of American life. "We wanted something appealing," he explained, "and we thought of a tiny bit of a mouse that would have something of the wistfulness of Chaplin—a little fellow trying to do the best he could."[5]

Disney's Chaplin-like mouse stood out even more in his very first cartoon, a riff on Charles Lindbergh's 1927 record-setting transatlantic flight.[6] Lindbergh was nothing like the Tramp. America's greatest

---

[3] Rojek, *Celebrity*, 18.
[4] See Jim Cullen, *The American Dream: A Short History of an Idea that Shaped a Nation* (Oxford: Oxford University Press, 2003), 59–131.
[5] Neal Gabler, *Walt Disney: The Triumph of the American Imagination* (New York: Alfred A. Knopf, 2007), 153.
[6] Michael Barrier, *The Animated Man: A Life of Walt Disney* (Berkeley: University of California Press, 2007), 57.

aviator was handsome and graceful, an unimpeachable hero who quite literally loomed above the grind of everyday life. But Mickey Mouse, plainly dressed and naïve, was determined to reach that high station. In the cartoon, Mickey opens a thick flying manual, rifles through the introduction, turns to a page with Lindbergh's portrait, captioned "Aces of Aces." Mickey studies Lindbergh's image while "Yankee Doodle" patriotically sounds in the background. Confident that he can replicate Lindbergh's most critical skills, Mickey Mouse ruffles his hair to mimic the airman's iconic appearance and jumps into his airplane, ascending without Lindbergh-like success.

There is more to this triad than a series of contrasts. Americans by and large agreed that Charlie Chaplin, Charles Lindbergh, and Mickey Mouse were the "greatest" in their respective arenas. They were useful metaphors for an American modern ambition that lacked discrete definition.[7] Their greatness was subjective, "attributed;" not objective, "achieved." That is, until they weren't great anymore. For reasons pertaining to individual contingencies and broader circumstances, each of these real and fictional figures was demoted from their top rankings of modernity's very best exemplars. The factors that downgraded Chaplin, Lindbergh, and Mickey Mouse represent how changes in American life mediated conversations and calculations around "greatness."

***

Charlie Chaplin was born in London in 1889. He persevered through a very sad childhood by shining in stage performances in London's West End. Throughout Chaplin's childhood, comedy companies discovered and rediscovered him. Each occasion elevated Charlie Chaplin to a higher tier of the British theater circuit.

In 1910, Chaplin and his older brother, Sydney, both worked for the Fred Karno London Company. Karno taught Chaplin pantomime. It was an artform that had caught on by necessity. Britain had banned dialogue in all but a handful of licensed theaters in the eighteenth century. Most venues were forced to improvise, to develop a repertoire of movements that led to prolonged sketches that held the interest of a public that could not afford a seat to watch Shakespeare at one of the talking-sanctioned venues. Britain's middle-class public took to the silent theater and marveled at the thoughtful motions and gesturing.

---

[7] Christine Stansell, *American Moderns: Bohemian New York and the Creation of a New Century* (Princeton: Princeton University Press, 2010), 6–8.

They embraced it as a core feature of the Victorian burlesque movement that added elaborate costume, opera music, and dance to lampoon the stagecraft of Britain's "stuffier" upper-class ranks.

The rise of colorful clowns and muted storytelling extended the mime's reach. Pantomime remained a staple in the middle-class music halls and paved inroads in the speech-licensed Theatre Royal sites that were the initial impetus to develop that silent genre. Circus performances pushed pantomime to add acrobatics and elevated the slapstick elements of the miming shows. Fred Karno's comedy company was the very best, recruiting trained gymnasts to elevate the performances. These elements complicated Karno's expertise: the fine art of "gesture acting." Having fully and intentionally blurred the lines of high art and slapstick, Karno's advertisements could boast "grand performances" full of "clever comedians," "catchy music," and "wonderful scenery" without fear of contradiction.[8]

There was ample space for Karno's stylings along America's vaudeville circuit. He regularly dispatched comedy troupes to the United States. In 1910, Karno sent Charlie Chaplin to perform with the "Number 2 Company." Some wondered whether he should have chosen Sydney Chaplin to headline the troupe. But Karno understood there was risk involved. In prior ventures, a number of his actors had defected to the American vaudeville scene; Sydney, reckoned Karno, was too valuable to lose. He had more experience than his younger brother. But Charlie had started to gain a following, doing his best pantomiming as an effervescent drunk. Charlie brimmed with potential, and Karno knew that. He signed the young Chaplin to a three-year contract just before Charlie left for New York. He hoped the long-term deal would dissuade Charlie from pursuing an American dream.

Charlie Chaplin impressed his American audiences, despite a decidedly mediocre lot that surrounded him. "Chaplin will do all right for America," offered a New York magazine writer, who also opined that it was "too bad" about the rest of the London company's sketches. Another critic had the same contrast in mind. "Now Charles Chaplin is so arriving a comedian," offered this writer, "that Mr. Karno will be forgiven whatever else the act may lack."[9] Karno had hoped that the regular showgoers would interpret the situation more generously. The troupe's

---

[8] Robinson, Chaplin, 92–99.
[9] See Robyn Karney and Robin Cross, *The Life and Times of Charlie Chaplin* (New York: Smithmark, 1992), 42.

routines placed Chaplin's uncouth character in the audience, permitting him to interrupt and interact with the other sketches from beyond the stage. The effect was meant to elevate the performances that did not formally feature Chaplin.

Charlie Chaplin honored his agreement with Fred Karno and remained a part of the troupe throughout the tour. But he returned to England, unhappy and underappreciated. Chaplin left Karno in his second American campaign. He was courted by an upstart, Keystone Studios, during a stop along the Midwestern vaudeville circuit. Keystone featured heavy doses of slapstick and Chaplin's drunkard gags seemed to fit into that genre. Chaplin, on the other hand, was eager to evolve the mimetic gesturing techniques he had learned from Fred Karno and play in more serious roles. "I dreamed that I was the great romantic actor of the age—the Ideal Romeo of the Photo-Shakespearean," he once confessed. "When I arrived in California I prepared to don the doublet and hose of the 14th century lovers. You can imagine my feelings when I was told that the first character I would play would be a man with a limp and a backache, trying to carry a trunk and balance a scuttle of coal on his head while climbing a greasy step ladder."[10]

Chaplin persevered. He always did. He resolved that he would make the most of the chance, even if it was to be something far removed from Shakespeare. Chaplin remained indignant about Keystone's gag-driven writing and must have known from the start that his tenure at the studio was to be short-lived. What is more, he could not pass up the financial windfall. Keystone offered to increase Chaplin's weekly rate from $60 to $150 and guaranteed a full year's salary. The Karno management recognized at that point that Chaplin had the talent to become the "greatest film-actor of the day," and could not stand in the way of a cinema career.[11] Just as Fred Karno had feared, Charlie defected to the United States.

Chaplin flourished in motion pictures and, by extension, the United States. In 1914, he appeared in thirty-six films for Keystone Studios. Women and men happily traveled to their local nickelodeon and paid the nickel fee to see Chaplin's movies. Through his Tramp persona, Chaplin forged a character for America's working and middle classes. Keystone imbued the Tramp with a slapdash humor that endeared

---

[10] See Lewis Jacobs, "Charles Chaplin: Individualist," in *Present Tense: The Arts of Living*, vol. 2, ed. Sharon Brown (New York: Harcourt, Brace and Company, 1941), 318–19.

[11] "Why Charlie Chaplin Left Us," *Answers* 55 (August 12, 1915): 272.

him to children. Grown-ups were absorbed in the films, as well. The Tramp was no clown, despite the preposterous attire and silly mustache. Chaplin's contribution, the Tramp's boldness to take chances and interrupt social norms on a farm, in a boxing ring, or board room, appealed to adult audiences who wondered inside themselves whether they had the audacity to challenge an employer or stand up to an intimidating bully. The Tramp was a manifestation of that fantasy. Chaplin's Tramp was relatable because he inaudibly conveyed the grievances that "poor" and "middle" America had for the upper class. His disheveled look and uneven posture suggested to the filmgoers more about the incongruities of modern life than it did about their own humble situations.[12]

The Tramp was an American everyman who aspired for affluence, status, and love. Its capacity to resonate attributed greatness to Chaplin. In America's Progressive Era, the wealth gap between the "self-made men" and their employees was widening and much more evident as huge masses of people crammed into denser urban centers. Chaplin had tapped into the frustrations about the difficulties to achieve what later became known as the "American Dream." The theater critic Walter Kerr offered that the "secret of Chaplin, as a character, is that he can be anyone."[13] No less than Sigmund Freud observed that Chaplin was a "great artist; certainly he always portrays one and the same figure: only the weakly, poor, helpless, clumsy youngster for whom, however, things turn out well in the end."[14] Freud overstated the ubiquity of Chaplin's happy ending routine but the major aspect of Chaplin's Tramp character was on the mark.

In his first films, Chaplin liked to point out social tensions: he parodied poets with lowbrow comedy, crossed a classical violinist with a drunk vagabond. Chaplin was advancing the miming traditions from Britain, harnessed in earnest by Fred Karno. In the first series of castings, Chaplin's Tramp was the "little fellow" – a factory worker, boardinghouse tenant, caretaker, custodian, or waiter – who tried his very best to "make it." In his misadventures and shortfalls, the Tramp still "won" because he heroically dared to collapse the very cultural barriers that his audiences could never attempt to break through.

[12] See Richard Ward, "Even a Tramp Can Dream: An Examination of the Clash Between 'High Art' and 'Low Art' in the Films of Charlie Chaplin," *Studies in Popular Culture* 32 (Fall 2009): 103–16.
[13] Walter Kerr, *The Silent Clowns* (New York: Knopf, 1979), 85.
[14] Robinson, *Chaplin*, 466.

Charlie Chaplin was an outright American cultural sensation in his adopted land. His silent miming had given voice to a sentiment in the United States that had prior to him lacked a language to properly articulate. The cult around him bordered on deification: "There is another large class of people in our country who still regard Charlie Chaplin as the great American hero and burn their incense at his altar."[15] Certainly, Chaplin had experienced fame in Britain. Before departing for his extended work in the United States, Chaplin had self-knowingly understood that he was the "greatest actor in London."[16] His self-evaluation was embellished, but the British fame had prepared him to nurture a "spark of interest" among the public.[17] However, Chaplin was, all told, unprepared for the prominence he would attain among American audiences. Once he acquired it, Charlie would not loosen his grip on the greatness he had achieved. Soon enough, Chaplin departed Keystone Studios for a competitor that offered him more directorial control and an opportunity to make millions.

The Tramp had made Chaplin into a very rich man, and he recognized the impression that the character made in this historical moment (Figure 3.1). Newspapers syndicated a Tramp comic strip. Fans could purchase Tramp toys and dolls. The merchandising provided Chaplin with a new metric to evaluate his impact. "I knew the extent of my success in Los Angeles by the long lines at the box offices," recalled Chaplin. "I did not realize to what magnitude it had grown elsewhere. In New York, toys and statuettes of my character were being sold in all the department stores and drugstores. Ziegfeld Follies girls were doing Chaplin numbers, marrying their beauty with mustaches, derby hats, big shoes and baggy trousers, singing a song called 'Those Charlie Chaplin Feet.'"[18]

Today, this is standard fare for the highest echelon of Hollywood. Charlie Chaplin was the very first, and every aspect of his celebrity stature was unprecedented. It was, according to one Chaplin biographer, a "great Chaplin explosion."[19] Fairs held Chaplin-impersonation contests to draw out families to their amusements. The young Walt

---

[15] F. B. Pearson, "Education for Civic Efficiency," *Ohio Educational Monthly* 66 (August 1917): 312.
[16] Charlie Chaplin, *Charlie Chaplin's Own Story* (Indianapolis: The Bobbs-Merrill Company, 1916), 155.
[17] Charles J. Maland, *Chaplin and American Culture: The Evolution of a Star Image* (Princeton: Princeton University Press, 1989), 27.
[18] Charles Chaplin, *My Autobiography* (New York: Simon and Schuster, 1964), 173.
[19] Robinson, *Chaplin*, 158.

FIGURE 3.1 Charlie Chaplin, dressed as "the Tramp" in the 1936 film *Modern Times*. Chaplin was viewed as the greatest filmmaker – not narrowly the greatest comedian – in the world. Courtesy of Bettmann/Getty Images.

Disney was said to be the "second-best Chaplin in Kansas City." Just a teenager at the time, Disney took pride in his talent. "I'd get in line with half a dozen guys," he recalled. "I'd ad lib and play with my cane and gloves. Sometimes I'd win $5, sometimes $2.50, sometimes just get carfare."[20]

But Chaplin was peerless. Hollywood declared that he was the "greatest laughmaker the world has ever known."[21] Each film's release "reestablished his reputation as the world's greatest fun maker."[22] No one had surpassed him. Every production improved upon his own precedent. But Chaplin found those assessments too limiting. He eschewed any descriptions that reduced him to a comedian or clown. These sorts of synopses missed his truest intentions. Chaplin routinely

[20] "Mr. and Mrs. Disney," *Ladies' Home Journal* 58 (March 1941): 146.
[21] "Charlie Chaplin will Soon Don Khaki Garb," *Los Angeles Times*, April 15, 1918, 1.
[22] See, for example, "Twelfth St.," *Independent*, October 30, 1920, 13; and "Charlie Chaplin in Greatest Film at the Forsyth," *Atlanta Constitution*, November 11, 1918, 8.

published various versions of the same self-reflective argument that suggested the key to his success in comedy was his understanding of the human condition.[23] Humor was how he exploited that intuition in his films. Chaplin once summed it up pithily for an interviewer: "I prefer to think of myself as a mimetic satirist."[24]

The highbrow critics preferred Chaplin's take on his work. The elites counted him among a shortlist of "geniuses" or "artists." Insiders gushed that Chaplin had "read Shakespeare from beginning to end" and that he was "familiar with the works of George Eliot and other noted writers, and is a stickler for poetry."[25] The logic was clear: Chaplin's artful comedy was informed by the arts. Along these lines, explained the actress Minnie Maddern Fiske, since the "test of an artist's greatness is the width of his human appeal, then Charlie Chaplin must be entitled to a place amongst the foremost of all living artists."[26] The eminent man of letters, Benjamin de Casseres, reported much of the same after a long meeting with America's leading filmmaker. His conclusion was that Chaplin had found a way, despite his earliest frustrations, to do Shakespeare while clowning as the Tramp:

In many hours' easy conversational talk with Chaplin I discovered a spirit of a very rare vintage—a poet, an esthete; a dynamic and ultra-advanced thinker; a man with a thousand surprising facets; a man of many accomplishments; a man infinitely sad and melancholy; a man as delicate as violin strings that register the world-wail and the world-melody; a Puck, a Hamlet, an Ariel—and a Voltaire.[27]

No one could measure up to Charlie Chaplin. One observer surmised that Chaplin was "probably more important than anybody else on earth." His justification for that august claim: "What other man on earth has been loved, respected and admired, at the same time, by French intellectuals, isolated Esquimaux, Iowa Babbits, jazz-maddened New Yorkers, Bulgarian peasants, Scotch Presbyterians, New Guinea cannibals, German scientists, English statemen, real estate brokers, dentists, kindergarten teachers, and the entire race of artists?"[28] Chaplin was simply omnipresent.

---

[23] See, for example, Charlie Chaplin, "What People Laugh At," *American Magazine* 86 (November 1918): 34, 134–37.
[24] Benjamin de Casseres, "The Hamlet-Like Nature of Charlie Chaplin," *New York Times*, December 12, 1920, BR3.
[25] Stanley W. Todd, "The Real Charlie Chaplin," *Motion Picture Classic* 3 (September 1916): 44.
[26] Robinson, *Chaplin*, 220.
[27] Casseres, "The Hamlet-Like Nature of Charlie Chaplin."
[28] Ralph Barton, "Picking on Charlie Chaplin," *New Yorker*, January 23, 1927, 17–18.

Chaplin's greatness suited the modern moment. He had struck a most powerful chord with Americans who had come up against too many barriers to climb up the nation's social ranks. In May 1929, the Academy of Motion Picture Arts and Sciences held its first awards ceremony. This was the original Oscars. It was a short affair held at the Roosevelt Hotel in Hollywood. In all, the Academy nominated candidates for a dozen awards "for outstanding achievements for the past year." In this inaugural program, each winner was presented with a foot-high bronze and gold statuette. Chaplin was nominated for acting, writing, and directing, and would likely sweep all three categories for his 1928 film, *The Circus* (the film's ironic plot centered on the Tramp's ineffectualness as a circus clown). Rather than make the first Oscars an overly Chaplin affair, the awards committee figured that Charlie "should be considered separately from the other award classifications," so that others could be recognized, as well.[29] Chaplin, then, received a "special award," allowing likely less-deserving artists to accept prizes in the more traditional categories at the first Academy Awards. For his part, Chaplin was pleased with the special honor, content that the award signified his "greatness" as America's leading comedian, film star, and foremost social critic of the paradoxical Modern Age.[30]

* * *

On May 21, 1927, Charles Lindbergh landed at Le Bourget, encircled by throngs of awestruck Parisians. His arrival had caused the "first modern traffic jam."[31] Lindbergh had taken off a day earlier from Roosevelt Field in New York. Americans had monitored the earliest stages of Lindbergh's attempt to become the first man to fly an airplane across the Atlantic Ocean. They tracked his progress as far as Nova Scotia before his plane faded into the aqua horizon. No one saw him again until he sailed over England, en route to Paris. By then, Lindbergh was transformed into a hero. His landing was the stuff of legends. The twenty-five-year-old cut a youthful, handsome figure, and he limberly climbed his long legs out of his cramped monoplane. "Well," said Lindbergh, according to one of a handful of several recountings of his first moments in Paris. "I did it."

---

[29] "Film Efforts Rewarded," *Los Angeles Times*, February 18, 1929, 1–2.
[30] See Bruce Davis, *The Academy and the Awards: The Coming of Age of Oscar and the Academy of Motion Picture Arts and Sciences* (Waltham, MA: Brandeis University Press, 2022), 96–97.
[31] Modris Eksteins, *Rites of Spring: The Great War and the Birth of the Modern Age* (Boston: Houghton Mifflin Company, 1989), 242.

"Did what?" asked a journalist. Lindbergh was not ignorant of his achievement. The pilot was acutely aware that he was the first aviator to fly from the United States to Continental Europe. What the writer questioned was Lindbergh's ability to attribute deeper meaning of his aeronautical adventure. "He had no idea of what he had done."[32] This unnamed journalist meant Lindbergh no disrespect. To the contrary, the young man's penchant for self-effacement and genuine naïveté over his very own European-styled status is what had rendered Lindbergh's accomplishment authentically American, what had raised his motives beyond "suspicion." Then again, it is challenging to discern precisely from his short article what this journalist found so "great" about Lindbergh's voyage. "He had fired the imagination of mankind," proffered the writer, indicating just a little more sophistication than Charles Lindbergh might have himself supplied about his impact on the world.

The whole thing portended trouble from the start. The problem was that the transatlantic race was conceived without a noble purpose in mind. The contest to travel by air from "New York to Paris or Paris to New York" was hatched in May 1919 by Raymond Orteig. Two months prior, Orteig had attended a special dinner at the Waldorf-Astoria Hotel in New York. The event was meant to honor Eddie Rickenbacker. Rickenbacker was "America's ace of Hearts," the commander of the 94th Aero Squadron during World War I. Orteig owned the Hotel Lafayette, an unofficial headquarters for airmen during the conflict. That connection brought the hotelier to Rickenbacker's celebratory banquet. Orteig later recalled that Rickenbacker's call to "do your share," although unconnected to a transatlantic aspiration, had inspired him to invest in air travel.[33] Speakers lined up to laud Rickenbacker and defend the aircraft industry that many believed had little purpose other than producing flying killing machines. World War I was all but decided, rendering airplanes, so thought the masses, much less useful. Aviation was reduced to a gimmick, and many Americans were not sanguine about its prospects. Stunt pilots barnstormed and performed aerial tricks. Short-distance airmail was expensive, and engineers had not yet figured out how to efficiently produce larger planes capable of carrying cargo. Commercial air transport was inconceivable, even as a cherished war hero such as Rickenbacker vouched for its promise.[34]

---

[32] "An American Viking of the Air," *Outlook* 146 (June 1, 1927): 139.
[33] Richard Bak, *The Big Jump: Lindbergh and the Great Atlantic Air Race* (Hoboken, NJ: John Wiley & Sons, Inc., 2011), 29.
[34] W. David Lewis, *Eddie Rickenbacker: An American Hero in the Twentieth Century* (Baltimore, MD: Johns Hopkins University Press, 2005), 226–27.

The first step was long-distance travel, something that the evening's toastmaster suggested could be accomplished if the world's two leading aviation powers, the United States and France, could join forces and figure out together. The defenders of aviation intrigued the French-born Orteig, who was aggrieved that the relationship between France and the US had frayed a few months earlier at the Paris Peace Conference that formally ended World War I.[35] Orteig was keen on doing his part to maintain connections between the two nations. The businessman had the same cause in mind many years earlier when he had recast the Martin Hotel as the Hotel Lafayette and added French cuisine to its fine dining menu. Orteig immediately pledged membership to the Aero Club of America. Several months later, he wrote to the Aero Club, insisting that he had just the contest to ensure the long-term usefulness of airplanes:

Gentlemen: As a stimulus to the courageous aviators, I desire to offer through the auspices and regulations of the Aero Club of America a prize of $25,000 to the first aviator of any allied country crossing the Atlantic, in one flight, from Paris to New York or New York to Paris, all other details in your care.[36]

The inherent "greatness" of the transatlantic mission was a work in progress. Insiders within the aviation industry would have to admit during a sober moment that Lindbergh's journey "had no noticeable, statistical effect on the public's attitude toward flight."[37] By contrast, the contribution of Charlie Chaplin, one of just a handful of human beings who rivaled Lindbergh's fame in the late 1920s, was much clearer: Chaplin had given the motion picture a purpose and artform. He made people laugh and think. The case for Lindburgh's greatness required more considered attribution.

What was the purpose of a transatlantic flight? Raymond Orteig was clear about his intentions: the benefactor solely wished to leverage aviation for diplomatic relations. "I had read so much about flights from Canada to Ireland, and New York to Azores, Lisbon, and England," Orteig told a reporter after he had endowed the race. "I wanted to offer some inducement for a flight which would include France."[38]

---

[35] John F. Ross, *Enduring Courage: Ace Pilot Eddie Rickenbacker and the Dawn of the Age of Speed* (New York: St. Martin's Press, 2014), 278.

[36] Richard J. Beamish, *The Boy's Story of Lindbergh, the Lone Eagle* (Chicago: The John C. Winston Company, 1928), 165.

[37] John Lardner, "The Lindbergh Legends," in *The Aspirin Age, 1919–1941*, ed. Isabel Leighton (New York: Simon & Schuster, 1949), 191.

[38] C. R. Roseberry, *The Challenging Skies: The Colorful Story of Aviation's Most Exciting Years, 1919–1939* (Garden City, NY: Doubleday, 1966), 26.

However, Americans required more altruistic motivation to make meaning of the competition. More adept men poured in other, more fulfilling significance to the so-called Orteig Prize. The French flying ace, René Fonck, added "universal peace" to the goals of the transatlantic contest. Fonck had no doubt noticed that the world had been suffering from a horrible bout of cynicism. Despite its promise, the Progressive Age had begot the devastation of World War I, leaving a rising generation jaundiced about the humanitarian intentions of its leaders. Fonck's argument to his listeners was to place their trust in technology since people had failed to deliver on peace. He imagined that the race would demonstrate air travel's power to increase lines of communication. Sturdier airplanes could carry larger cargo and transport goods and people from one site to another. Both Fonck and another challenger for Orteig's purse, Richard Byrd, held that commercial aviation was central to check the economic forces that led nations to the battlefield.[39] Byrd's financial backers added the "cause of science" to the airmen's "interest of world peace."[40]

Neither war hero won the Orteig Prize. Instead, the barnstormer airmail messenger, Charles Lindbergh, claimed it upon touchdown in Le Bourget. Lindbergh had achieved a modicum of fame for his flying finesse in the prairielands of the American Midwest but not much farther than that. Beyond the detection of the media, Lindbergh studied how the prior challengers had faltered. He perfected his air machine through a thorough investigation of eleven earlier transatlantic attempts that had led to eighteen fatalities. Upon entering the race, Lindbergh did not speak about his aspirations for world peace or the advancement of science. He had unabashedly registered for a chance to claim the sizable prize.[41] Wealth was certainly a feature of the Modern Age, but not one that Americans preferred to boast about.

Lindbergh's pathbreaking flight had caused an absolute sensation in Europe and the United States. Much of that had to do with the mystique that had surrounded him. Lindbergh was an unknown Midwesterner, son of a forgettable congressman from Minnesota, traveling in a small white plane. Prior aspirants had tried with larger engines in bulkier machines, and with copilots on board. Lindbergh, then, was, to most observers, an inscrutable mystery.

---

[39] René Fonck, "My New York-Paris Flight," *Aero Digest* 8 (June 1926): 330.
[40] C. R. Roseberry, *Glenn Curtiss: Pioneer of Flight* (Syracuse, NY: Syracuse University Press, 1972), 366.
[41] Joe Jackson, *Atlantic Fever: Lindbergh, His Competitors, and the Race to Cross the Atlantic* (New York: Farrar, Straus and Giroux, 2012), 129.

After thirty-three and a half hours, a "movement of humanity," over 150,000 women and men, gathered near the Paris airfield as Lindbergh fell from the skies in the *Spirit of St. Louis* (Figure 3.2). Ambassador Myron Herrick rescued Lindbergh from the Parisian masses. Everyone wanted to touch him, some dislodged pieces of Lindbergh's airplane as keepsakes. At least ten people were hospitalized. Herrick coordinated Lindbergh's hero tour, hosting him at his residence and escorting the pilot to France's Aero-Club. Herrick arranged for Lindbergh's travel to Belgium where he was knighted into the Order of Leopold by King Albert I and then spirited to London for an audience with King George V at Buckingham Palace. Herrick's efforts were duly noticed by Ernest Hemingway, who was residing in Paris at the time: "Isn't it fine what the American embassy's doing for Lindbergh. It's as if they'd caught an angel that talks like Coolidge."[42]

FIGURE 3.2 Charles Lindbergh standing beside *The Spirit of the St. Louis* shortly after his transatlantic flight in May 1927. Courtesy of Bettmann/Getty Images.

---

[42] Edmund Wilson, *The Twenties: From the Notebooks and Diaries of the Period*, ed. Leon Edel (New York: Bantam Books, 1976), 317.

Less than three weeks after the transatlantic flight, Lindbergh returned to the United States. President Calvin Coolidge reserved the right to be the first to welcome Lindbergh, bestowing upon him the Distinguished Flying Cross. The American press was quick to anoint Lindbergh the "world's greatest aviator," although no one seemed capable of stating so precisely what his feat "proves, if anything."[43] Upon a visit to Los Angeles, the local press feted Lindbergh as "America's favorite son" who performed the "greatest feat ever accomplished by an airman" that "established him as the world's greatest aviator."[44] Most Americans were sure that Lindbergh had achieved something truly "great" but could not elaborate on the accomplishment much more than that. "Enthusiasm and acclaim," observed a writer for the *New York Times*, had "run through the nation like an infection." Yet, shared that same editorialist: "There has been no complete and satisfactory explanation."[45]

The American intellectual, John Erskine, suggested that Lindbergh had emerged as a powerful and broadminded "metaphor" for the Modern Age.[46] That was not the original intent. Raymond Orteig's narrow original explanation for establishing the airplane race did not capture the pandemonium. It was not possible that the whole world had so embraced Charles Lindbergh for improving relations between France and the United States.

It was up to Lindbergh, then, to add further definition to his achievement. But reading into the intentions of the young pilot did not yield much. Lindbergh had not dedicated his preparation to anything more than the pursuit of Raymond Orteig's cash prize. He sensed that he needed to add something more to his rationale. Lindbergh now insisted, as earlier aviators had suggested about their own attempts to soar above the Atlantic, that his 3,600-mile, thirty-three-and-a-half-hour flight had represented the success of "American science and genius which had given years of study to the advancement of aeronautics."[47] His father

---

[43] "Lindbergh: Sociological Note," *Baltimore Sun*, May 23, 1927, 10. See also "As 'Hero of Paris' Lindbergh is Feted by French Nation," *Boston Globe*, May 25, 1927, 1; and "Lindbergh Feted by French Fliers," *New York Times*, May 25, 1927, 2.

[44] "Col. Lindbergh, American," *Los Angeles Times*, September 20, 1927, A4.

[45] "A Tribute to Character," *New York Times*, June 11, 1927, 18.

[46] John Erskine, "Flight: Some Thoughts on the Solitary Voyage of a Certain Young Aviator," *Century Monthly* 114 (September 1927): 514.

[47] John W. Ward, "The Meaning of Lindbergh's Flight," *American Quarterly* 10 (Spring 1958): 14.

had publicly opposed America's entry into World War I, and perhaps this was the reason Lindbergh leaned into science rather than peace to underscore his Atlantic mission. Whatever his motivation, Lindbergh's explanation satisfied his public. In short order, the handsome Charles Lindbergh "had become the most photographed man in the world."[48]

His supporters augmented the scope of the Lindbergh metaphor. American statesmen such as President Coolidge presented Lindbergh as a peacekeeping science experiment. This was the opinion of Charles Evan Hughes, whose positions included New York Governor, US Secretary of State and, in time, Chief Justice of the Supreme Court. "We are all better men and women because of this exhibition in this flight of our young friend," said Hughes of Lindbergh. "Our boys and girls have before them a stirring, inspiring vision of real manhood. What a wonderful thing it is to live in a time when science and character join hands to lift up humanity with a vision of its own dignity."[49] Lindbergh was modernity incarnate: packed with wonder and ambition and freighted with bombastic blurry language and contradictions.

Americans became further invested in thickening the Lindbergh metaphor. Some celebrated the transatlantic voyage as a symbol of youthful spirit. Theodore Roosevelt Jr. compared Lindbergh to other mythical American young people: a "lineal descendent" of Daniel Boone and Davy Crockett. Others interpreted the young man's reservedness as humility and liked to believe that his emergence had undercut charges of American arrogance.[50] Ambassador Herrick, the young aviator's initial handler upon touchdown in France, placed Lindbergh's importance in religious terms, a creed that became known as the "Lindbergh religion." Herrick was Colonel Charles Lindbergh's first prophet. Herrick believed that Lindbergh was a godsend, meant to restore the world's peacemaking credibility after World War I.[51] "He was the instrument of a great ideal," stated Herrick about Lindbergh, "and one need not be fanatically religious to see in his success the guiding hand of providence."[52] Herrick refused to reduce Lindbergh's work as "merely the triumph of a great adventure," something akin to "great sporting and commercial

---

[48] A. Scott Berg, *Lindbergh* (New York: G. P. Putnam's Sons, 1998), 158.
[49] Charles A. Lindbergh, "Lindbergh's Own Story: The History of the Atlantic Flight as Told by Himself," *Current History* 26 (July 1927): 534.
[50] See "Col. Charles Lindbergh," *Los Angeles Times*, September 20, 1927, A4.
[51] See Eksteins, *Rites of Spring*, 242–74.
[52] Myron T. Herrick, "Foreword," in *We*, ed. Charles A. Lindbergh (New York: G. P. Putnam's Sons, 1927), 5–6.

achievements." 1927 had its share of those: for instance, Babe Ruth was the first to smash sixty home runs in a single baseball season and Al Jolson starred in *The Jazz Singer*, the first feature-length "talkie" movie.

Lindbergh's prophets insisted that their idol transcended mortal fascinations. Herrick instead preferred to understand Lindbergh as a "God-sent messenger of help, smiling defiance of [his] faith at an all too skeptical world."[53] Some went further in the worship of the Lindbergh creed. He was a "demi-god, the personification of human achievement." Others dubbed him a "New Christ," insisting that Lindbergh was in some measure connected to a Second Coming.[54] The accolades were always couched in vagaries.[55]

The journalist Silas Bent was troubled that the press had fawned over Lindbergh, that the newspapers counted him "among the great pioneers of history" or that his airborne trek was the "greatest feat of a solitary man in the records of the human race." Bent represented an incredulous minority that deigned to question Lindbergh and his accomplishment. "The truth of the matter," concluded Bent, "was that Lindbergh made his flight not only for the cash prize, but for its exhibition value."

Silas Bent must have known that his judgment would be received as a most unpopular opinion. Letter-writers dismissed his take on the matter, supposing that "if our religious press tells us that our wild enthusiasm for such traits of character as the world adored in Lindbergh is incompatible with the Christian religion, then we cannot expect our young people, whose aspirations are naturally high and fine and who instinctively detect and despise any insincerity, to be drawn to the Christian religion."[56] This was Lindbergh's greatness, a metaphor for an allusive partnership between modernity, diplomacy, technology, and faith. No one could cogently offer an explanation of how these forces could coexist. The same was the case for Charles Lindbergh's flight from New York to Paris. His plane's touchdown at Le Bourget somehow gave confidence that mankind would experience a soft landing into an uncertain future. It was a moment of indescribable greatness that papered over the unexplainable feelings of a burgeoning Modern Age.

***

---

[53] Ibid., 6, 10.
[54] Christopher Gehrz, *Charles Lindbergh: A Religious Biography of America's Most Infamous Pilot* (Grand Rapids, MI: Wm. B. Eerdmans Publishing Co., 2021), 61–62.
[55] Silas Bent, "Idol Worship: 1927," *Christian Advocate*, December 8, 1927, 1496.
[56] Florence Emily Cain, "Idol Worship: 1927," *Christian Advocate*, January 12, 1928, 62.

In March 1928, Walt Disney was jobless, riding a train from Chicago to California. The twenty-five-year-old cartoonist had started his homeward journey in New York. He had traveled to Manhattan to reason with Universal Pictures, to explain to the film executives that cartoons had a future and that he and his staff deserved to be paid better to bring about that animated vision. It did not work. Disney was beside himself, in disbelief that a film distributor had brokered a deal behind his back with Universal and convinced Disney's staff that they were better off without him. Worst of all, Walt Disney and animator Ub Iwerks no longer owned their first successful cartoon, Oswald the Lucky Rabbit. Disney later recalled that Oswald was "going over," meaning doing well at that time.[57] The truth of that matter was that Oswald was a relative hit, faring far better than Disney's and Iwerks' earlier "Alice Comedies." The newspapers compared Oswald to Felix the Cat, the standard-bearer of the nascent animated cartoon industry.

Disney did not quit. The painful experience with Universal Studios, and his lack of political savvy to convince the executives to follow his lead, confirmed to him that his next project needed to be his own. All Walt Disney required was a new character. Smaller creatures had worked well for the first generation of American animators. Disney decided on a mouse because felines were too overrepresented in the cartoon industry. Canines evoked far too much violence and he had already tried his luck with a rabbit. Along the journey Disney wired his brother that he was "coming home with a great new idea." By the time he returned to his wife, Lillian, in Los Angeles, Disney had already scripted the scenario for the Lindbergh-inspired short silent cartoon called *Plane Crazy*. Disney had moved on from Oswald and excitedly told his wife about Mortimer Mouse and his attempt to fly like Charles Lindbergh. Lilly found the name Mortimer "too sissy." Disney asked whether "Mickey" was passable. "It sounded better than Mortimer," she replied.[58]

Disney was sure that Mickey Mouse was his big break. Iwerks and a small crew of artists produced thousands of black-and-white drawings. Disney started to shop the cartoon, to "make the name of 'Mickey Mouse' as well-known as any cartoon in the market," as Iwerks got to work on a second Mickey film. In the middle of that second production, Disney called things to a halt. He had not yet found a buyer

---

[57] Walt Disney, "Growing Pains," *American Cinematographer* 22 (March 1941): 107.
[58] Lillian Disney and Isabella Taves, "I Live with a Genius," *McCall's* 80 (February 1953): 104–105.

for the Lindbergh lampoon but urged his artists to redirect their attention to a third project: a "talkie" cartoon. He was inspired by Al Jolson's pathbreaking film, *The Jazz Singer*. It was the first movie with lip-synchronous singing and speech. "That's it. That's it," Disney told his family. "It looks realistic, it'll be realistic. That's what we've got to do. Stop all these silent pictures."[59]

Disney stopped peddling *Plane Crazy* and brainstormed *Steamboat Willie*. The seven-and-a-half-minute animation set on a sidewheeler riverboat was the very first occasion that Mickey saved Minnie from his nemesis, Pete. Disney set the sound by playing the animation on a projector while synchronizing the accompanying music. He recorded one of the illustrators playing "Turkey in the Straw," just as Mickey and Minnie cranked a goat's tail – the goat had swallowed a songbook and ukulele – like a phonograph. Disney tasked a different artist to produce sound effects with his mouth. Another banged pencils while Walt provided the voice for Mickey Mouse. It took a good deal of technological finesse to match the video with the audio. On November 18, 1928, *Steamboat Willie* premiered before an unremarkable feature film in New York. The first ever motion picture critic, Mordaunt Hall, was the first to opine on Disney's inaugural "sound cartoon:"

On the same program is the first sound cartoon, produced by Walter Disney, creator of "Oswald the Rabbit." The current film is called "Steamboat Willie," and it introduces a new cartoon character, henceforth to be known as Micky [sic] Mouse." It is an ingenious piece of work with a good deal of fun. It growls, whines, squeaks and makes various other sounds that add to its mirthful quality.[60]

Mickey Mouse was a sensation. "Everybody was talking about it and raving about the funny actions this mouse character did," recalled a motion picture insider. Those in charge of Felix the Cat recognized that "Disney put us out of business with his sound."[61] Disney next arranged *Plane Crazy* to audio and released it five months after *Steamboat Willie*. Critics reviewed it very favorably, albeit they were unprepared to comment on Mickey's and Minnie's romantic relationship: "Disney has derived some breezy situations, one or two of them a bit saucy but, considering the animal characters, permissible."[62]

---

[59] Neal Gabler, *Walt Disney: The Triumph of the American Imagination* (New York: Alfred A. Knopf, 2007), 115–16.
[60] Mordaunt Hall, "The Screen," *New York Times*, November 19, 1928, 16.
[61] Gabler, *Walt Disney*, 128.
[62] "Plane Crazy," *Variety*, April 3, 1929, 11.

The press liked to compare Mickey Mouse to Charlie Chaplin. They had a lot in common. Their films focused on the "little fellow who is fighting the big fellow."[63] The philosopher Walter Benjamin jotted down a note to himself that "All Mickey Mouse films are founded on the motif of leaving home in order to learn what fear is."[64] The pairing delighted Disney, who freely admitted that Chaplin was his inspiration. For his part, Ub Iwerks tried to steer Mickey into less trampy roles, parts that resembled Douglas Fairbanks' heroic portrayals of Zorro and Robin Hood. Disney's take, of course, prevailed.[65] Like Chaplin, Mickey was cast in a myriad of roles – some everyday characters, others eccentric – that placed him in underdog situations. Disney meant for this to increase his cartoon's appeal beyond any social or economic niche, so that everyone could find the "Mickey in us."[66] Mickey Mouse was a changemaking aspiration like all American great people and things. Like Chaplin before him and Lindbergh afterward, Mickey Mouse's greatness was more attributed than evidently achieved. In the first eleven years of existence, one critic made an unofficial audit of the characters Mickey Mouse had played. The list was Chaplin-like:

Gaucho, deckhand, farmer, impresario, teamster, musician, explorer, swimmer, cowboy, fireman, convict, pioneer, taxi driver, castaway, fisherman, cyclist, Arab, football player, inventor, jockey, storekeeper, camper, sailor, Gulliver, boxer, exterminator, skater, poloist, circus performer, plumber, chemist, magician, hunter, detective, clock cleaner, Hawaiian, carpenter, driver, trapper, horseman, whaler, and tailor.[67]

By 1931, Mickey Mouse cartoons were standard fare in eighty percent of America's 15,000 movie theaters. Walt Disney organized a team of thirty artists to sketch each film. Mickey had a feature comic strip syndicated in sixty newspapers in the United States and twenty others overseas. His likeness, considered by many a work of "art," was featured in galleries at the Chicago Art Institute, Harvard's Fogg Art Museum, and

---

[63] Edward Wood, "The Magic of Mickey Mouse," *Picture Show* 27 (September 24, 1932): 10.
[64] *Walter Benjamin: Selected Writings*, vol. 2, eds. Michael W. Jennings, Howard Eiland, and Gary Smith (Cambridge: Harvard University Press, 1999), 545.
[65] Jeff Ryan, *A Mouse Divided: How Ub Iwerks Became Forgotten and Walt Disney Became Uncle Walt* (New York: Post Hill Press, 2018), 57–62.
[66] Walt Disney, "The Cartoon's Contribution to Children," *Overland Monthly* 91 (October 1933): 138.
[67] Lewis Jacobs, *The Rise of the American Film: A Critical History* (New York: Harcourt, Brace and Company, 1939), 498.

the Los Angeles County Museum.[68] Stores carried Mickey Mouse toys, dolls, storybooks, safety razors, and candy boxes. Born five months before Mickey, the illustrator Maurice Sendak once wrote about growing up with animation's greatest invention, with all the impressive trappings of modern merchandising:

> He was our common street friend. My brother and sister and I chewed his gum, brushed our teeth with his toothbrush, played with him in a seemingly endless variety of games and read about his adventures in comic strips and storybooks. Best of all, our street pal was also a movie star, in the darkened theater, the sudden flash of his brilliant, wild, joyful face—radiating great golden beams—filled me with an intoxicating, unalloyed pleasure.[69]

Some complained. The opera singer Florence Austral believed that Mickey had distracted the masses from her high art world. Others informed Ms. Austral that they could "think of nothing in modern entertainment for which Mozart could be more fitly neglected."[70] A disgruntled moviegoer protested that Disney was a menace and "if I had any kids, they'd go to see Mickey Mouse only over my dead body."[71] But that same dissatisfied individual admitted that he had surveyed America's most prominent experts on education, and no one agreed with him. "For my money, Mickey Mouse is really the only true art that has come out of Hollywood," said actor Maurice Evans during a radio discussion with Eleanor Roosevelt. Mrs. Roosevelt, in turn, recalled another ardent admirer: "My husband always loved Mickey Mouse and we always had to have it in the White House."[72]

Mickey Mouse's success encouraged Walt Disney's studios to produce other cartoons. Within discrete social circles, it was satisfactory for moviegoers to confess that the "Three Little Pigs" compared to Mickey. But it was, perhaps understandably, a "heretical sect which considers the 'Silly Symphonies' by far the greater of Disney's products."[73] In 1932, the Academy of Motion Picture Arts and Sciences issued a special award to Walt Disney for the creation of Mickey Mouse. They had

---

[68] See Steven Watts, *The Magic Kingdom: Walt Disney and the American Way of Life* (Boston: Houghton Mifflin Company, 1997), 123–24.
[69] Maurice Sendak, "Growing Up with Mickey," in *A Mickey Mouse Reader*, ed. Garry Apgar (Jackson, MS: University Press of Mississippi, 2014), 191.
[70] C. A. Lejeune, *Cinema* (London: Alexander MacLehose & Co., 1931), 84.
[71] Frederick McCord, "Is Walt Disney a Menace to Our Children," *Photoplay* 45 (April 1934): 92.
[72] "Postscripts & Afterthoughts," *Time* 57 (April 30, 1951): 44.
[73] Gilbert Seldes, "Mickey-Mouse Maker," *New Yorker*, December 19, 1931, 25.

been mulling how to acknowledge Mickey since birth. "For years there has been discussions within the academy ranks of acknowledging the genius of Walt Disney."[74] Disney provided cover for the true awardee. No cartoon carried with it the intangible grandeur and greatness of Mickey Mouse.

***

Walt Disney's creature was more than just an animated mouse personifying and rehearsing the very best of Charlie Chaplin's routines, but with sound. Truth to tell, Mickey Mouse's greatness was far more baffling than Chaplin's or Lindbergh's. America acknowledged that Mickey was manmade, the handywork of Walt Disney and Ub Iwerks. His energy was also their concoction; Disney had so cleverly devised a method to bring music and sound into the animated shorts. However, the popular perception had it that it was Mickey and not his inventors who summoned millions of people to the movie houses. Disney was not great. Walt was secondary, the Hollywood artist who had "created the greatest of all film stars: Mickey Mouse."[75]

Disney encouraged the separation of Mickey Mouse from him: "We have become great pals, Mickey and I," quipped Disney, aware of the inherent schizophrenia. "And I'm not fooling when I say that he is just as much a person to me as anyone I know."[76] Pundits focused on the fictional character, asking for the "reason why Mickey Mouse has such a tremendous hold on the cinema public?"[77] Walt Disney claimed ignorance on that existential question. "Sometimes I've tried to figure out why Mickey appealed to the whole world," offered Disney. "Everybody's tried to figure it out. So far as I know, nobody has. He's a pretty nice fellow who never does anybody any harm, who gets into scrapes and through no fault of his own, but always managed to come up grinning."[78]

Other Americans deigned to account for Mickey Mouse's greatness on multiple grounds. First, Mickey had achieved a level of international

---

[74] "Walt Disney Honored by Academy Special Awards," *Washington Post*, December 4, 1932, A1.
[75] O. Bristol, "Walt Disney," *Picture Show* 33 (August 10, 1935): 7.
[76] Walt Disney, "'Mickey Mouse': How He was Born," *Windsor Magazine* 74 (October 1931): 642.
[77] Wood, "The Magic of Mickey Mouse," 10.
[78] "Mickey Mouse: Changed, but He Doesn't Look 50," *Chicago Tribune*, November 15, 1977, A6. The religion scholar Martin Marty traced the quote to the 1930s, in a German magazine. See Martin E. Marty, "On Religion," *New York Times*, December 3, 1977, 23.

fame, more than Edgar Allen Poe or Charlie Chaplin had obtained. By 1932, Disney's mailroom staff opened 6,000 letters each week. Many were addressed to Mickey Mouse. However, German fans sent to "Michael Maus." From France, he was known as "Michel Souris." "Mikki Maus" in Russian, and "Topolino" in Italian. In Spain, "Miguel Ratoncito." Japanese followers knew him as "Miki Kuchi."[79]

A second explanation for Mickey's greatness was more profound than his international reputation and fully set him apart from Chaplin and other Hollywood greats: Mickey Mouse provided an escape from the economic drudgeries of the Great Depression. From 1929–1939, the world's gross domestic production fell by 15 percent. A quarter of Americans lost their jobs, and many became homeless. The stock exchanges collapsed. Banks failed. People lost faith in the real world. Mickey emerged as a reliable albeit fictional pal. The Freudian psychoanalyst Abraham Brill was perhaps the first to notice the grand utility of Mickey's fantasy world. This was particularly the case for grown-ups. Brill described the adult who watch Mickey and "forgets all about his drab, routine problems and merges back into a period of life when everything could still be attained through fantasy."[80]

Part of Mickey's fantasyland had to do with Disney's painstaking investment in the animation. The peerless art of each Mickey Mouse cartoon suggested to an increasing number of Americans that the very best animators could overcome the blemishes of real life. "In his pictures," wrote one critic of Walt Disney, "every movement, whether of flora or fauna, is correlated; every leaf, every whisker, every eyelash, every swerve, every bound is imbued with significance, drama or humour."[81] Filmgoers marveled that Disney shorts appeared seamless and made them ponder whether the live action motion pictures could overcome the now all-too-noticeable film splices and imperfect scene transitions that were made in the cutting room.

It was humorous during the first decade of the mouse's "life" to point out that despite his impact and popularity, Mickey Mouse was not real. Walt Disney and others liked to jest that Mickey was the single unpaid film star in Hollywood; that he was the most dependable actor since he would never leave for another studio; and that he

---

[79] "Mickey Mouse's New Affiliation," *New York Times*, June 26, 1932, X3.
[80] "Dr. Brill Analyzes Walt Disney's Masterpieces," *Photoplay* 45 (April 1934): 92.
[81] Sydney Tremayne, "Then it Can't Be All Sex-Appeal," *Britannia & Eve* 4 (January 1932): 106.

accumulated the most international fame and yet had never shaken hands with a world leader. Yet, there was something deeper to this. Mickey Mouse's world was fantasy, much better than the real world that reminded audiences, to some degree or another, of the crushing and pervasive economic hardship wrought by the Great Depression. "Charlie Chaplin must contend with a more or less material world," admitted an astute commentator. "Mickey Mouse and his companions," on the other hand, "live in a special cosmos of their own in which the nature of matter changes from moment to moment."[82] One could debate who was more famous: Chaplin or Mickey Mouse? However, what truly had separated Mickey from Charlie was historical circumstance. In the 1930s, Chaplin's live action social criticisms painfully reminded audiences of their personal plight. Mickey Mouse was a tonic, a temporary respite from that hard reality (Figure 3.3).

FIGURE 3.3 Walt Disney and Mickey Mouse board a plane to headline the 1933 World's Fair in Chicago. Courtesy of Bettmann/Getty Images.

[82] Creighton Peet, "Miraculous Mickey," in *A Mickey Mouse Reader*, 17.

The Great Depression confirmed what humankind already knew: people were imperfect. Films, because they featured real life individuals, had lost some luster. Some of the most popular movies of the decade were those that transported audiences into a different reality: *The Wizard of Oz*, *Gone with the Wind*, and *The Adventures of Robin Hood*. Films that depicted real life were not as much in vogue. "The human figure has always stood in the way of cinema progress. The silly affairs of men, their silly civilized gestures, their schooled faces, their shapeless clothed bodies, lacking both form and texture, have occupied the camera lens for years past, just as to-day their flat passionless voices are monopolising the microphone."[83] The same critic extolled animation: "Mickey Mouse has achieved that perfect blend between visual and aural impulses."[84] His films were the stuff of magic.

All these tributes preceded Mickey Mouse's technicolor debut in 1935. By then, more than 500 million people had paid to view the marvelous mouse in their local nickelodeons. Mickey was in the estimations of many the "evolutionary product with everything that ever was made for the screen in his ancestry and with Charlie Chaplin as his closest human relative."[85] Mickey Mouse was an antidote to the anxieties of the humdrum of the Depression, a vision of how to overcome the real world. He was the "sublimest thing that flashes across the screen."[86] Mickey "represents the modern fairy tale."[87] His cartoons went "beyond simple artistic design."[88] The zoologist Stephen Jay Gould and essayist John Updike agreed that the fantastical appeal of Mickey Mouse had to do with the symmetrical roundness of his face. Gould pointed out that while Ub Iwerks had from the beginning drawn Mickey Mouse with endearing features, the growing number of artists assigned to Mickey films quickly evolved him, softening his "ratty character" in favor of an adorable "childlike appearance."[89] Updike homed in on the simplicity and balance of the multiple circles that made up Mickey's face. His ears, argued Updike, "properly belong not to three-dimensional space but to an ideal realm of notation, of symbolization, of cartoon resilience

---

[83] Lejeune, *Cinema*, 89.
[84] "The Barn Dance/Draughtsman ... Walt Disney," in *A Mickey Mouse Reader*, 8.
[85] Terry Ramsaye, "Mickey Mouse: He Stays on the Job," in *A Mickey Mouse Reader*, 56.
[86] Wood, "The Magic of Mickey Mouse," 11.
[87] Harry Carr, "The Only Unpaid Movie Star," *American Magazine* 11 (March 1931): 55.
[88] Pierre Scize, "The Cinema," in *A Mickey Mouse Reader*, 13.
[89] Stephen Jay Gould, *The Panda's Thumb: More Reflections in Natural History* (New York: W. W. Norton & Company, 1980), 98.

and indestructability."[90] The Depression proved that people could lose fortunes, feel pain, and break down, physically and mentally. Mickey Mouse, on the other hand, stayed above all that. He promised hope and change. This was his greatness.

* * *

The greatness of Chaplin, Lindbergh, and Mickey Mouse were tightly tethered to historical circumstances. Their so-described greatness was attributed to them due to the social needs of their moment. Historical change also held the power to loosen their grasps on greatness. Evaluated this way, attributed greatness was far more tenuous than the achieved variety. Perhaps the same might have been said of Robert E. Lee if "greatness" held the same amount of cultural currency on the eve of the Civil War. One can imagine the disappointment of a Yankee upon learning that Lee, a hero of the Mexican–American War, chose to fight for the Confederacy rather than the Union. Lee, of course, was a far more formative figure in the Civil War than Chaplin, Lindbergh (although he, more than the other two), and Mickey Mouse were in twentieth-century politics. Through his military record, Lee had achieved something that could not be so easily removed from his enduring legacy.

The value of studying these three figures is that they rose and fell in an American century obsessed with defining and redefining greatness. Earlier individuals such as George Washington, Ralph Waldo Emerson and Edgar Allan Poe had preceded this epoch. Their achievements were essentially fixed by the time Henry McCracken and others emerged in the twentieth century with designs on canonizing and popularizing America's greatest people. The pathbreaking work by historian Annette Gordon-Reed on Thomas Jefferson's relationship with a slave, Sally Hemings, is the exception that proves the rule.[91] By contrast, Chaplin, Lindbergh, and Mickey were in their "lifetimes" anointed great symbolic exemplars of progress and change. Each inspired hope during the bleak years of the Great Depression. Hence, attributed greatness. After that, though, they roused sensations that achieved just the opposite. These reconsiderations of greatness point to aspirational pragmatism implicit in the coronation of American greatness.

The most well-known instance is Lindbergh. His politics during World War II destroyed his reputation. Lindbergh's sister-in-law

---

[90] John Updike, *More Matter: Essays and Criticism* (New York: Random House, 1999), 202.
[91] Annette Gordon-Reed, *Thomas Jefferson and Sally Hemings: An American Controversy* (Charlottesville, VA: University of Virginia Press, 1997).

quipped that "in just fifteen years he had gone from Jesus to Judas!"[92] Lindbergh was the most visible pitchman of the pro-isolationist and short-lived America First Committee. Founded in 1940, the group lobbied for the United States to withstand pressures to enter World War II. Once a reticent hero, Lindbergh revealed a new and aggressive persona to keep American soldiers out of "Europe's affairs." Several factors account for Lindbergh's transformation: his own father had adopted a similar position before World War I; his social circle after the transatlantic flight expanded to include intellectuals with eugenic-aligned beliefs; and he had spent the preceding years in Europe, self-exiled after the tragic kidnapping of his infant son.

Lindbergh had evinced some of his isolationist politics before the birth of the America First movement. In 1936, he and his wife, Anne Morrow Lindbergh, attended the contentious 1936 Berlin Olympics as special guests of Hermann Göring, head of the Nazi air force. In 1938, Göring summoned Lindbergh back to Germany to receive the Service Cross of the German Eagle for his contributions to aviation. Göring presented the award to Lindbergh on behalf of Adof Hitler, amid heightened political tensions and just a month before the devastating Kristallnacht pogroms. The ceremony was done without fanfare and all Lindbergh offered in response was "thank you." However, the presentation raised ire: "How can any American accept a decoration at the hand of a brutal dictator who, with that same hand, is robbing and torturing thousands of fellow human beings?" asked Secretary Harold Ickes, a member of President Franklin Roosevelt's cabinet.[93] Anne Lindbergh's best-selling 1940 pamphlet that described Germany and Russia as the "wave of the future" did not assuage matters.[94]

The Lindberghs returned to the United States in 1939 and revealed an added personal point to his political positioning. For two decades, Lindbergh had enjoyed a caliber of fame predicated on the promise of aviation. He and others had claimed that the transatlantic flight from New York to Paris had augured a scientific revolution and world peace. Instead, Americans read about the threats of Nazi air strikes throughout Europe. Airplanes had reverted into killing machines, and Lindbergh's reputation sank into something far less than greatness. Writing just before the start of World War II, Lindbergh declared that "aviation seems almost

---

[92] Berg, *Lindbergh*, 433.
[93] "Ickes Hits Takers of Hitler Medals," *New York Times*, December 19, 1938, 5.
[94] Berg, *Lindbergh*, 406.

a gift from heaven," a "tool specially shaped for Western hands."[95] But by the time his writing appeared Germany had annexed Poland and most readers had given up hope in that theology of manmade flight.

His defense of aviation introduced a disturbing aspect of Lindbergh's thinking. He called the "Western" protectors of aviation the "White race" who had to soar above the "pressing sea of Yellow, Black, and Brown."[96] Americans were troubled that Lindbergh had linked their stock with the Nazis, that theirs was a "common heritage." This was a trope that drew from Francis Galton's eugenics and recalled Herbert Spencer's hope for the United States to rise to the top of Aryanism. Congress was nonplussed. Lawmakers summoned Lindbergh to hearings, where senators questioned why the now-infamous airman had not condemned Hitler. Senator James Byrnes of North Carolina censured Lindbergh for an immoral indifference toward the "flagrant violations of the rights of peaceful little nations; the cruel and bitter persecution of God-fearing men, women and children because of their religion, race or political opinions; the burning of books, the bombing of helpless women and children fleeing in terror from their homes; the parachute spies and the torch troops."[97]

The public pundits piled it on. Letter-writers to Lindbergh expressed vitriol, declaring "What an unpatriotic dumb bell you are."[98] Others labeled Lindbergh an antisemite for his abject refusal to condemn Hitler's plan to murder Europe's Jews. Eleanor Roosevelt told reporters that "If I had received a medal from Hitler, as Col. Charles A. Lindbergh did, I would have returned it long ago."[99] The playwright Robert Sherwood called Lindbergh a "Nazi with a Nazi's Olympian contempt for all democratic processes."[100] Lindbergh's dwindling lot of defenders preached free speech and pointed out that polls still indicated that most Americans were opposed to the United States entering the war and that Lindbergh was a modern-day Isaiah, a brave prophet who refused to surrender to the niceties of political speech.[101]

---

[95] Charles A. Lindbergh, "Aviation, Geography, and Race," *Reader's Digest* 35 (November 1939): 64.
[96] Ibid.
[97] James Francis Byrnes, "Answers to Charles Lindbergh," *Palestine Post*, June 25, 1940, 3.
[98] Berg, *Lindbergh*, 415.
[99] "First Lady Hints Lindbergh Should Return Nazi Medal," *Washington Post*, May 2, 1941, 6.
[100] "Calls Lindbergh 'a Nazi,'" *New York Times*, December 12, 1940, 18.
[101] See, for example, "More Lindbergh Letters—Writers Uphold Flier's Stand—Rap on Dorothy Thompson," *Boston Globe*, May 4, 1941, B12.

The Rise and Fall of the Great Changemakers

Lindbergh's final fall from greatness took place on September 11, 1941. In Des Moines, Iowa, Lindbergh delivered his most explicit remarks for the America First Committee, the single occasion that he said anything publicly about Jews' role in political affairs. Anne Morrow Lindbergh cautioned her husband and "dread[ed] the reaction on him."[102] But Charles Lindbergh was incorrigible. He did not listen to the warnings that his calls for continued isolation from world affairs had become packed with racism and separated American Jews' interests from the rest of US citizens:

> I am not attacking either the Jewish or the British people. Both races, I admire. But I am saying that the leaders of both the British and the Jewish races, for reasons which are as understandable from their viewpoint as they are inadvisable from ours, for reasons which are not American, wish to involve us in the war. We cannot blame them for looking out for what they believe to be their own interests, but we also must look out for ours. We cannot allow the natural passions and prejudices of other peoples to lead our country to destruction.[103]

The Des Moines speech irrevocably ruined Lindbergh's public persona. His biographer listed the rhetorical gestures that captured Lindbergh's transformed reputation: He had gone from "Public Hero No. 1" to "Public Enemy No. 1;" was the "symbol of anti-Semitism in this country;" and the "most dangerous man in America."[104] One politician called Lindbergh's speech the "most un-American talk made in my time by any person of national reputation." New York Mayor Fiorello La Guardia described the discourse as a "carbon copy of a Nazi paper."[105] The pro-isolationist newspapers had to confess that after the Des Moines debacle, Lindbergh's "name henceforth will be associated with those who believe in the creed of hate, of bigotry and of intolerance." Intuiting the pragmatism and contingencies of attributed greatness, an astute observer forecasted that Lindbergh's "usefulness as a public figure is ended."[106]

Two months later, on December 7, 1941, Japanese airplanes bombed the US naval base at Pearl Harbor. On the following day, Congress declared war on Japan. Lindbergh and the America First Committee canceled an upcoming rally in Boston and released a statement that

---

[102] Ibid., 425.
[103] *American Antiwar Speeches, 1846 to the Present*, ed. Jesse Stellato (University Park, PA: Pennsylvania State University Press, 2012), 117.
[104] Berg, *Lindbergh*, 428.
[105] "Lindbergh Address Condemned by Mayor," *New York Times*, September 19, 1941, 12.
[106] "The Lindbergh Speech in Des Moines," *Jewish Record* 4 (December 1941): 638.

conceded that "by force of arms we must retaliate." On December 11, the America First Committee voted for dissolution. Eager for absolution, Lindbergh sought recommission, but the US Air Force rejected his request. Charles Lindbergh's politics, the failed erstwhile promises of aeronautics, and the historical turn of world circumstances had totally removed Lindbergh from his high station. After World War II, Americans started to refer to Gen. Jimmy Doolittle as the "world's greatest aviator." Doolittle had led decisive airstrikes on Japan after Pearl Harbor and received the Medal of Honor for changing the US's fortunes in the Pacific.[107] Doolittle was a deserving hero. But it was a more complex set of forces that withdrew Lindbergh from the rank of the greatest aviator of all time.

***

World War II had a very significant impact on Mickey Mouse, but it had nothing to do with diplomatic improprieties. In December 1941, Walt Disney secured contracts to produce animated films for the US Navy and Department of Treasury. He was relieved. A year earlier, *Pinocchio* had disappointed, and *Fantasia* had flopped. Disney was in debt and his large staff was ready to strike. The government work was a financial life preserver and had energized America's leading animator. However, the government did not want Mickey Mouse to star in these commissioned movies. Mickey was no longer a scrappy everyman. He had become an unassailable figure who hardly ever erred. He had evolved into that fanciful persona to help his audiences rise above the drudgeries of the Great Depression. But the government hired Disney to produce films that leaned into the scary reality of a world war. Disney required a cartoon character that could face the battlefields and struggle along with Americans as they grappled with the dilemmas of a "warfare state."[108] Disney's "mind was seething with new plots and shenanigans for Donald Duck."[109] Mickey was an afterthought.

It was already apparent that Donald had been vying to topple Mickey as Walt Disney's most important cartoon character. Donald Duck was born on April 29, 1934, the brainchild of Walt Disney and Dick Lundy. The studio required a more mischievous character since Mickey Mouse was no longer permitted, according to Walt Disney and public opinion, to play

---

[107] Jody Jacobs, "World's Greatest Aviator," *Los Angeles Times*, June 22, 1973, H6.
[108] See James T. Sparrow, *Warfare State: World War II Americans and the Age of Big Government* (New York: Oxford University Press, 2011).
[109] Sidney Carroll, "Disney – Our Secret Weapon," *Esquire* 19 (March 1943): 62.

rambunctious roles. Mickey was by now more Fairbanks than Chaplin. The Mickey Mouse Club had by 1932 reached one million members, and those youngsters and their parents expected Mickey to comport with politeness and incur good fortune. "Every time we put him into a trick, a temper, a joke, thousands of people would belabor us with nasty letters." By contrast, Donald was "so easy." The writers applied all the canceled Mickey gags to Donald. "Donald became our ham, a mean, irascible little buzzard. Everyone knew he was bad and didn't give a damn."[110] The critics complained that the ideologization and protection of Mickey's image had transformed him "into something like an international bore"[111]

Caught in this tension, Disney hatched the testy Donald Duck, a cartoon character that could once again embrace hijinks and humor that had once ingratiated Mickey Mouse and Charlie Chaplin to American audiences. Decked out in his sailor outfit, Donald Duck, raspy voiced and hot-tempered, debuted in "The Wise Little Hen." He did well and was promptly promoted to a slate of Mickey-featured films. In February 1935, Donald shared the spotlight with Mickey in Disney's first color cartoon.

The newspapers picked up on the "duckward" trend. His fan mail rivaled Mickey's.[112] On the radio program frequencies "Donald Duck, we would say, stole the show from Mickey Mouse."[113] "It's manifest how fast growing is the vogue of Donald Duck, the volubly irate gander who bids fair to par Mickey as Disney's favorite creation."[114] The Disney animators and storytellers took to Donald because there was too much at stake when focused on Mickey. "We began to have an awful hard time defining stories for Mickey," admitted one writer. "[He] began as a mischief maker, but he developed right off the bat into a little hero type, and you couldn't knock him around too much."[115]

In 1937, the studio had to alter the script for "Mickey's Inventions" because the plot included ample doses of machines pulverizing the protagonist. Instead, the animators changed the film to "Modern Inventions," riffing on a recent Chaplin film, and swapped Mickey for

---

[110] Irving Wallace, "Mickey Mouse and How He Grew," *Collier's* 123 (April 9, 1949), 21.
[111] William Troy, "Puppets – Two Styles," *Nation* 140 (May 8, 1935): 556.
[112] "Walt and Donald (Disney and Duck) Both Had Modest Start," *Daily Republican*, April 28, 1941, 5.
[113] Larry Wolters, "Donald Duck Star of Disney Radio Program," *Chicago Tribune*, January 4, 1938, 19.
[114] Abel, "Shorts," *Variety*, February 12, 1936, 16.
[115] Marcia Blitz, *Donald Duck* (London: New English Library, 1979), 13.

Donald. The cartoonist Carl Barks approved. "It was lots of fun with Donald. With Mickey it would have been kind of dangerous, because Mickey always had to be right," recalled Barks. "He always had to come out the winner. With the duck I had a comedian that I could treat badly and who I could make fun of."[116]

Mickey Mouse remained the face of Walt Disney Studios, even as other animated stars proved more useful to the bottom line. But thinking in financial terms, some started to refer to Disney as the "father of Snow White," the studio's – or anyone else's – first full-length animated movie. There was amply good reason to elevate Disney's very first princess flick. *Snow White and the Seven Dwarfs* netted almost $7 million in worldwide receipts, making it the highest-grossing American movie until it was unseated by *Gone with the Wind*. Still, commentators marveled that "with fawns and nymphs and princesses to choose from," Walt Disney stayed "enamored with the mouse."[117]

World War II finally convinced Disney to think otherwise. Reeling from massive debt, Disney dedicated nine-tenths of his staff to animating war films: "His whole vast studio—with Donald Duck and all the rest—are working now for Uncle Sam."[118] Mickey Mouse was relegated to two films per annum. The US government pitched Disney to produce propaganda to support the Allies. He owed far too much to the banks to turn the opportunity down. In January 1942, Donald appeared in a film meant to promote prompt payment of taxes, an act, the film let on, that was just as valiant as flying fighter jets and marching in combat units. It was inconceivable that Mickey would delay payment of income tax. Donald, on the other hand, would have to be convinced, just like the lion's share of US citizens. In August, Disney premiered "Saludos Amigos" (Greetings, friends) to acquaint and bind Americans and Latin Americans during a moment in which the State Department feared that South American governments might align with Hitler.

In February 1943, Disney came to terms with Donald's ascendance and Mickey's fall from stalwart greatness. He was visiting Harvard University to seek scholarly guidance on how to best "debunk" Hitler's racial theories.[119] What Disney was quite certain about, he told

---

[116] *Carl Barks Conversations*, ed. Donald Ault (Jackson, MS: University Press of Mississippi, 2003), 143.
[117] Dorothy Ducas, "The Father of Snow White," *Los Angeles Times*, June 19, 1938, 12.
[118] J. P. McEvoy, "Walt Disney Goes to War," *Los Angeles Times*, July 5, 1942, H9.
[119] "Disney, Hooton to Hold Conference on Nazi Ideology," *Harvard Crimson*, February 4, 1943, 1.

reporters, was that his next series of anti-Nazi films would star Donald Duck and not Mickey Mouse. "We needed someone tougher. A guy who wasn't a gentleman."[120] Disney had surmised that his American viewers during wartime required the feistier – and therefore, more "masculine" – Donald Duck. Disney liked that Donald was a "little mischief" and a bona fide "roughneck."[121] Donald had recently starred in "Der Fuehrer's Face," a film that depicted Donald in a dream, overworked on a Nazi assembly line. Donald is forced into overtime, assembling warheads. His only break comes to perform the Nazi salute. Finally, he awakes from that nightmare, dressed in star-spangled nightwear, and the film ends with Donald embracing a golden statuette of the Statue of Liberty.

This was no scene for Mickey Mouse. He was too pristine to work with munitions and, even within the context of a bad dream, Mickey could never grapple with siding between the forces of good and evil. But real-life people had to handle warheads and struggled with the politics of World War II. For them, Donald Duck resonated far better.

In 1947, a Gallup Poll canvassed Americans to ascertain their favorite cartoon character. The survey placed Donald Duck in first place, ahead of Warner Brothers' relative upstart, Bugs Bunny. Gallup ranked Mickey Mouse in third place.[122] The results did not surprise Walt Disney, who, in the postwar period, resigned to Mickey Mouse's middling fate. He spoke about his beloved Mickey in apologetics. "Sure," admitted Disney. "After 120 pictures, it's only natural for them to get a little tired of The Mouse. It's tough to come up with new ideas, to keep him fresh and at the same time in character."[123] Yet, it was not merely fatigue that had demoted Mickey Mouse from his high station. Stripped of the qualities that had made him a star, Mickey was no longer all that useful to Americans (Figure 3.4). His attributed greatness was a curious historical-contingent casualty of World War II.

***

America's postwar fear of Communism changed Charlie Chaplin's fortunes. In truth, Chaplin wasn't a Communist. However, the Federal Bureau of Investigation alleged he was a crypto-Communist. Officials

---

[120] Marjory Adams, "Disney Tells Why Donald Replaced Mickey as 'Tough,'" *Boston Globe*, February 6, 1943, 3.
[121] "Donald Duck Explained," *Cincinnati Enquirer*, February 8, 1943, 13.
[122] Frank Nugent, "That Million-Dollar Mouse," *New York Times*, September 21, 1947, 61.
[123] Ibid.

FIGURE 3.4 Certainly by 1951, Walt Disney had embraced the perception that Donald Duck had overtaken Mickey Mouse as America's "greatest" cartoon. Courtesy of Hulton Deutsch/Getty Images.

hated that Chaplin associated with the composer Hanns Eisler, an actual card-carrying Communist, and offered money to help Eisler and others flee the country if members of Congress's Un-American Activities Committee summoned them in order to interrogate their political beliefs. Interested parties also loathed that Chaplin flouted their concern over indigenous Communist threats. In a 1947 press conference, Chaplin responded to a reporter's request to "define your present political beliefs." Chaplin's answer was clear but mockingly verbose:

Well, I think that is very difficult to do these days, to define anything politically. There are so many generalities, and life is becoming so technical that if you step off the curb—I think you need a guidebook—if you step off the curb with your left foot, they accuse you of being a Communist. But I have no political persuasion whatsoever. I've never belonged to any political party in my life.[124]

[124] Kevin J. Hayes, *Charlie Chaplin Interviews* (Jackson, MS: University Press of Mississippi, 2005), 105.

On another occasion, Chaplin explained that "I am not a Communist, but I am pretty pro-Communist."[125] Chaplin claimed he was an "internationalist" who abhorred war, a position made widely apparent in his 1940 film, *The Great Dictator*. That was another point of frustration for Chaplin's detractors; his films and the Tramp figure, more specifically, always seemed to satire the ills of American capitalism and the United States' political interests. His movies and banter helped J. Edgar Hoover and the FBI build a large file on the comedian that registered evidence of Chaplin's "Red sympathies."[126]

Chaplin never did provide the smoking gun. Neither Hoover nor the indefatigable members of Congress's Un-American Activities Committee could prove Chaplin was guilty of anything more than irreverence and antiauthoritarianism. Without much to go on, Hoover clung to peripheral matters such as Chaplin's infidelities (these accusations were all true) to make the case for the comedian's pernicious influence on the American public. Chaplin's biographer reviewed the FBI's files on his subject and was struck by the "degree of sloppiness and stupidity that many of the reports reveal." He surmised that an "inordinate amount of time seems to have been devoted to processing hearsay, rumours, poison-pen letters and cranky unsolicited correspondence."[127]

Lack of evidence did not halt the FBI's attempts to ruin Chaplin. Politicians called for Chaplin to distance himself from Hollywood actors and directors with known Communist sympathies. Instead, Chaplin flouted those pleas and joked about his associations with Russians and liberals. Friends and critics had warned Chaplin that his penchant for political commentary during World War II made him vulnerable and visible to partisan watchdogs. He would not be silent, however. Chaplin's son, Charles Jr., explained that his father's irreverence stemmed from the senior Chaplin's feeling that he "belonged here in America, with its promise of freedom in thought and belief and its emphasis on the importance of the individual."[128] His friendships with American Communists and distaste for the officials that sought to get rid of them was borne out of his defense for American individualism.

Chaplin's posture just further raised the ire of the opposition. In June 1947, Rep. John Rankin of the House's Un-American Activities

[125] David J. Langum, *Crossing Over the Line: Legislating Morality and the Mann Act* (Chicago: University of Chicago Press, 1994), 194.
[126] Robinson, *Chaplin*, 556.
[127] Ibid., 557.
[128] Charlie Chaplin Jr., *My Father, Charlie Chaplin* (New York: Random House, 1960), 340.

Committee called on the US attorney general to "deport Charlie Chaplin." Rankin was troubled by Chaplin's latest film, *Monsieur Verdoux*. The congressman from Mississippi charged that Chaplin's films were "loathsome" and his "very life in Hollywood is detrimental to the moral fabric of America."[129] A week later, Rankin appeared before Congress again to deride Chaplin and read a letter from a film censor in Tennessee that alleged "Charlie Chaplin is a traitor to the Christian American way of life" and an "enemy of decency."[130]

Chaplin responded. He described Rankin's tactics as a "Fascist technique."[131] To members of the House Un-American Activities Committee, Chaplin dared them to subpoena him and reiterated: "I am not a Communist. I am a peacemonger."[132] The committee never formally summoned Chaplin to Capitol Hill.[133] Chaplin remained in a deadlocked cold war with Hoover's FBI and Rankin's Un-American Activities Committee for the better part of a decade.

The battle first took a toll on Chaplin's fame. At the start of the 1950s, American journalism was populated by a "generation that has heard plenty about Chaplin, but never seen him."[134] His movies were no longer in wide circulation among a public that preferred the "talkies." His reputation among young people centered on Chaplin's (supposed) politics and contained little about his pathbreaking work as a filmmaker.[135] The American media was either ignorant of Chaplin or thoroughly against him. One journalist told Hoover that "I'd like to run every one of those rats out of the country and start with Charlie Chaplin."[136]

The trouble for Chaplin's opponents was that the greatest comedian did not provide the grounds for expulsion. Instead, government officials waited to shut Chaplin out rather than kick him out. In September 1952, Chaplin's family boarded a ship to England, where he would debut his forthcoming film, *Limelight*. While aboard, US Attorney General James McGranery rescinded Chaplin's re-entry permit to the United States under the US Code of Laws on Aliens and Citizenship that stipulated barring

---

[129] *Congressional Record: Proceedings and Debates of the 80th Congress, First Session* (Washington, DC: United States Government Printing Office, 1947), 6895.
[130] Ibid., 7308.
[131] "Rankin Demands Chaplin Expulsion," *Los Angeles Times*, June 13, 1947, 2.
[132] Robinson, *Chaplin*, 590–91.
[133] "Doubt Chaplin will be Called in Red Inquiry," *Chicago Tribune*, October 18, 1947, 2.
[134] "Who Is this Charlie Chaplin?" *Answers*, November 4, 1950, 118.
[135] See A. H. Weiler, "By Way of Report," *New York Times*, December 14, 1947.
[136] Richard Carr, *Charlie Chaplin: A Political Biography from Victorian Britain to Modern America* (London: Routledge, 2017), 236.

non-citizens on the grounds of "moral, health or insanity or for advocating Communism or associating with Communist or pro-Communist organizations." This piece of legislation offered more room to incriminate Chaplin who was not a Communist but certainly had a record of supporting friends who were in fact aligned with Communism. McGranery ordered the Immigration and Naturalization Service to hold Chaplin for questioning if he attempted to reenter the United States. Chaplin learned about McGranery's announcement aboard the liner and cabled his lawyer to find out what the attorney general "had in mind."[137] Upon reaching London, Chaplin declared that he wanted to return to the US since "I have millions and millions of friends in America—and a few enemies."[138] Negotiations stalled; neither side would budge. The actor's surprise turned quickly into bitterness. Chaplin stayed in exile in Europe for two decades.

***

The formation of the Hollywood Walk of Fame in 1960 tested Chaplin's enduring greatness against his fallout from fame. E. M. Stuart of the Hollywood Chamber of Commerce conceived of the idea – admittedly borrowed from the concrete handprints outside of the Grauman's Chinese Theatre – to excavate 15,000 square feet of sidewalk on Hollywood Boulevard and Vine Street, insert lighting cables underground beneath brass stars and charcoal-colored terrazzo. The initial plan was to assign 500 stars to the "most prominent figures" in the film industry.[139] The Chamber of Commerce convinced the local store owners on Hollywood and Vine to assume responsibility for the $1,151,000 budget.

In February 1958, the Motion Picture Producers Association provided the Chamber of Commerce with an initial list of 1,529 candidates for the Walk of Fame. Charlie Chaplin did not make the cut. Harry Sugarman, president of the Hollywood Improvement Association, told reporters that "opinion was divided" and that Chaplin's "name could be added later." Sugarman assured that "no one is trying to rewrite the history of the entertainment industry." He then provided a stark example to prove his earnestness: "Hitler's name can't be erased from the pages of history, but I doubt if anyone is interested in aggrandizing him further."[140] A comparison between Chaplin and Hitler did

---

[137] "Chaplin to Return Here, He Declares," *New York Times*, September 23, 1952, 9.
[138] "Crowds Welcome Chaplin to London," *New York Times*, September 24, 1952, 3.
[139] "Group List Names for Hollywood Fame Walk," *Los Angeles Times*, August 28, 1957, A6.
[140] "Chaplin Left Out of 'Walk of Fame,'" *Independent*, February 20, 1958, 32.

not portend well for the comedian. Two months later insiders leaked that the businesses situated along the Walk of Fame route had vetoed Chaplin. "There was no other way," said a Chamber of Commerce official. "Some property owners said that if Chaplin went in they wanted out. And since the property owners are footing the bill we did not want to jeopardize the project."[141]

Prominent Hollywood stars defended Chaplin. Sam Goldwyn, Mary Pickford, Stan Laurel, and Buster Keaton told United Press International that they disagreed with Chaplin's politics but also opposed the ban. "If there's anybody entitled to be in a motion picture hall of fame, Mr. Chaplin has probably done more than anybody I know," declared Goldwyn. "Furthermore, I don't believe he's a Communist. I believe he's a capitalist, and I know him better than anybody else."[142]

Others argued for Chaplin while accepting the FBI's allegations as absolute fact. Mary Pickford's defense of Chaplin mirrored the logic of earlier champions of Edgar Allan Poe's bid into NYU's Hall of Fame. "We may disagree heartily with Charlie's political views, but we make ourselves ridiculous to the rest of the world by ignoring the world's greatest comedian." By far the most astonishing defense came from Adolphe Menjou, one of the more prominent Hollywood supporters of the House's Un-American Activities Committee. In Menjou's estimation, Chaplin's greatness was just far too great to suppress: "I think he's too great to keep his name off despite the fact that he has a hole in his head politically."[143] The lobbying efforts failed. The Los Angeles City Council approved a final list of stars in October 1958 and left Chaplin's name off it.

Charlie Chaplin Jr. took the matter to court. Chaplin Jr. was a middling actor, unable to step beyond his father's shadow. In his memoir, Chaplin Jr. recalled a conversation with a group of New York reporters, a brief episode that confirms the burden of living up to his father's unreachable standard:

"I am going to be a great actor," I told them solemnly.
  I was bragging, perhaps. But it wasn't just bragging. I was thinking about a man who was the greatest comedian in the world. I was his son with his name. So I had to be good. More than anything else in the world I wanted him to be proud of me.[144]

---

[141] Murray Schumach, "Chaplin Left off Film Honor Roll," *New York Times*, April 26, 1960, 40.
[142] Rick Du Brow, "Chaplin Argument Rises," *Eureka Humboldt Standard*, May 26, 1960, 30.
[143] Ibid.
[144] Chaplin Jr., *My Father, Charlie Chaplin*, 51.

In July 1960, Chaplin Jr. sued the Los Angeles City Council, the Hollywood Chamber of Commerce, and the Hollywood Improvement Association for "malicious libel," of personal and professional damages related to ignoring his father's career, "a milestone in the history of picture making."[145] Chaplin Jr. asked the courts to compel the Chamber of Commerce to provide his father a star on the Walk of Fame and compensate the son $400,000 for the "degradation and humiliation to him and his family."[146] As a professional, Chaplin Jr. claimed the omission to his father had exposed him, Chaplin Jr., to "contempt, ridicule and obloquy in his community and throughout the rest of the world, and caused him to be shunned and avoided, and tended to injure him in his profession and occupation as an actor and motion picture artist."[147]

Chaplin Jr.'s lawyers argued that no fair assessment of Chaplin's greatness among Hollywood's elite could deny him a "rightful place" on the Walk of Fame. Mack Sennett, a former and formidable silent film actor, supported the claim. "That's ridiculous," testified Mack about Chaplin's ban. "This is a matter of art, not politics," he reasoned. "Charlie was the greatest comedian we ever had on the screen."[148] His erasure from that position, figured Sennett, could only be due to personal malice.

But Chaplin no longer was Hollywood's greatest actor. The defense told the courts that the Los Angeles City Council was only guilty of a "failure to pay a compliment." By way of analogy, continued that logic:

To publish a written statement that the great Presidents of the United States were Washington, Lincoln, Theodore Roosevelt, Wilson and Franklin Roosevelt does not libel Hoover or Truman. Perhaps it might hurt their feelings, but it is not libelous.[149]

In an earlier epoch, Chaplin was much more than a Truman or Hoover. He was the single most important filmmaker in US history. However, the Cold War had done much to dethrone Chaplin. Without a lot of

---

[145] "Aver 'Malice & Prejudice' Erased Charles Chaplin from Hollywood Walk," *Variety*, July 27, 1960, 3.
[146] Ibid.
[147] Court Materials for Charles Chaplin Jr. vs. Hollywood Chamber of Commerce, Case No. 751589. Archives and Records Center, Superior Court of California, County of Los Angeles, Los Angeles, CA.
[148] "Mack Sennett Speaks Up for Chaplin in Dispute," *Ventura County Star-Free Press*, August 27, 1960, 14.
[149] Court Materials for Charles Chaplin Jr. vs. Hollywood Chamber of Commerce, Case No. 751589.

contemplation or consideration for Chaplin's erstwhile standing, Superior Judge Ellsworth Meyer dismissed Charlie Chaplin Jr.'s libel case against the Hollywood Walk of Fame.[150]

***

America eventually restored Chaplin's greatness. Once again, historical contingencies were the determinant of change. In the late 1960s, vigorous opposition to the Vietnam War convinced many in the United States to question the government's decision making. The loss of faith in leadership "encouraged the public to think of Chaplin as a political victim instead of a political villain."[151] The very same thing, I will explore, happened to Muhammad Ali. Chaplin's legacy was suddenly much more usable. The liberal French government honored him as a Commandeur de la Légion, the nation's highest civilian honor. The United States was therefore due for some contrition to its adopted son, the "wronged genius" of Hollywood.[152]

Chaplin was finally bequeathed a space on the Walk of Fame in 1972. Some still complained that he was a "traitor" but most welcomed Chaplin back "home."[153] Amenable to participate in an American forgiveness tour, Chaplin agreed to return to the United States at the invitation of the Academy of Motion Picture Arts and Sciences. The Academy decided to award Chaplin with a second lifetime achievement award, this for the "Incalculable effect he has had in making motion pictures the art form of this century."[154] New York City announced a "Salute to Charlie Chaplin" event at Lincoln Center.[155] In Los Angeles, the owners of the Taft Building on the corner of Hollywood Boulevard and Vine Street commissioned a large sculpture of Chaplin to stand outside, near the route of the Walk of Fame.[156]

The restoration of Chaplin's attributed greatness compelled the Walk of Fame to reconsider. The executive committee of the Hollywood Chamber of Commerce stubbornly voted to maintain the ban, but enough members approved a motion to poll the entire board.[157] The final vote

---

[150] "Chaplin Son Loses Suit on 'Fame Walk,'" *Los Angeles Times*, October 14, 1960, 28.
[151] Maland, *Chaplin*, 336–37.
[152] Ibid.
[153] "They Haven't Given Up—Letter Writers Assail Chaplin," *Los Angeles Times*, April 9, 1972, 20.
[154] Judith Kinnard, "Chaplin May Attend Oscar Ceremony," *New York Times*, January 14, 1972, 18.
[155] "Charlie Chaplin Returns after 20-Year Absence," *Baltimore Sun*, April 4, 1972, A1.
[156] "Romanelli Will Sculpt Chaplin," *Los Angeles Times*, March 2, 1972, G14.
[157] "Banning of Chaplin," *Washington Post*, February 7, 1972, B3.

for Chaplin tallied 30–3 in his favor.[158] A spokesman for the reinstated greatest filmmaker supplied the Chamber with disappointment. "Mr. Chaplin appreciates the insertion of his star in the Hollywood Walk of Fame but regrets to advise the Hollywood Chamber of Commerce that he will not be able to accept their kind invitation."[159] Instead, officials hired a Chaplin impersonator dressed in a derby, a tight-fitting jacket, and a pair of baggy pants. This, too, was useful to attribute an image of American-style greatness.

[158] Joan Sweeney, "Silent Screen Great Chaplin Voted Star on Walk of Fame," *Los Angeles Times*, February 12, 1972, C1.
[159] "Chaplin Gives Chamber 'Thanks, But No Thanks,'" *Progress Bulletin*, March 27, 1972, 20.

4

How the Babe Became the Greatest (and the Roosevelts, Too)

Ty Cobb was baseball's first all-time great. He advanced a child's game into something more grown up but didn't alter the sport so much as to transform it into something unrecognizably brand new. Children liked to mimic Cobb's exaggerated gestures and repertoire of swings in a pickup game of stickball. Like other American greats, Cobb showed how his craft could be done much better. In the Age of Edison, Cobb incrementally changed baseball into a scientific, replicable, smart man's game. Years later, his critics would minimize Cobb because his team squandered three American League pennants and never won the World Series.[1] But during his playing career, no one held that against him. Cobb was baseball's greatest player even though the Detroit Tigers were never, at least during Cobb's time, the sport's best team. He was a peerless individual ball player and that was a far more crucial indicator of success than the standings printed in the sports columns. Cobb was fast, strong, and until he developed glaucoma, possessed the best hand-eye coordination in the sport. America valorized Cobb for his cleverness and an uncanny knack for outsmarting his opponents.

Cobb retired in 1928 after a twenty-four-year career in Major League Baseball. He was, at that moment, baseball's greatest of all time, judged against other remarkable players.[2] A year earlier, Babe Ruth hit sixty home runs and his New York Yankees, the so-called Murderers' Row,

---

[1] E. A. Batchelor, "Ty Cobb as I Knew Him," in Ty Cobb and Al Stump, *My Life in Baseball: The True Record* (Garden City, NY: Doubleday, 1961), 12. Much later, Cobb was said to have opined and regretted this championship shortcoming. See Ed Bang, "Cobb Never Achieved His Greatest Ambition," *Sporting News*, January 17, 1962, 11.

[2] See Paul Gallico, *Farewell to Sport* (New York: Alfred A. Knopf, 1938), 334–35.

swept aside the Pittsburgh Pirates to win the World Series, capping one of the most dominant baseball seasons ever. Yet, Cobb, by most accounts, was still measured greater than Ruth. Even Claire Merritt Ruth was, before she married the Babe, "quite certain that as a great as Babe Ruth was, he would never equal my friend from Georgia, Ty Cobb."[3] America coveted Cobb's hard work and clever strategies. They admired his hustle on the ball field, even as his tactics roughed up defenders standing in the base path. No one denied Ruth's production, but many of the sportswriters found him unrelatable. They claimed that his mighty swings were too effortless and godlike to comprehend. The Babe's record of frivolous off-field antics and off-color company rendered him a rather undesirable model for America's young and impressionable children. Most about Ruth couldn't be copied; the parts that were weren't all that aspirational.

It didn't last, although not much had changed on the baseball field to force a revote. By the middle of the twentieth century Babe Ruth was recognized as the single greatest baseball player who had ever lived. Readers of Bernard Malamud's 1952 novel, *The Natural*, understood very well that Walter "The Whammer" Whambold, the American League slugger that Roy Hobbs seeks to displace as the "greatest there ever was in the game," was based largely on Ruth.[4] America had humanized Ruth's accomplishments and forgiven his indiscretions. Writing on the eve of World War II, the social theorist Leo Löwenthal had anticipated the rise of Ruth and other famed people who were famous for entertaining rather than a tangible worldly contribution. In opinion polls, Ruth was the only "idol of consumption," a celebrity marked by his contribution to leisure, that ranked among the great "idols of production," people who had achieved some concrete on behalf of civilization.[5] In February 1950, under two years after the Babe had died, the majority of 393 sportswriters polled by the Associated Press agreed that Babe Ruth was baseball's greatest player. Among the leading sports scribes, Ruth outdueled Cobb by a wide margin of 253–116; five others shared the remaining twenty-four ballots.[6]

---

[3] Claire Ruth and Bill Slocum, *The Babe and I* (Englewood Cliffs, NJ: Prentice-Hall, Inc., 1959), 24.
[4] Bernard Malamud, *The Natural* (New York: Harcourt Brace and Company, 1952), 108.
[5] Leo Löwenthal, "Biographies in Popular Magazines," in *Radio Research, 1942–1943*, eds. Paul F. Lazarsfeld and Frank N. Stanton (New York: Arno Press, 1979), 516.
[6] "Babe Ruth Named Greatest Player in Baseball for Past Fifty Years," *New York Times*, February 5, 1950, 1.

Ty Cobb was disappearing. In September 1955, contestants on a television gameshow failed to identify Cobb, even after they were provided with ample clues and then removed their blindfolds to see the retired athlete right in front of them. Once he was revealed to them, one of the contestants, now recalling Cobb's seedier reputation, added to the gameshow host's narration of Cobb's records that he "spiked a lot of second basemen, too."[7] The remark reminded the audience that Cobb was a tough competitor and took considerable license to remain on top, on and off the baseball diamond. Yet, Cobb's invisibility wasn't just about his bully persona (and racist proclivities).

He intuited this, at some level. Still very much living in the past, perhaps in denial, Cobb shared that "people tell me I was the greatest player who ever lived. And maybe I am—as far as the way I played baseball." Even still, Cobb admitted "I wish I could have been more like the Babe. When he died, an entire nation mourned."[8]

Cobb misunderstood. The sentiments that informed the nationwide grieving, sanctification, really, for Ruth, triggered his elevation above Cobb. Ty Cobb was totally eclipsed by a reimagined Babe Ruth, a wholesome, hardworking American "everyman" whose charity – eventually incorporated as the Babe Ruth Foundation, Inc., founded in 1947 – was principally earmarked for underprivileged children who would come of age in the 1950s as, in Tom Brokaw's formulation, America's "Greatest Generation."[9] The Greatest Generation defeated Hitler and stymied the Great Depression. They moved to bigger houses in the suburbs, held salaried jobs rather than laboring for an hourly wage. These women and men of the 1950s owned new cars and sat down to eat beside televisions broadcasting Elvis Presley (from the waist up), James Dean, and a host of sitcoms that extolled the virtues of their newfound, so-called traditional family values. They built big churches and attended college to show that Americans were more pious and wiser than their Soviet counterparts in the burgeoning Cold War. Americans in the 1950s mythologized the recent past and their contemporary moment to suggest that, as a collective, they'd fulfilled a grand American destiny. It was a "boom decade" for halls of fame; Americans built no fewer than twenty-five

---

[7] Richard Bak, "Three Strikes: Golden Years Were Bittersweet for the Georgia Peach," *Detroit Free Press*, August 23, 2005, D1.
[8] See Tom Stanton, *Ty and the Babe: Baseball's Fiercest Rivals* (New York: Thomas Dunne Books, 2007), 236.
[9] See Tom Brokaw, *The Greatest Generation* (New York: Random House, 1998).

such edifices in the 1950s.[10] These new museums matched the transformation of Babe Ruth in the American imagination. Ruth's singular greatness wasn't anchored in aspirational change, the usual measure of greatness of Ty Cobb and most other erstwhile great Americans. Babe Ruth had become the greatest of all time because he had come to represent what was already great, so figured the overconfident lot, about America.

The turn from Cobb to the Babe suggests something very different than, say, the transition from Mickey Mouse to Donald Duck or Charlie Chaplin to a cast of more patriotic film stars. No, the rise of Babe Ruth and, for that matter, Franklin and Eleanor Roosevelt, to the ranks of the very greatest was part of a larger realignment of "greatness" in America. Instead of identifying great people as an exercise of what Americans could be, the search for greatness was transformed into a nostalgic act meant to confirm and defend the values and feats of a confident and perhaps complacent people. When a disgruntled generation beseeches its descendants to recall the good old days, they're drawing from a 1950s notion. The same for those women and men who long for a disappeared great generation, or a politician who promises to make America great again. In each claim, there are echoes of this curious epoch.

* * *

First, Ty Cobb. In April 1910, Charles Comiskey coronated Cobb on the eve of his fifth campaign in the Major Leagues. By then, the twenty-three year-old Detroit Tiger outfielder had led the American League in batting average for three consecutive years. He ranked at the top in most offensive categories, including home runs (nine) during the prior season. The svelte, six-foot tall batsman was the liveliest hitter in the so-called Dead Ball Era of baseball. Comiskey, the owner of the Chicago White Sox, conceded that Pittsburgh's Honus Wagner fielded better at a more demanding position, shortstop, than Cobb, however skillfully, patrolled rightfield. Yet, Comiskey determined, no one was a better all-around player. "I pick the Detroit man because he is, in my judgment, the most expert man of his profession."[11] Ty Cobb hit, bunted, and ran the bases better than anyone else had. His was a

---

[10] See Paul Soderberg, Helen Washington, and Jaques Cattell Press, *The Big Book of Halls of Fame in the United States and Canada* (New York: R. R. Bowker Company, 1977), xiii, 21–22.

[11] Charles A. Comiskey, "Ty Cobb Best of Diamond Heroes," *Chicago Tribune*, April 17, 1010, C1.

learned, somewhat scientific, expertise of baseball. Charlie Comiskey and Cobb's other rivals had to admit that the Tiger outfielder just knew the game much better than anyone else.

Some criticized Comiskey on the grounds that it was premature to announce any athlete as baseball's greatest ever. Professional baseball was still a work in progress. The World Series was just nine years old, and the sacrifice fly was but a toddler. The backlash against Comiskey was that if anyone deserved to be dubbed the greatest, however tentatively, it was the Pittsburgh Pirates' "seasoned racer," Honus Wagner, not Cobb, the comparatively "young colt."[12] Wagner had played a similar style of baseball a decade before Cobb reached the professional ranks. These observers did not have the benefit of historical hindsight to recognize that Americans intuited greatness as a remarkable and new notion of changemakers. They would have been equally bemused to learn that three decades later Cobb and Wagner were among the inaugural Baseball Hall of Fame inductees made up of "recent" ballplayers and that the "old-timers" of the prior century were fully overlooked for honors.[13]

Cobb was uninterested in that quarrel. When asked about it, he called Comiskey's praise the "greatest compliment any ball player could receive." He shrewdly avoided further controversy: "I hope I will some day be the player Wagner is."[14]

Cobb overcame the tentativeness. The endorsement opportunities that came with his success on the baseball field leveraged his high station among the sport's legends. For a share in its profits, Ty Cobb permitted the Tuxedo Tobacco Company to boast in its circulars that "The World's Greatest Ball Player Smokes the World's Best Tobacco."[15] Likewise, Cobb authorized an iron supplement company to refer to him as a "Super-man" and the "World's Greatest Baseball Player."[16]

By the 1920s, most baseball players and writers agreed Cobb had overtaken Wagner. On August 30, 1925, Mayor John Smith of Detroit hosted a testimonial dinner for Ty Cobb. The aged baseball player had just completed his twentieth season as the Detroit Tigers' center fielder and the team's most pivotal player. The gala was hailed as the "greatest event of its kind," hosted at Navin Field, the ballpark where Cobb

---

[12] "Greatest Baseball Player," *Washington Post*, April 23, 1910, 6.
[13] James C. O'Leary, "Many Old-Time Baseball Stars Appear Overlooked," *Boston Globe*, December 21, 1936, 10.
[14] "Cobb Feels Highly Honored," *Chicago Tribune*, April 18, 1910, 10.
[15] See full-page advertisement in *Literary Digest* 50 (January 23, 1915): 174.
[16] See near-full-page advertisement in *Chicago Tribune*, August 20, 1916, 796.

had set almost a hundred Major League Baseball records. The "Georgia Peach" – Cobb's nickname, an homage to his birthplace, ever since the writer Grantland Rice bestowed it upon him in 1904 – held the sport's top marks in games played, runs, hits, and best overall batting average. Most agreed that there was no one so disciplined in the batter's box or smarter while circling the basepath than Tyrus Raymond Cobb. From 1907 to 1919, Cobb won twelve batting titles, nine of them in consecutive fashion. There were a host of statistical categories that he very nearly topped. Cobb ranked second in career stolen bases (Billy Hamilton), doubles (Tris Speaker), and triples (Sam Crawford). At the banquet, the president of the American League described Cobb as the "greatest ball player of all time." Charlie Comiskey's opinion was by this time a postulate of baseball know-it-alls. Connie Mack, a legendary ball player and manager, offered a similar assessment of Cobb, counting him the very best among other greats such as Eddie Collins, Tris Speaker, and Walter Johnson.[17] Cobb was so good that he made Mack and others forget about Pittsburgh's Wagner. Missing from everyone's list was the home run champion, Babe Ruth.

The total omission of George Herman Ruth was a product of the moment. 1925 was a very disappointing year for Ruth and the New York Yankees. It was the only time in a stretch of about sixty years that the Yankees had lost more games than won. Ruth missed a third of the season, likely due to alcoholism. In games he played, the Babe hit for a lower average and slugged fewer home runs, compared to his usual powerful accomplishments. The lowest ebb occurred in St. Louis. The Yankees were in town to play the Browns and Ruth was late for batting practice, reportedly for indulging too much in the St. Louis nightlife. The ball club fined Ruth a hefty amount and suspended him, too.

***

It would require great cultural forces to supplant Cobb. In the 1920s and 1930s, Americans made meaning of baseball through Ty Cobb. He reigned over America's pastime in "Cobbensian fashion."[18] He had perfected, so it was explained, the science of baseball. He studied opposing pitchers and improvised his bat swings – his preference, all things considered, was to chop his bat with a short, sharp motion – depending on

---

[17] "Cobb Called Greatest of All Time," *Washington Post*, August 31, 1925, 14.
[18] See Peter Williams, *The Joe Williams Baseball Reader: The Glorious Game, from Ty Cobb and Babe Ruth to the Amazing Mets* (Chapel Hill, NC: Algonquin Books, 1989), 14.

the situation. On principle, Cobb never allowed a pitcher to face him on consecutive occasions in the same batting stance. Cobb had a penchant for getting on base and a knack for reaching home plate. No one before or since boasts a better lifetime batting average. He had accumulated more hits than anyone until the ageless Pete Rose bested Cobb in 1985. Cobb held the record for runs scored until Ricky Henderson broke that hallowed record in 2001, albeit with the benefit of more at-bats available to him than Cobb.

A sportswriter's description of Cobb's game was illustrative of the public's admiration. On one occasion in New York – and there were many like it – Cobb laid down a bunt so precisely that the third baseman did not bother to challenge the speedy man and throw to first base. Cobb wreaked havoc on the basepath, panicking the defense with his keen decision making. An "average player would have stopped at second" after the Tigers' next hitter lined a pitch into short centerfield. Cobb wasn't average, however. With steely decisiveness, he curved around the top of the baseball diamond and set his sights on third. The outfielder hurled the ball to the infield, and it reached the third baseman just as a "geyser of dust" erupted on top of him; one of Cobb's "old tricks." The ingenious Cobb overslid the base to avoid the third baseman's tag, "but he twisted his body and came back to touch it with his hand." The umpire ruled Cobb safe. After that, the Georgian raced to steal home plate. He almost made it there on the pitcher's windup and scored on an infield out because the hitter made inadvertent contact with the pitch.[19]

Americans appreciated that Cobb's cerebral approach evolved baseball rather than revolutionized it. It made the sport more relatable that its best players succeeded through acquired skill rather than supernatural abilities. Pundits wrote about the "slow evolution of the sport" that "displayed itself in batting, in the form of the bunt, the place hit and various other manifestations of skill." The intelligent and painstaking Cobb was the very best at this. Other ballplayers studied Cobb's habits and batting stances supposing that it was the Georgia Peach's intellect and preparedness rather than sheer talent that advanced him above the competition. It was, therefore, the consensus opinion that "Ty is the greatest batter who ever lived" precisely because he had "as much to do with this batting evolution as any one man." Through Cobb, this sportswriter and others developed maxims that held implications for more than just professional baseball: "The chief value of brains is in

[19] Ibid., 14–15.

the learning of new things, day after day, and this is what Ty Cobb was popularly believed to be able to do."[20]

Baseball held within it a formula to succeed in America, so long as you were a white man. The philosopher Morris Cohen intuited this when he described baseball as a "religion" meant for the masses. For Cohen, baseball's appeal was its ability to cultivate a "brotherhood" that all could join so long as they applied sufficient pluck.[21] In line with this, Grantland Rice, the dean of sports journalism, presented Cobb as an American everyman, capable of great things because he was so determined to become great. "Cobb saw that he was only a fair base-runner," related Rice, "so he went forth alone, to slide and practice by himself, hours at a time. He kept plugging at this art until he knew that he could handle himself around the bases."[22] Rice had it that Cobb's resolve led him to the processes to hit better against left-handed pitching and a host of other tactical imperfections that the honest Cobb reversed during his career.

The press preferred Cobb's approach over Ruth's. As the baseball purists interpreted it, the Babe's mammoth home runs and Cobb's slick bunts and targeted line drives had similar outcomes: each led to runs scored. But Cobb's strategy-driven play personified the virtues that Americans looked for in baseball. These included, wrote the scholar Michael Kimmel, "autonomy and aggressive independence" as well as "obedience, self-sacrifice, discipline, and a rigid hierarchy."[23] By contrast, Ruth's unprecedented power and upward swing "follows no set rule" and "flouts accepted theories." Ruth, they charged with derision, "throws science itself to the winds and hews out a rough path for himself by the sheer weight of his own unequalled talents."[24] A baseball manager called Ruth a "freak type."[25] Another big leaguer jested that "I am not so certain now that Ruth is human."[26] The comment likely drew from recent reports of Ruth's upbringing in a Baltimore

---

[20] Leverett T. Smith Jr., *The American Dream and the National Game* (Bowling Green, OH: Bowling Green University Popular Press, 1970), 196.
[21] Morris R. Cohen, "Baseball," *The Dial*, July 26, 1919, 57–58.
[22] Grantland Rice, "The Swelled Head: Stories of Men Who Have Suffered from It," *American Magazine* 88 (October 1919): 203.
[23] Michael S. Kimmel, *History of Men: Essays on the History of American and British Masculinities* (Albany, NY: State University of New York Press, 2005), 68.
[24] See Smith Jr., *The American Dream and the National Game*, 190–91.
[25] See Joseph Durso, *The Days of Mr. McGraw* (Englewood Cliffs, NJ: Prentice-Hall, Inc., 1969), 206.
[26] Chet Thomas, "Babe Ruth the Super Player," *Baseball*, November 1920, 586.

orphanage, a backstory that made the Babe seem otherworldly rather than a rags-to-riches American tale.[27] Baseball traditionalists fumed that the homerun was "one of the least difficult hits known to batting in baseball" and that Ruth had "degenerated [the sport] into a mere tug of brute force."[28] The Babe's peerless power was perceived as irreplicable. He threatened to empty baseball of its greater meaning for the American dream and everyday life.

Still, Babe Ruth deserved more credit than was provided to him in the greatest-of-all-time conversations generated by Cobb's milestone dinner. By 1925, Babe Ruth was a household name, his personal life the subject of nearly as many bylines as Henry Ford. The public cared so much because of his baseball dominance. The Babe had led the league in home runs for six of the past seven years. In 1919, Ruth had set the record for most home runs in a single season (twenty-nine) and then eclipsed the mark twice over (fifty-four in 1920, then fifty-nine homers a year later). Ruth's strength with a heavy baseball bat had made him the sport's "biggest drawing card," so admitted none other than Ty Cobb.[29] Ruth was also a good outfielder and had been an even better left-handed pitcher before his hitting prowess rendered him an everyday player (pitchers need breaks in between outings) in the starting lineup.

However, the debate between Ty Cobb and Babe Ruth rendered baseball statistics rather meaningless (Figure 4.1). Of supreme importance to the experts was Cobb's peripatetic efforts to get on base and then his circuitous adventure to return to home plate. Ruth's capacity to shortcut the process and do it all with a single swing carried no appreciable real-life application. "Like most lovers of baseball I like to see long hitting," wrote one sportswriter, "but I got more than enough of it in 1920 and 1921."[30] In other words, he found Ruth a trifle boring. To quell any minor resistance against Cobb, this sports scribe expressed remorse for the popular, unstudious attention paid to the home run. He longed for the triple, "about the nicest hit of all, a line drive of terrific force, well placed between the outfielders, combining with nice judgment and speed of foot in base running." This was Cobb's trademark. The journalist

---

[27] See Jane Leavy, *The Big Fella: Babe Ruth and the World He Created* (New York: HarperCollins, 2018), 33–55.
[28] See John E. Dreifort, *Baseball History from Outside the Lines: A Reader* (Lincoln, NE: University of Nebraska Press, 2001), 127–28.
[29] See Elliott Tripp, *Ty Cobb: Baseball and American Manhood* (Lanham, MD: Rowman & Littlefield, 2016), 310.
[30] See Dreifort, *Baseball History from Outside the Lines*, 128.

FIGURE 4.1 Ty Cobb and Babe Ruth examine a baseball bat during the 1927 season. Courtesy of the National Baseball Hall of Fame and Museum.

predicted that the anomalous Ruth would cease to be the "dominant influence." He prayed with fervor for a time when the "bubble of home run popularity is exploded, then the three bagger along with other suppressed baseball features will come into its own."[31]

[31] F. C. Lane, "What's Wrong with the Three Base Hit?" *Baseball*, June 1922, 304.

The irony is that some credited Babe Ruth's home run onslaught with "saving the national pastime" during a very dark situation.[32] In October 1919, the heavily favored Chicago White Sox lost the World Series to the Cincinnati Reds. Soon enough, it was reported that a ring of bookies and members of the Chicago club, the so-called Black Sox, fixed the competition, even though a jury later acquitted all parties. The scandal roiled the public. Major League Baseball established a commissioner's office to ensure the integrity of the sport. That wasn't enough. "Baseball needed a Superman," recalled the writer Grantland Rice, "a man who could capture the imagination of the public—who could restore America's faith in baseball." In 1920, Babe Ruth slugged fifty-four home runs into the bleachers. With each blast, Ruth restored the faith. "The public wanted to see the ball smashed out of the park—where there couldn't be any question of inside baseball."[33] During that season, Yankees manager Miller Huggins led a campaign to elevate Ruth above Cobb on the premise of popularity. The Babe "busts the ball" and "appeals to everybody." Cobb's strategy-minded style was too "scholarly" and limited to the "students of baseball." In Huggins's estimation, "all those interested in the game are not students; most of them miss the fine points, the inner dope."[34] Yet expert sportswriters still maintained that the older but durable Cobb, with all his grit and gamesmanship, rendered him baseball's greatest man.[35]

Baseball players and insiders continued to pick Cobb over Ruth, even after the latter's historic sixty-home run season in 1927 and his mythical (likely didn't happen) "called shot" against the Chicago Cubs in the 1932 World Series. These things seemed to remind Americans that Ruth's records were "lessonless" milestones achieved by someone whose strength was just too far beyond mortal men. He was a "demi-god greater than paganism," wrote Silas Bent, the same reporter who covered Charles Lindbergh's Atlantic flight.[36]

Most self-appointed judges made it a two-person contest.[37] The editors of the *Sporting News* recognized Cobb as the "greatest player the

---

[32] Hy Hurwitz, "Ruth, Wagner and Cobb Again Lead the List," *Boston Globe*, January 9, 1936, 17.
[33] Grantland Rice, *The Tumult and the Shouting: My Life in Sport* (New York: A. S. Barnes & Company, 1954), 106.
[34] "Ruth Is Hero Where Once Cobb Reigned," *Sporting News*, August 12, 1920, 3.
[35] See, for example, "Ty Cobb Again Boosts His Batting Average," *Baltimore Sun*, August 15, 1920, 20.
[36] Bent, "Idol Worship," 1497.
[37] There were exceptions. When asked to share his personal ranking, the Yankee first baseman, Lou Gehrig, chose Wagner over Cobb. His selections elicited a query about

sport has yet produced." Ruth was the "artisan," but Cobb was the "artist," the "brainiest player" and that it was his "imagination more than his body that set him apart."[38] Dan Daniel proclaimed "Ty Cobb the greatest of all time." Daniel qualified that "Babe Ruth must be rated the hardest hitter of all time—though not the greatest hitter."[39] The umpire Billy Evans wrote, when asked to decide: "Ty Cobb I would rate the greatest ball player of all time ... Babe Ruth I would rate a close second to Ty Cobb."[40] In 1931, a syndicated column reported the findings of a panel of players and managers that ranked Cobb as the very best. Figured one baseball insider: "But picking the greatest player that ever lived is easy, I think. I pick Ty Cobb. I guess every one will do the same."[41]

* * *

That Babe Ruth didn't receive any consideration during the 1925 season was due to off-field troubles. The contrast between the news of Cobb's twentieth anniversary celebration and Ruth's supposed demise was startling. Certain members of the press exercised some self-imposed amnesia about Cobb's rough play on the basepath and his bigotry off it. One magazine paired Ruth and Cobb, respectively, as the "naughty boy and the good boy."[42]

Others recollected a bit better, but the message rang the same. Hearst's top sportswriter marveled at how "both headlines were flung across the

---

his famed New York teammate. "Ruth?" quipped Gehrig, anticipating the question. "Oh, I guess he belongs up there somewhere, maybe next to Cobb." See "Lou Gehrig Pays Debt to Ruth by Placing Third to Wagner, Cobb," *Evening Report*, February 1, 1937, 6. There were some other exceptions. Grantland Rice couldn't decide between the two in 1933 while a limited poll of major leaguers produced that same year found that most preferred Ruth. In 1930, Connie Mack picked Christy Mathewson as his greatest of all time but then changed his mind to Ruth in 1934. Ruth's manager, Miller Huggins, who had sided with Ruth in 1920 decided on Honus Wagner over Cobb and Ruth in 1929. See Grantland Rice, "Ruth and Cobb Rated at Top of Baseball's All-Time List by Rice," *St. Louis Globe-Democrat*, August 15, 1933, 7; A. K., "Greatest of All Time, Thought Fred Clarke," *San Francisco Examiner*, February 10, 1929, 35; "Mack Says 'Matty' was Greatest of All Time," *Boston Globe*, March 15, 1930, 9; "Ruth Idol of Most A. L. Players," *Miami News*, March 6, 1934, 14; and "Give Me Ruth," *Brooklyn Eagle*, July 6, 1934, 19.

[38] "Press Voices Fans' Regret Over Ty Cobb's Retirement," *Rock Island Argues*, November 15, 1926, 6.
[39] Daniel M. Daniel, "Classifying the Champions," *Paterson News*, January 11, 1927, 16.
[40] Billy Evans, "Cobb, Speaker and Ruth are Named by Billy Evans as Greatest Outfielders of Last 25 Years," *Public Opinion*, February 18, 1930, 4.
[41] C. William Duncan, "Who Is Baseball's Greatest Player?" *Miami Herald*, July 5, 1931, 30.
[42] "Spanking Baseball's Baby and Petting Its Paragon," *Literary Digest*, September 19, 1925, 58.

front pages of newspapers on the same day." Cobb wasn't perfect, gushed Frank Menke. He'd "lost it" on occasion and had gotten "involved in a few jamborees." "Jamborees," as it were, was a journalistic understatement. Cobb's rap sheet included assault of a black groundskeeper and his wife for attempting to shake his hand, bludgeon of a heckler at a game between Cobb's Tigers and the New York Highlanders and inciting a duel with umpire Billy Evans (the same Evans who later rated Cobb above Ruth) under the grandstands after Evans had taken exception to Cobb's profanity-laced complaints about the officiating during a loss to the Washington Senators. He also ignited skirmishes with rivals who alleged that he slid into basemen with an intention to injure them with his cleats. Rumors abounded that Cobb filed the spikes of his shoes to punish any defender who dared block his path. He was arrested for an altercation with a hotel elevator operator, although reports differ as to whether Cobb was the provocateur, and if his actions were racially motivated. Yet, it is certain that Ty Cobb was a Jim Crow racist, at times a rude teammate, and a bully – no doubt about it. Frank Menke was aware of these blemishes but still insisted that Cobb "has been an honor to baseball, a credit to the game and the greatness that has been his is something that he has shared with baseball itself."[43]

During the Prohibition Era, Ruth's infractions weighed more sinful. Menke charged that Babe Ruth was a disgrace. The Babe was "transformed," "ruined" and "reduced to common clay" by "clubbing greatness" and outsized fame. The writer reviewed the sparse facts of Ruth's troubled childhood: his time spent in a Baltimore orphanage and the care he received from a small group of Catholic priests to set him on a better path. Ruth should have gained sufficient inspiration from his own life's story to stay out of trouble as a famous adult. Menke narrated Ruth's case as a cautionary tale of squandered opportunity, the very reason that the US Senate had passed the Eighteenth Amendment to prohibit alcohol. "The mighty blows he delivered on the ball field, the wild hurrahing that came to him, the cheers of legions," charged the writer, "all eventually made Ruth come to feel that he was bigger than the game itself, and being bigger, there were no rules and no regulations that he need observe." Conversely, the 1920s witnessed the enabled rise of the Ku Klux Klan and other racist groups to which Ty Cobb was not a card-carrying member but certainly shared a point of view.

---

[43] Frank G. Menke, "On the Sports Trail," *Palladium-Item*, September 7, 1925, 9. For a fuller discussion of Cobb's incidences and "unpopularity," see Tripp, *Ty Cobb*, 255–292.

Their perspectives were permitted to fester by an American public that believed there were harsher moral matters to quell.

Ty Cobb predicted that his top status would not endure. He anticipated that Ruth would overtake him, that it was just a matter of time before Ruth's power game became the norm in professional baseball. In 1924, he told Grantland Rice that the "old game is gone," while the pair watched Babe Ruth during batting practice at Yankee Stadium. "We have another game, a newer game now. In this game, power has replaced speed and skill. Base running is about dead." Rather than plot a move around the basepath, surmised Cobb, the runners "wait for somebody to drive 'em home."[44] For his part in the rivalry, Ruth also prepared for Cobb's star to descend. In his annual player ratings published in the newspapers, the Babe stopped including Cobb among his "all-stars" in 1922.[45] Whether his omission was motivated by his dim assessment of Cobb or the latter's insults hurled at Ruth (Cobb liked to insinuate that Ruth's unworthiness was connected to what he alleged to be African American facial characteristics) is indeterminable.[46]

But Cobb remained atop the field, at least for another decade. In February 1936, the newly established National Baseball Hall of Fame announced its inaugural class of "immortals," decided by 226 members of the Baseball Writers' Association. All but four voters cast ballots for Ty Cobb making him the top vote-getter, ahead of Babe Ruth and Honus Wagner. The New York press imagined the "amazed eyes of [the] committee" upon learning that "Cobb was enthroned as the greatest of all stars."[47] That much was melodrama. In truth, No one was surprised by the vote. Walter Johnson and Christy Matthewson were the other three to receive the requisite 75 percent of total votes from the judges.[48]

Cobb learned of the honor during a round of golf. "I am overwhelmed. I am glad they feel that way about me. I want to thank them all."[49] Jimmy Cobb once testified that his father was "prouder of that

---

[44] Rice, *The Tumult and the Shouting*, 25.
[45] "Will Babe Ruth Pick Hornsby? Fans Already Picking Favorites," *Harrisburg Telegraph*, August 18, 1926, 11.
[46] See Edmund F. Wehrle, *Breaking Babe Ruth: Baseball's Campaign Against Its Biggest Star* (Columbia, MO: University of Missouri Press, 2018), 59–60.
[47] "Ty Cobb Tops Hall of Fame Ball Players," *Brooklyn Eagle*, February 3, 1936, 10.
[48] "222 Ballots Name Ty Cobb No. 1 Immortal in Baseball Hall of Fame," *Baltimore Sun*, February 3, 1936, 10. For a fuller history of the first Baseball Hall of Fame vote, see James A. Vlasich, *A Legend for the Legendary: The Origin of the Baseball Hall of Fame* (Bowling Green, OH: Bowling Green State University Popular Press, 1990), 41–53.
[49] "Thanks!" *Cincinnati Enquirer*, February 3, 1936, 15.

Hall of Fame vote than of anything else connected with his baseball career."[50] It is puzzling, then, that Cobb did not make more of an effort to attend the festivities when the inaugural classes were enshrined in 1939. He made it in time for the banquet and complained that train delays prevented him from participating with Ruth and the other inductees (he later suggested that his bitterness toward baseball commissioner, Kenesaw Landis, played a factor in his tardiness).[51] Later in life, however, he made it a habit of reminding friends that "I know who was voted *first* to the Baseball Hall of Fame."[52]

Everyone seemed to still prefer Cobb. Even Ruth relented as the two men became friendlier in retirement. "The old boy," said the Babe of Cobb, "was the greatest player I ever saw or hope to see." Ruth used the same logic to laud Cobb that the sportswriters had deployed to boost the Detroit outfielder over the Yankee great. "I had a reputation for being a slugger and I guess I could hit 'em pretty far at that, but that guy Cobb could do everything—better than any player I ever saw. Old Georgia Peach was a great hitter, a spectacular fielder, a wonderful thrower and, oh boy, how he could run."[53]

***

Babe Ruth died on August 16, 1948, at Memorial Hospital in New York. He was fifty-three, a victim of a rare form of cancer. Ruth's remains were first transported in a black draped casket to Yankee Stadium – the "House that Ruth Built," as termed by the sportswriter Fred Lieb – to permit his fans to file past and pay their last respects. A few days later his body was removed to St. Patrick's Cathedral for a requiem mass and a hero's funeral. Six thousand women and men – family members, teammates, the mayor, and the governor – crammed into the cathedral. Inside, Cardinal Francis Spellman, who had rehearsed much of the same a year earlier on "Babe Ruth Day" at Yankee Stadium, prayed that the "Divine Spirit that inspired Babe Ruth to overcome hardships and win the crucial game of life animate many generations of American youth to learn from the example of his struggles and successes loyally to play their positions on all American teams." Spellman emphasized Ruth's hard work, the adversity he had overcome to emerge as a great man. He wasn't

---

[50] See Charles C. Alexander, *Ty Cobb* (New York: Oxford University Press, 1984), 217.
[51] Ibid., 218.
[52] Charles Leerhsen, *Ty Cobb: A Terrible Beauty* (New York: Simon & Schuster, 2015), 308.
[53] "Babe Ruth Calls Ty Cobb Greatest Player Ever to Don Spikes," *Washington Post*, August 24, 1945, 12.

some superpowered, unduplicated phenomenon. He was hardworking, just as industrious as Ty Cobb. Outside, rain poured on 75,000 people who lined the sidewalks on Manhattan's Fifth Avenue. They filled ten city blocks. More than 100,000 stood along the 30-mile route that the funeral cortège took to deliver Ruth to the Gate of Heaven Cemetery in Westchester.[54] New Yorkers wanted one last gaze at a person who had inspired them, on and off the baseball field (Figure 4.2).

One of the last to leave the cathedral was Philadelphia Athletics manager, Connie Mack. Back in 1925 at the Cobb event in Detroit, Mack couldn't fathom placing Ruth in Ty's class. Mack wished to remain in the holy site to wait out the rain. He stood beside the sportswriter, Dan Daniel, yet another pundit who had earlier put in writing his preference for Cobb over Ruth. That was, after all, the consensus opinion until, well, just now. Mack and Daniel huddled in the rear of the cathedral, surrounded by a group of priests. One cleric asked

FIGURE 4.2 An estimated 75,000 mourners, young and old, lined New York's streets in the rain to watch the funeral motorcade in honor of Babe Ruth in August 1948. Courtesy of Al Gretz/Getty Images.

[54] Alexander Feinberg, "75,000 Go to Babe Ruth's Funeral and Stand in Rain Along Fifth Ave.," *New York Times*, August 20, 1948, 1.

Mack to rank Babe Ruth in the "all-time rating of baseball." Mack did not hesitate. "Well, the Babe certainly was in a class by himself," he explained. Anticipating a learned rebuttal, Mack launched into a dissertation on how "Ruth and Cobb were different types."[55] Daniel disagreed. The comparison between Ruth and Cobb was no longer, to him, a worthy debate. Daniel confessed to Mack his conversion to Ruthianism and proceeded to make a statistical argument for Ruth's case as baseball's very greatest. Cobb was a distant second.

Then Daniel moved beyond the numbers. "The most vital testimony in proving that Ruth was the greatest ball player of all time," he determined, "is not found in the records." He spoke about Ruth's affection for children, recalling the Babe's humble roots, and painted a blatantly whitewashed portrait of the Babe as a model celebrity citizen. The priests had just heard a similar eulogy uttered by Cardinal Spellman. Soon after departing the church, Daniel recorded his conversation with Connie Mack and the St. Patrick's clergy in a book tribute to Ruth. No longer in the cathedral, Daniel still found it fitting to sermonize that statistics "fail to tell the tremendous things that he did for the game." Daniel spoke of how "baseball inspired the growing American boy largely because of the achievements of the Babe." By contrast, Cobb was – it's unclear if the pun was intended – a "ruthless player" and, alluding to Ty's racism, irascible with that "hot Dixie temper."[56]

Cardinal Spellman and Dan Daniel invested their sentimental remarks in Ruth's pull-yourself-up-by-your-bootstraps biography. Suddenly, America was intrigued by Ruth's humanity and thought there was something to learn from his personal experiences. Little is known about Ruth's childhood, save for the half-truths relayed in a serialized autobiographical, ghostwritten column in 1920.[57] There wasn't much of a demand for information of this sort because, after all, so many had already deemed Ruth superhuman, beyond any earthly historical investigation. Little on Ruth's backstory appeared during the balance of his career and retirement. Sportswriters tended to draw from that initial sketch. The sportswriter Tom Meany, for instance, relied on it in his 1947 book-length ode to Ruth; or as he put it, "one man's impressions of the greatest baseball figure who ever lived."[58] In his final months,

---

[55] Dan Daniel, *The Real Babe Ruth* (St. Louis, MO: C. C. Spink & Son, 1948), 73.
[56] Ibid., 74.
[57] Leavy, *The Big Fella*, 46–48.
[58] Tom Meany, *Babe Ruth: The Big Moments of the Big Fellow* (New York: Grosset & Dunlap, 1947), 9.

How the Babe Became the Greatest

Ruth's family agreed to terms with E. P. Dutton to publish an "authentic story" of the Babe's life. The publisher rushed the project, owing to Ruth's diminishing health. The first chapter, "This Is How It Begins," corrects the public record, again revising just a very thin literature on Babe Ruth's early years.[59] Ruth confessed that "I was a bad kid," sent to St. Mary's Industrial School because his parents couldn't put up with him, and then reformed with the support of his Catholic teachers. The section reads like an ethical will: Ruth imploring his young readers to recommit to the "greatness" of America, to reengage with the sentiment of an idyllic bygone era:

But baseball won out. Through baseball, I got the second break of my life ... In this great land today baseball is providing breaks for other youngsters, some of them as hard and unknown as I was. It is a great calling for a boy, but it is only one of countless fields which an American boy can enter and try his hand at.

Too many youngsters today believe that the age of opportunity has passed. They think it ended about the time people stopped reading Horatio Alger.

There are more opportunities today than when I was a boy. And all of these opportunities are open to every type of American. The greatest thing about this country is the wonderful fact that it doesn't matter which side of the tracks you were born on, or whether you're homeless or homely or friendless. The chance is still there. I know.[60]

Eulogies and tributes to Ruth in the years directly after his death tended to remember Ruth's work outside the batter's box. He was "more beloved by the crowd than any man who ever stepped upon a diamond," ran a typical refrain. Not to miss a chance to recall his origins, the same editorial reminded readers that the "beginning of his life gave him a bond with the common people. He had it tough to begin with. He was brought up in an orphanage and a priest encouraged him to be a ball player."[61] As well, the passage of time had remedied Ruth of his alcoholism and womanizing. Instead, memoirists recalled Ruth's penchant for fun. The scarce mention of his nightlife routine was raised to demonstrate just how far he had matured later in life. This was a trick of the trade for media brass that needed, however schizophrenically, to separate the personal lives of celebrities from an idealized version.[62]

---

[59] Bob Considine, *The Babe Ruth Story* (New York: E. P. Dutton, 1948), 11–22.
[60] Ibid., 18.
[61] "Babe Ruth Was More than a Great Baseball Player," *Atlanta Journal*, August 16, 1953, 2F.
[62] P. David Marshall, *Celebrity and Power: Fame in Contemporary Culture* (Minneapolis, MN: University of Minnesota Press, 1997), 187–89.

Ruth was being reborn as a transcendent American figure. Baseball wasn't even the most important aspect of his storied life. Grantland Rice memorialized him as an "emblem, a symbol."[63] Others jovially feted the Babe as a "fun-loving immortal."[64] True, the Associated Press voted him, in a relative landslide, the greatest ball player of the first half-century. Yet, the crux of the renewed discussion around Babe Ruth had to do with nostalgia. If they had to assess baseball greatness based on crude numbers, confessed the editors of the *Sporting News*, Cobb remained the "all-time No. 1." Like Dan Daniel, the magazine pleaded that facts and figures were insufficient because "Ruth was not merely a ball player." He was the "idol of the youngsters of America." More than that, though, "Ruth was the greatest exemplar in baseball history," not due to his home run swing or World Series triumphs. No, he was the greatest of all time, a "patron saint," as a baseball player, because Babe Ruth "made over the game to suit the modern tempo of American life, and the modern love for action."[65]

Of course, this was total revisionism. Cobb's methods far better matched the prevailing tempo and tenor of American life. In economic terms, Cobb played the white-collar "thinking man's game" while Ruth was the blue-collar slugger, a powerful laborer. He was a good factory worker but hardly cut out for management. While he never had much success at it, Cobb coached the Tigers in his final seasons as the club's top player. By contrast, the Yankees turned down Ruth's overtures in 1934 to manage the New York team. Throughout Ruth's power surge in the 1920s, sportswriters rarely, if at all, made any broader connection to "action." To the contrary, during this interwar period Americans and practically everyone else eschewed such language, exhausted by the war-themed images that had taken so many lives during World War I. The revival of action language came about as anxieties rose concomitant with the emergence of Hitler's Third Reich. Like the boxer Joe Louis (nicknamed the Brown Bomber), the Yankees, as the "Bronx Bombers," became a popular symbol of American wartime self-confidence. Yet, this moniker, coined by Dan Daniel, didn't appear until 1936, once Ruth had left the team and handed the spotlight to the Yankees' next great baseball hero, Joe DiMaggio.[66]

---

[63] Grantland Rice, "Babe Ruth Greatest Figure Sports World Has Ever Known," *Boston Globe*, August 17, 1948, 8.
[64] Harold Kaese, "Babe Ruth: A Fun-Loving Immortal," *Boston Globe*, August 16, 1958, 11.
[65] "Game Made Ruth – And He Remade Game," *Sporting News*, August 25, 1948, 10.
[66] Duke Goldman, "Paragon vs. Prodigy: The Cultural History of Joe DiMaggio and Mickey Mantle as Yankee Brand Icons," in *The New York Yankees in Popular Culture: Critical Essays*, ed. David Krell (Jefferson, NC: McFarland & Company, Inc., 2019), 60.

**

The golden age of Babe Ruth's greatness came about during a period that Tom Brokaw aptly popularized as the "Greatest Generation." This term, I would argue, is no coincidence. Said Brokaw on an NBC political talk show in 1994, "I think this is the greatest generation any society has ever produced."[67] Brokaw had in mind the legacies of the women and men born during the Great Depression, some of whom served in the Normandy D-Day landings in World War II, and many more who worked very hard in the immediate postwar period to rebuild the United States. With "missionary zeal," Brokaw produced a book for the Greatest Generation, a critically acclaimed best-seller.[68] His was part of a larger phenomenon among Americans to wax nostalgic about the 1950s.[69] Painting with a purposefully broad brush, Brokaw highlighted the likes of servicewomen, salesman, and airplane engineers. He had in mind the American everyman and went to great lengths to describe the better-known individuals as no different from the American rank and file. Like a scrapbook, Brokaw produced dozens of chapters, each a vignette of the lives of everyday Americans, famous US politicians, and financial powerbrokers whose lives intersected by virtue of their total commitment and sacrifice to procure America's so-described greatness.

The mythologizing of the 1950s began early on – actually *during* the 1950s. Historians write about the "instant nostalgia" created in this epoch when radio disc jockeys coined the phrase "golden oldies" to identify popular songs produced just a few years prior.[70] Tellingly, a department store vice president censured "those Ty Cobb of retailing-store executives who wistfully speak of 'the good old days' of 25 or 30 years ago." He called their dismissal of the present financial conditions, but likely not realizing its Fordian implications, "bunk."[71] Most Americans celebrated their moment as a "new invention," eager to show up the anti-capitalist Soviet Union in the early stages of the Cold War. The gross national product grew by 250 percent since the end of World War II. Almost two-thirds of Americans held middle-class

---

[67] Brokaw, *The Greatest Generation*, xxx.
[68] See, for example, "The Class of '45," *New York Times*, December 27, 1998, BR7.
[69] See Janelle L. Wilson, *Nostalgia: Sanctuary of Meaning* (Lewisburg, PA: Bucknell University Press, 2005), 67–87.
[70] William H. Young and Nancy K. Young, *The 1950s* (Westport, CT: Greenwood Press, 2004), 179.
[71] Ed Stanton, "'Good Old Days' in Retailing Termed Purely Fictional," *Women's Wear Daily*, August 17, 1953, 1.

incomes, although the disparity between white Americans and African Americans remained very significant.[72]

A big part of 1950s America was the family. It was the "first wholehearted effort to create a home that would fulfill virtually all its members' personal needs."[73] In this period, Americans married younger and with the help of increased income and the G. I. Bill, bought homes, typically, in the suburban hinterlands. By the end of the decade, 62 percent of American families owned single-family homes, compared to 43 percent in 1940. Three-quarters had enough money to afford a car and about nine out of ten households owned a television and likely tuned into programs – *Father Knows Best*, *The Adventures of Ozzie and Harriet*, *Leave it to Beaver*, *Make Room for Daddy*, and *The Donna Reed Show*, to list a few – that stressed middle-class, family values.[74] These television shows and the suburban environs they aimed to depict were mostly white, as African Americans and other minority groups struggled to keep apace in this mythologized decade of American greatness. Moreover, TV programs created "flashbulb" collective memories and experiences that fortified the values transmitted by famous faces, who were in turn, noted social scientists at that time, "given a special place in the commercially organized fantasies of the nation."[75]

***

Americans required symbols that captured their newfound self-proclaimed greatness. The earlier aspirational changemaker model would not do since little, anymore, required changing. The point was to embrace a new slate of figures that exemplified America's readymade state. Two of the more prominent examples were Franklin and Eleanor Roosevelt. Both had been recast from changemakers to nostalgia-laden American "common people." Some judged that this wasn't a stretch. In FDR's lifetime, his advisors wondered aloud "what traumas or

---

[72] See Stephanie Coontz, *The Way We Never Were: American Families and the Nostalgia Trap* (New York: Basic Books, 2016), 24–26.
[73] Elaine Tyler May, *Homeward Bound: American Families in the Cold War Era* (New York: Basic Books, 2008), 13–14.
[74] Coontz, *The Way We Never Were*, 24.
[75] See Erving Goffman, *The Presentation of Self in Everyday Life* (Garden City, NY: Doubleday, 1959), 31; and James W. Pennebaker and Becky L. Banasik, "On the Creation and Maintenance of Collective Memories: History as Social Psychology," in *Collective Memory and Political Events: Social Psychological Perspectives*, eds. James W. Pennebaker, Dario Paez, and Bernard Rimé (Mahwah, NJ: Lawrence Erlbaum Associates, 1997), 3–19.

epiphanies had transformed a Hudson Valley patrician into a champion of the common people of America?"[76] By the brink of the 1950s, Roosevelt had been elevated to the hallowed station of great American statesmen that only George Washington and Abraham Lincoln dared to tread. There had been some precedents to this, but none who had persisted too long before descending to a middling, or at least a more modest rank. Washington and Lincoln were the exception, so it was believed, who proved a general rule of the "tendency of natural leaders to avoid public life for business and the law."[77]

Until Lincoln and the Civil War, Washington was the unequivocal leader of the pack.[78] The best anyone could do, as Henry Cabot Lodge made clear in his high esteem for Benjamin Franklin was second place: "Franklin was the greatest American of his time, with the exception of Washington."[79] In 1925, Gutzon Borglum had drawn criticism when he announced that his carvings of "empire-builders" on Mount Rushmore in South Dakota would feature Thomas Jefferson and Theodore Roosevelt alongside the standard bearers: Washington and Lincoln. Although he had "never claimed to be selecting the four greatest men in American history," Borglum had to go to significant lengths to justify Jefferson and Roosevelt, and at times explained how his renderings still preserved the peerlessness of the other, more distinguished pair.[80] The decision to include the recently deceased Roosevelt had been more controversial than Jefferson, although that was only because of the uptick in Jefferson's popularity brought about by Roosevelt in his presidential discourses and the many public speeches delivered by the politician, creationist, and several-time presidential hopeful, William Jennings Bryan.[81]

---

[76] See H. W. Brands, *Traitor to His Class: The Privileged Life and Radical Presidency of Franklin Delano Roosevelt* (New York: Doubleday, 2008), 12.

[77] Arthur M. Schlesinger, *Paths to the Present* (New York: The Macmillan Company, 1949), 93.

[78] See R. B. Bernstein, *The Founding Fathers Reconsidered* (Oxford: Oxford University Press, 2009), 115–67.

[79] Henry Cabot Lodge to James M. Beck, July 17, 1923, Reel 84, Henry Cabot Lodge Papers, Massachusetts Historical Society, Boston, Massachusetts. Cited in See Huang, *Benjamin Franklin*, 136.

[80] See Gilbert C. Fite, *Mount Rushmore* (Norman, OK: University of Oklahoma Press, 1952), 47–48. See also, John Taliaferro, *Great White Fathers: The Story of the Obsessive Quest to Create Mount Rushmore* (New York: PublicAffairs, 2002), 208; and Rex Alex Smith, *The Carving of Mount Rushmore* (New York: Abbeville Press, 1985), 129–32.

[81] See Merrill D. Peterson, *The Jefferson Image in the American Mind* (New York: Oxford University Press, 1960), 259–60.

Abraham Lincoln and George Washington were peerless because all the other US presidents, being as they were fallible human beings, had foibles. It was in certain circles blasphemous to harp all that much on the greatest presidents' respective humanities. In 1885, John Bach McMaster had hoped that from the pens of future historians, when it came to Washington, "shall read less of the cherry-tree and more of the man."[82] One reviewer found McMaster's formulation troubling, supposing that the "towering excellence and nobility of George Washington is too much for some people." The writer agreed that it was "silly to suppose or maintain that Washington was faultless" but understood McMaster's call for reevaluation of Washington as "mean."[83]

There was a posthumous competition between the two at the top, and it suggested that more was in the mix than their own bona fides. Lincoln's resonance was framed in contemporary terms. Or, as the historian Daniel Boorstin wrote about the phenomenon, "We revere them," referring to the likes of Lincoln and Washington, "not because they possess charisma, divine favor, a grace or talent granted them by God, but because they embody popular virtues." In the throes of war and grave human rights concerns, issues that similarly defined the mid nineteenth and mid twentieth centuries, Lincoln loomed the largest. "We admire them," wrote Boorstin, mostly about Lincoln, "not because they reveal God, but because they reveal and elevate ourselves."[84] In political campaigns during the 1940s, "Abraham Lincoln was quoted more than any other man."[85] In January 1945, the American Institute of Public Opinion reported that 42 percent of Americans thought Lincoln was a "greater man." Just 22 percent preferred Washington while the balance remained either uncertain or believed they were "equally great."[86] The most common explanations for selecting Lincoln over Washington were freighted with contemporary timbre: because he was "more of a humanitarian" and that he was the "people's President," "more down to earth," and

---

[82] John Bach McMaster, *A History of the People of the United States*, vol. 2 (New York: D. Appleton and Company, 1885), 452–53.

[83] Leonard Irving, "Do We Know George Washington?" *Magazine of American History* 29 (March 1893): 223.

[84] Daniel J. Boorstin, *The Image or What Happened to the American Dream* (New York: Atheneum, 1962), 50.

[85] Dixon Wecter, *The Hero in America: A Chronicle of Hero-Worship* (New York: Charles Scribner's Sons, 1941), 4.

[86] Hadley Cantril, *Public Opinion, 1935–1946* (Princeton: Princeton University Press, 1951), 562.

"demonstrated the principles of true democracy."[87] In any case, the "Lincoln cultists" and "Washington cultists" agreed that criticism was "unholy," and that "if the Father of his Country is godlike, the Great Emancipator is Christlike."[88]

In April 1945, President Roosevelt died and became an archetypical American. "America was to be many things, and Franklin represented most of them."[89] A half-year later, the American Institute of Public Opinion asked "who is the greatest person, living or dead, in world history?" In this poll, FDR garnered 28 percent of the vote. Lincoln collected 19 percent and came in second. Jesus Christ registered in third place and George Washington, an indicator of a downward trend, finished in fourth.[90]

Roosevelt was posthumously projected as the American everyman, symbolic of the so-called Greatest Generation that enlisted in World War II and rebuilt the American economy after the elongated Great Depression. His New Deal and faith in the American spirit during World War II prophesied the passage into a splendid postwar age of picket fences, paternal reverence, hard work, and widespread middle-class incomes. America required a version of Roosevelt that jibed with these images. The public therefore ignored FDR's Harvard pedigree and his family's vast wealth. Instead, Americans focused on Roosevelt's health struggles. In his lifetime, FDR was careful to hide his use of a wheelchair in public. In his death, during the immediate postwar period and throughout the 1950s, Americans celebrated Roosevelt's perseverance in leading the nation while handling his disability. FDR's wheelchair became a symbol of determined grit, the personification of the great American everyman.[91]

The scholarly elite basically concurred with the public consensus about FDR, even as they refused to prise the very top slot away from Lincoln. The Harvard historian Arthur Schlesinger surveyed fifty-five scholars and determined in the pages of *Life* magazine that Roosevelt

---

[87] Ibid. For an even earlier, rarer indication of Lincoln's rise above Washington, see Arthur H. Vandenberg, *The Greatest American: Alexander Hamilton* (New York: G. P. Putnam's Sons, 1921), 3–25.
[88] Thomas A. Bailey, *Presidential Greatness: The Image and the Man from George Washington to the Present* (New York: Appleton-Century, 1966), 4.
[89] Henry Steele Commager, "Franklin Still Speaks to Us," *New York Times*, January 15, 1956, SM10.
[90] Cantril, *Public Opinion, 1935–1946*, 565.
[91] See Sara Polak, *FDR in American Memory: Roosevelt and the Making of an Icon* (Baltimore: Johns Hopkins University Press, 2021), 173–81.

was among the "Great" presidents. Lincoln was the only unanimous decision. Washington and Roosevelt captured the next spots while those polled extended the top tier to Woodrow Wilson, Thomas Jefferson, and Andrew Jackson. Rather than identifying them as unbridled changemakers, Schlesinger surmised that his colleagues picked this lot out of their reverence for progressiveness mixed with tradition. "The six great Presidents often seemed politically ahead of their times," wrote Schlesinger, "but they had to be careful not to get too far ahead."[92]

Schlesinger's report caused something of a sensation. Much later, the historian recalled, quite correctly, that the "main sticking point was the classing of Franklin Roosevelt among the six 'greats,' next to Lincoln and Washington."[93] Schlesinger kept hundreds of letters, many that advised him to read John Flynn's *Roosevelt Myth*. Flynn's thick and controversial monograph accused FDR of kowtowing to Stalinism, an accusation, among many, that, to the major New York publishers, rendered the book unsellable.[94] After a lesser publishing house produced Flynn's work, book reviewers condemned it as scholarly screed; among these, the young Arthur Schlesinger Jr. called the book "simply hysterical."[95] Flynn's tome did not sell very well but it was popular among a swath of Americans who wrote to Schlesinger Sr. with indignation. One writer shared with the historian a long note he penned to *Life* to cancel his subscription, expressing annoyance that Henry Luce, an avowed Republican, and the magazine's well-known publisher, printed a ranking that celebrated far more Democrats than Republican-affiliated US presidents.[96] Another letter-writer simply supposed that Schlesinger was "really working in the Kremlin's propaganda mill."[97] He blamed Luce for printing the gratuitous nonscientific study on the eve of the 1948 presidential election and considered the transgression a consequential part of the upset of Republican Thomas Dewey against Harry

---

[92] Arthur M. Schlessinger, "Historians Rate U.S. Presidents," *Life*, November 1, 1948, 73.

[93] Arthur M. Schlesinger, *In Retrospect: The History of a Historian* (New York: Harcourt, Brace & World, 1963), 109.

[94] See John E. Moser, *Right Turn: John T. Flynn and the Transformation of American Liberalism* (New York: New York University Press, 2005), 166–79.

[95] Arthur Schlesinger Jr., "John T. Flynn on the F. D. R. Era," *New York Herald Tribune*, November 7, 1948, 2.

[96] B. Kesselheim to Life Magazine, November 4, 1948, Box 422, Folder 1, Arthur M. Schlesinger Jr. Papers, MSS-17775, New York Public Library Manuscripts and Archives Division, New York, NY.

[97] Unsigned letter to A.M. Schlesinger, November 15, 1948, Box 422, Folder 1, Arthur M. Schlesinger Jr. Papers.

Truman. A politically conservative editorialist published the same theory about the recent presidential election and called the declaration of FDR's greatness an instance of "historical sacrilege."[98]

The common charge was that FDR was a changemaker, and a radical one at that. This was not the stuff of American greatness – at least it was no longer the key ingredient. The United States had entered the calmer and more plentiful 1950s despite Roosevelt's "misguided" politics. American capitalism had overcome FDR's heavy taxations and the expensive welfare programs that, in their view, impeded the American economy rather than, as liberals deemed it, nursed it back to financial health. The most far-fetched conspiracies held that Roosevelt purposely provoked Japan's attack on Pearl Harbor to force Congress to take a "most un-American" turn and involve itself in foreign affairs. Critics warned that Roosevelt's was a bad legacy to usher into the 1950s and blamed the dead president for the expanded government oversight and America's involvement in the Korean War.[99]

But plenty of others agreed with Schlesinger's tallies. This group, the one best represented in popular surveys, believed that Roosevelt's political calculations had been guided by American knowhow. They thought that FDR's presidential decisions were cut from a variety that any sensible patriot would have made, just as so many other Americans embraced choices and sacrifices to steer the nation into a more prosperous postwar period. Theirs was the shared "rendezvous with destiny" that Roosevelt had predicted, and Tom Brokaw later interpreted as going "well beyond the outsized expectations" of the symbolic exemplar who had pronounced them at the 1936 Democratic National Convention.[100] A gentleman from Cedar Rapids, Iowa, wrote to Schlesinger to thank him for the material to respond to his neighbors who hold an "inordinate hatred" for FDR.[101] "Isn't it amazing, and faith-renewing," shared another writer, "to see the people registering, almost as if by instinct, the perception and perspective of the historians!"[102] As the 1950s drew to a close, Arthur Schlesinger Jr. worried in a piece on the "Decline of Greatness" that his generation

---

[98] Malcolm W. Bingay, "Twisting History," *Detroit Free Press*, November 3, 1948, 6.
[99] See James T. Sparrow, *Warfare State: World War II Americans and the Age of Big Government* (Oxford: Oxford University Press, 2011), 242–60.
[100] Brokaw, *The Greatest Generation*, 12.
[101] M. W. O'Rieley to Arthur M. Schlessinger, November 8, 1948, Box 422, Folder 1, Arthur M. Schlesinger Jr. Papers.
[102] Phil Forke to A. M. Schlessinger, November 15, 1948, Folder 1, Box 422, Arthur M. Schlesinger Jr. Papers.

was slipping under decidedly un-Rooseveltian leaders.[103] Yet, the elder Schlesinger remained more sanguine than his son about America's prospects. Schlesinger Sr. repeated his polling experiment in 1962, this time with a slightly larger pool of seventy-five historians. He was gladdened that, owing to FDR's repeated high rank with Lincoln and Washington, the "longer perspective adds weight to the previous judgment."[104] The response to this second iteration, notwithstanding some "subdued muttering," likewise confirmed Roosevelt's near-supreme station among America's greatest presidents.[105]

***

Eleanor Roosevelt's march to greatness was slower and steeper than her husband's. Unlike FDR, she lived long enough to conform her image to a new American postwar standard. It wasn't easy. In the weeks preceding her husband's presidential inauguration in March 1933, the press pilloried Mrs. Roosevelt for accepting hefty honoraria for speaking engagements and displaying a "lack of dignity" by commenting on an assortment of controversial political subjects. The journalists had hoped Roosevelt would behave like one of her First Lady predecessors, Grace Coolidge, who had reportedly "not wish[ed] to be more than the mistress of the White House."[106]

Eleanor Roosevelt polled particularly poorly among gentlemen. They resented her political activities, something she was forced to do after her husband's paralytic illness in 1921. In short order, Mrs. Roosevelt recognized she was very good at it, and quite valuable to the causes she supported: from the Women's Trade Union League to Al Smith's New York gubernatorial reelection campaign. Her outspokenness made men uncomfortable. Months before FDR vied for his unprecedented third term in the Oval Office, many American men in May 1940 expressed hope that they had seen the very last of Eleanor in Washington, DC. More than half of men polled said that they "don't care," "don't know," or that Mrs. Roosevelt "should retire entirely from the public eye."[107] Her numbers rose, as did her husband's, after

---

[103] See Barry D. Riccio, "The U.S. Presidency and the 'Ratings Game,'" *The Historian* 52 (August 1990): 571–72.
[104] Arthur M. Schlesinger, "Our Presidents: A Rating by 75 Historians," *New York Times*, July 29, 1962, 143.
[105] Robert L. Bloom to the *New York Times*, July 31, 1962, Box 422, Folder 2, Arthur M. Schlesinger Jr. Papers.
[106] See David Michaelis, *Eleanor* (New York: Simon & Schuster, 2020), 280–81.
[107] Cantril, *Public Opinion, 1935–1946*, 557.

the United States entered World War II. Still, about 40 percent of Americans said they could find something very disagreeable about the First Lady. The most common gripes were that Roosevelt "butt[ed] in on her husband's business," was too eager to "take sides in public questions," and, relatedly, she "should stay home more."[108] These chauvinists were likely the kind who would have agreed with the cynical opinion shared in the newspapers at that moment: the "greatest woman is she who produces the best child. The two greatest women in American history during the past hundred [sic] years are the mothers of Abraham Lincoln and Thomas A. Edison."[109]

Most Americans were not antiwomen; they just preferred a decidedly un-Rooseveltian type. That much was evident whenever people considered "great" women, a conversation that took place in parallel to other greatness discussions since most of the people that Americans had assigned to the ranks of greatness were men.

The people who gave the deepest thought to great women were, in general, the feminists who championed suffrage and equal rights. They weren't all that smitten with Roosevelt either. Take, for instance, Bryn Mawr College's M. Carey Thomas Prize established in 1922 to honor an "American woman who had achieved real eminence in some line of work."[110] The prize was endowed by Bryn Mawr's alumnae association in honor of Thomas's twenty-eight year tenure as president of the all-women's college located in Philadelphia's western suburbs. Today, Bryn Mawr has scrubbed Thomas's legacy from the buildings formerly known as Thomas Library and Thomas Hall amid pressure to recognize and denounce her racist and antisemitic points of view.[111] Back then, however, Thomas was regarded as one of America's leading women educators, a suffragist, and an exemplar of greatness. Bryn Mawr College reasonably tapped Thomas as the first awardee of the prize upon her retirement.

Eleanor Roosevelt wasn't Bryn Mawr material and it cut both ways. She was born into a union of wealthy New York aristocrats. Roosevelt's biographer suspected that she had once aspired to enroll in Bryn Mawr, or perhaps another women's college such as Vassar College in

---

[108] Ibid., 559–60.
[109] Arthur Brisbane, "Today," *Austin Statesman*, December 28, 1932, 4.
[110] "Deed of Trust Creating the M. Carey Thomas Prize Fund," Box 1, Folder, 1, M. Casey Thomas Award Collection, Bryn Mawr College Archives, Bryn Mawr, PA.
[111] See Beatrice Forman, "College to Remove Name of Ex-Leader," *Philadelphia Inquirer*, March 22, 2023, B2.

Poughkeepsie, New York.[112] She was taken by the first wave of the feminist movement that lobbied for suffrage, advanced education, and jobs for women. But her maternal grandmother, a Victorian-inclined socialite, "humphed" at the prospect of her granddaughter attending such an institution. "All you need, child," said Grandma Mary Hall to young Eleanor, "are a few of the social graces to see you through life."[113] From the other perspective, the Bryn Mawr ladies valued women with formal education and, quite frankly, resented the stigma assigned to their schools by affluent elites such as the Roosevelts and the Halls. That they shared common social causes was contravened by the impression that women such as Roosevelt had ascended to their station by leveraging their husbands' credentials. They considered that path a political shortcut that ultimately undermined their feminist cause. For this breed of women leaders, the Thomas Prize for an "eminent woman" conjured up, contrary to Grandma Hall, an individual of worldly standing and an education that matched a great male counterpart.

The idea for the prize was inspired by President Thomas's work to establish grants and fellowships for European scholars to study and work at Bryn Mawr College. At her request, Bryn Mawr's alumnae endowed the prize to be "given to an American woman … for real eminence in any line of achievement," to model greatness and inspire young pupils at Bryn Mawr College and elsewhere in the United States.[114] Thomas, as a founding member of the award committee, was a stickler for the criteria and insisted that the "prize should be awarded only if there was a suitable candidate to whom to award it, that an award should be passed rather than made to a person not of the highest distinction."[115]

The committee members had to remind Thomas of her position after the latter recommended the Polish-born physicist Dr. Marie Curie because she was disappointed with the American-born candidates. "Let us open the prize as good internationalists to any woman," suggested Thomas. "Then at once we have Mme. Curie who would

---

[112] See Michaelis, *Eleanor*, 61.
[113] See Alfred Steinberg, *Mrs. R.: The Life of Eleanor Roosevelt* (New York: G. P. Putnam's Sons, 1958), 42.
[114] Alumnae Committee to Honor President Thomas, Meeting Minutes, February 4, 1922, Box 1, Folder 1, Casey Thomas Award Collection, Bryn Mawr College Archives, Bryn Mawr, PA.
[115] Dorothy S. White, "History of the M. Carey Thomas Prize Fund," July 23, 1930, Box 1, Folder 1, Casey Thomas Award Collection.

come over for it and several others of first rank – enough to last until the U.S. grows some more."[116] The committee begged Thomas for her forbearance and patience for American women.[117]

The committee wanted their prize to be Nobel-like, and studied the protocols of other august prizes to ensure that theirs reached the highest caliber.[118] This meant selectivity for new committee members. In May 1930, Eleanor Roosevelt – then the First Lady of New York, not of the whole United States – was nominated for an opening on the Thomas Awards Committee, but the members did not give her much thought, preferring, instead, the theater critic, Rosamond Gilder, and several other leading ladies.[119]

The much more important decisions about awarding the prize underwent even harsher scrutinization. Edith Wharton – whose regret that her parents forbade enrollment in a women's college was well-known by then and apparently sufficiently redemptive – was the first woman to win the Pulitzer Prize in Fiction (for her novel *The Age of Innocence*) but the Bryn Mawr ladies judged that "Mrs. Wharton's later work was less good." Dr. Florence Sabin's pioneering work on the origins of blood vessels was good enough to elevate her to the presidency of the American Association of Anatomists but the Thomas Award Committee concluded that she "might be a candidate in future years when her work on tuberculosis is completed."[120] In due course, the committee selected Jane Addams as the award's second recipient since the social scientist and activist's "right to receive it was indisputable."[121]

Jane Addams fit all the criteria of a great feminist changemaker. She was the founder of the Hull House in Chicago, a pioneering settlement organization that developed social service programs for poor, immigrant families. As a reformer and avowed suffragist, she ran in circles that included Emily Bach, Theodore Roosevelt, and Woodrow Wilson. As a philosopher, she debated progressivism with the likes of John

---

[116] M. Carey Thomas to Marion E. Park, May 30, 1927, Box 1, Folder 2, Casey Thomas Award Collection.
[117] See Dorothy S. White to Marion E. Park, June 9, 1927, Box 1, Folder 2, Casey Thomas Award Collection.
[118] See, for example, Curtis Bok to Constance G. C. Ludington, September 25, 1935, Box 1, Folder 4, Casey Thomas Award Collection.
[119] M. Casey Thomas Prize Committee Meeting Minutes, May 23, 1930, Box 2, Folder 13, M. Casey Thomas Award Collection.
[120] Ibid. Sabin later won the prize in 1935. See "Thomas Award Goes to Doctor F. R. Sabin," *College News*, October 23, 1935, 1.
[121] Ibid.

Dewey and George Herbert Mead. As a graduate of Rockford Female Seminary, she was a kind-of-kinswoman of the Bryn Mawr alumnae. On her own, Addams invented the social work profession and, in tandem with others, founded the American Civil Liberties Union.[122]

Bryn Mawr College made much of the "most important event," and made arrangements for NBC to broadcast the program on its radio networks.[123] The proceedings honoring Addams acknowledged that

> Jane Addams has ceased to be a figure of mere local importance and has become universal in her significance—a symbol of a whole period of human history, a symbol of thousands of men and women who have shared with her in the past and in the present and who will continue to share for all time in a labor of service to humanity.[124]

In line with other great Americans, Addams was hailed as a changemaker for her "scholarly and scientific achievements for social progress in American life."[125]

Public opinion agreed that Addams was America's leading woman, if not the "greatest woman in the world."[126] In 1922, the National League of Women Voters asked its constituents to name the "greatest living American women." Jane Addams appeared on nearly every list, ahead of suffragist Carrie Chapman Catt, artist Cecilia Beaux, and Edith Wharton.[127] The Bryn Mawr prize was among several marquee honors bestowed upon Addams, a remarkable list of accolades that boasted the Nobel Peace Prize in 1931. It was decried as something of an upset that a popular poll conducted by the *Ladies' Home Journal* in coordination with the National Council of Women placed Addams behind Church of Christ founder, Mary Baker Eddy, as the nation's "greatest woman."[128] In her native Chicago, Addams was by "universal consent," opined a local minister, "the greatest among modern women—lover of humanity, and a social statesman of sanity, saintliness and serene idealism."[129]

---

[122] See Louise W. Knight, *Jane Addams: Spirit in Action* (New York: W. W. Norton & Company, 2010), 65–103.
[123] "Jane Addams," *College News*, May 6, 1931, 2.
[124] Francis Perkins, "Address on the Occasion of the Presentation of the M. Carey Thomas Award," *Bryn Mawr Alumnae Bulletin* 11 (June 1931): 8–9.
[125] Ibid.
[126] "Jane Addams Believes U.S. Will Join League," *Globe*, September 16, 1921, 5.
[127] "Twelve Greatest Women," *New York Times*, June 25, 1922, xxi.
[128] See "Mary B. Eddy Voted 'Greatest Woman,'" *New York Times*, December 21, 1932, 21; and Loring A. Schuler, "Twelve and a Thirteenth," *Ladies' Home Journal* 50 (March 1933): 24.
[129] "Past Names 'Ten Greatest Women Today,'" *Chicago Tribune*, May 18, 1931, 19.

Withal, the reports on the National Council of Women's poll revealed just a "scattering [of] votes for Mrs. FDR."[130]

* * *

For a short time, Eleanor Roosevelt framed her public image to fit in the Jane Addams mold. She fancied herself ahead of her time, at least in the social circles that Roosevelt had frequented as a youngster. In her 1938 memoir, Roosevelt described her break from the Victorianism of her youth. "I became a much more ardent citizen and feminist than anyone about me," wrote Roosevelt about her first engagement with the suffragettes.[131] "You accepted invitations to dine and to dance with the right people only, you lived where you would be in their midst," she wrote about the protocol of her top-notch pedigree. "In short, you conformed to the conventional pattern."[132] Hers was also an upbringing in which "I took for granted that men were superior creatures and still knew more about politics than women."[133]

Roosevelt's point was that she had overcome the transgressive social elitist infelicities, as the Bryn Mawr feminists had perceived them. It was a far trickier ordeal to declare her political independence from FDR, even as she had, Washington insiders and gossipers were aware, separated her political agenda from her husband's ever since his extramarital affair with Lucy Mercer.[134] Eleanor Roosevelt omitted that detail in her memoir, of course. She did include the struggle of raising young, frustrated boys who lacked routine access to a very busy father. Her descriptions did not jibe with the scenes of a wholesome family unit displayed on television screens a dozen years later. The book, edgy for its time, rose to the top of the bestseller charts, especially in the Washington DC market.[135] Critics described it as a "frank, unaffected, courageous story of an American woman's life."[136]

Eleanor Roosevelt's memoir ingratiated her to American feminists. Her appointment as the inaugural chair of the United Nations'

---

[130] See "Mary B. Eddy Voted 'Greatest Woman.'"
[131] Eleanor Roosevelt, *This Is My Story* (New York: Harper & Brothers, 1937), 297.
[132] Ibid., 3–4.
[133] Ibid., 180–81.
[134] See Hazel Rowley, *Franklin and Eleanor: An Extraordinary Marriage* (New York: Farrar, Straus and Giroux, 2010), 179–209.
[135] See, for example, "Best Sellers of the Week Here and Elsewhere," *New York Times*, January 3, 1938, 19.
[136] Katherine Woods, "Mrs. Roosevelt's Own Story," *New York Times*, November 21, 1937, 95.

Commission on Human Rights after FDR's demise also helped. In December 1947, Bryn Mawr President Katherine McBride wrote to Roosevelt to inform her that the alumnae committee had selected her and Anna Lord Strauss of the League of Women Voters as corecipients of the M. Carey Thomas Award. McBride credited Roosevelt for her "great contribution to international understanding."[137] Some questioned Roosevelt's fit within the Bryn Mawr expectation of female and feminist greatness since she had made her mark "as wife of a president." However, the group, after minimal debate, finally came around to the position – the same argument embedded in her autobiography – that a "strong case can be made for [Roosevelt's] independence, courage, and wisdom in that connection."[138]

The trouble was that outside of Bryn Mawr College feminism no longer led the discussion about great women. Postwar America was drawn to a more "family friendly" woman. Many feared that feminism was an obstacle to reaching this ideal. The earliest supporters of Eleanor Roosevelt's station among America's greatest women wished to endow her image with postwar cultural currency (Figure 4.3). They described her as "America's busiest wife and mother."[139] The mounting groundswell for Roosevelt as the "greatest woman of our time" concomitantly denounced the "vicious tirade and abuse" that sought to cast her as an overbearing wife bent on injecting her feminist agenda to her husband's policies.[140]

Eleanor Roosevelt apparently intuited all this and refashioned her image to complement the idyllic American wife and mother. Gone was the self-portrait of a changemaking, reformer feminist. In 1949, Roosevelt published a second memoir that focused much more on her late husband and how she, as First Lady, negotiated motherhood "as life grew busier in the White House, my husband had less and less time for family affairs."[141] She didn't dare use "feminism" in the book-length self-description. This iteration presented Eleanor Roosevelt as a doting wife who cared for her ailing husband and did her very best to hide

---

[137] Katherine E. McBride to Eleanor Roosevelt, December 29, 1947, Box 1, Folder 5, Box 1, Folder 2, Casey Thomas Award Collection. See also Millicent Carey McIntosh to Margaret Paul, October 28, 1947, Box 1, Folder 5, Casey Thomas Award Collection.
[138] Merion Edwards Park to Katherine E. McBride, September 11, 1946, Box 1, Folder 5, Casey Thomas Award Collection.
[139] "Two of America's Greatest Women," *Women's Day* 1 (September 1938): 2.
[140] Ralph McGill, "The Greatest Woman of Our Time," *Atlanta Constitution*, September 14, 1947, 14B.
[141] Eleanor Roosevelt, *This I Remember* (New York: Harper & Brothers, 1949), 19.

FIGURE 4.3 Franklin and Eleanor Roosevelt at the former's presidential inauguration on March 4, 1933. Although it was a long process and had several iterations, the ceremony introduced America to two of its "greatest" individuals of the twentieth century. Courtesy of Library of Congress Prints and Photographs Division.

his wheelchair from public view, as to preserve his "manhood." In this installment, Roosevelt responded to her detractors who had claimed she was too independent and imposing. "The political influence that was attributed to me," wrote Roosevelt about the allegation, "was nil where my husband was concerned, largely because I never made the slightest effort to do what I knew I could not do."[142] America appreciated this more motherly version. "We are unfair to her," cried a book reviewer of the uncharitable assessments of Eleanor Roosevelt.[143] Another review praised the memoir of this "great and important figure," full of "an even riper wisdom" than the prior autobiography because it placed FDR at the "center of the stage."[144]

A third memoir cemented Roosevelt's case for maternal greatness. The 1958 volume doubled down on Roosevelt's family life, much to

[142] Ibid., 6.
[143] Elizabeth Janeway, "Franklin and Eleanor Roosevelt," *New York Times*, November 6, 1949, BR1.
[144] James H. Powers, "F. D., Wife, Rampageous Roosevelts," *Boston Globe*, November 20, 1949, A9.

the satisfaction of the American literary critics.[145] This final rendition painted a self-portrait of a gentle widow Christmas shopping for thirteen young grandchildren.[146] Most of her final autobiography documented her brave travel to Soviet Russia and many other locales as a reluctant diplomat, doing her very best to serve her country and the memory of her husband. Roosevelt's concluding remarks, meant to drum up courage to stand up to the Soviet Union, invoked FDR's famous remarks at his first presidential inauguration: "When we do that, we shall have nothing to fear."[147] She was a woman leader, forced by her situation, to carry on the mantle of her courageous, late husband.

Eleanor Roosevelt died in November 1962. Civil Rights leaders and heads of state, from Martin Luther King to Golda Meir, mourned the "greatest woman in the world."[148] Her family likewise recalled her as "one of the world's most revered women."[149] Everyday Americans, remembering her recast image as a mother to a nation, called her the "greatest woman of our time."[150] This was not the same image of her that was feted by Bryn Mawr College when its alumnae conferred the M. Carey Thomas Prize and welcomed Roosevelt "into a brave fellowship."[151] To the contrary, Eleanor Roosevelt had since rewritten herself into the American ideal, a symbol of greatness, of womanhood, that the people around her imagined they had already become.

***

Babe Ruth's now-peerless greatness – he was, by then, "head and shoulders over his closest rival" – symbolized the same spirit of Postwar America.[152] Unlike Ty Cobb, his image was increasing, not shrinking. "I am reminded of my husband a little more often than most widows because I see his name everywhere in the papers, increasingly every year," wrote Claire Ruth, with echoes of Eleanor Roosevelt. "The legend of

---

[145] See, for example, Margaret L. Coit, "Keeping Up with Mrs. Roosevelt," *New York Times*, September 14, 1958, BR1; and Malvina Lindsay, "The Unsinkable Mrs. Roosevelt," *Washington Post*, September 14, 1958, E6.
[146] Eleanor Roosevelt, *On My Own* (New York: Harper & Brothers, 1958), 7.
[147] Ibid., 234.
[148] See "Israel Saddened by Great Loss," *Jewish Advocate*, November 8, 1962, 1; and Martin Luther King Jr., "Epitaph for Mrs. FDR," *New York Amsterdam News*, November 24, 1962, 11.
[149] Patrcia Peabody Roosevelt, "Eleanor Roosevelt: A Great Lady's Last Brave Days," *Good Housekeeping* 164 (June 1967): 80.
[150] "Eleanor Roosevelt," *Ladies' Home Journal* 80 (November 1963): 8.
[151] "The M. Carey Thomas Award," *College News*, March 11, 1948, 2.
[152] Branch Rickey, "Some Old Baseball Ideas," *Life*, August 2, 1954, 82.

the Babe seems to be growing with time."[153] The press also marveled how ten years after his death, Ruth was "still [the] greatest baseball star."[154] For Mrs. Ruth, the inflated Babe Ruth of the 1950s was a source of comfort:

> I thought I was the only one who loved him. Now I know I wasn't. A nation loved him. Not just because he hit 714 home runs, and did all sorts of wonderful things on a baseball field. But because the people sensed that he was one of them. He had their faith and their weaknesses. They loved him because he was, above all else, a great human being.[155]

Her reflection was also a reminder that Babe Ruth was no longer a supernatural figure, an unduplicatable "accident" of paranormal baseball stardom.[156] That erstwhile description of Ruth was rather unhelpful to an American public who needed him, in mythical form, to be a palpable reflection of themselves.

Those widespread superlative feelings about Babe Ruth were most evident in the summer of 1961, as Yankees outfielder Roger Maris challenged Ruth's home run record. Before then, Jimmie Foxx and Hank Greenberg had come very close to toppling Ruth's record of sixty homers in a single season. On each occasion, the "worshipers of Babe Ruth" heaped "resentment of the false gods who have arisen from time to time and attempted to replace their idol atop the pedestal."[157] Ruth had anticipated that a future ball player would eclipse his mark, "and when it is broken, I'd like to see it done by a Yankee and keep it in the family."[158] The Yankee stars, Roger Maris or Mickey Mantle – the latter faded during the tail end of the 1961 season due to injuries – would have been an amenable replacement for Ruth if he had meant what he had said.

Instead, Maris reportedly received the "genteel malice of the American people."[159] It was much worse than that, however. Maris lost hair and

---

[153] Ruth and Slocum, *The Babe and I*, 12. Claire Ruth also fashioned her own image as an idyllic wife in a postwar America. She wrote: "Now that I was Mrs. Ruth, I felt Mrs. Ruth had a job to do. It's the job every wife does in one form or another, I imagine, no matter how many of them insist upon denying it. I had a few reforms to institute." See ibid., 96.

[154] "Babe Ruth, Dead Ten Years, Still Greatest Baseball Star," *Baltimore Sun*, August 17, 1958, 2D.

[155] Ibid., 208.

[156] On this description of Ruth, see Sidney Reid, "Meet the American Idol!" *The Independent* 103 (August 14, 1920): 170.

[157] Arthur Daley, "Consolation for Idolators," *New York Times*, August 22, 1961, 34.

[158] Ruth and Slocum, *The Babe and I*, 92.

[159] William Barry Furlong, "That Sixtieth Home Run," *New York Times*, August 20, 1961, SM53.

grew "tired" by the pressure and angst placed on him.[160] Baseball legends such as Joe DiMaggio and Hank Greenberg rooted for him, but Maris remained inhibited by baseball fans' allegations of deicide.[161] A few sports scribes tried to placate worried fans that "should the record of sixty be broken, in would only be a chip off the altar stone."[162] Ruth's greatness was everlasting by this point; it was noncontingent of any single record. Still, these women and men required reassurance of Ruth's vitality and the stability of American greatness. In the end, Ford Frick, Commissioner of Major League Baseball, mollified America. Before ascending the ranks of professional baseball administration, Frick was Ruth's former ghostwriter and avowed Babe Ruth fan.[163] In the heat of the home run chase, Frick ruled that unless Maris broke Ruth's record in 154 games – the American League had just extended the season to 162 games – the record books would reflect two distinct home run marks.[164] After Maris hit his sixty-first home run in the season's final contest, most chroniclers preferred to keep it as a single record but placed an inglorious asterisk by the name of the man who, despite the batting statistic, could never outshine Babe Ruth's greatness.[165]

Ruth was omnipotent. Ty Cobb was certainly not.[166] The Georgia Peach's legacy – "the story of his life" – was "marked by a streak of meanness as wide as a ball field."[167] Writers in the 1950s, in the thick of the Civil Rights Movement, focused on how Cobb "more than once became so irritated that he left the playing field, went up into

[160] See Tom Clavin and Danny Peary, *Roger Maris: Baseball's Reluctant Hero* (New York: Simon & Schuster, 2010), 197–98. See also Jane Leavy, *The Last Boy: Mickey Mantle and the End of America's Childhood* (New York: HarperCollins, 2010), 232–34.
[161] See "Hank Greenberg Roots for Mark in Homers by Maris or Mantle," *New York Times*, September 14, 1961, 35; and "Baseball Figures Oppose Frick Ruling," *Washington Post*, September 19, 1961, A18.
[162] Daley, "Consolation for Idolators," 34. See also Arthur Daley, "The Pause that Refreshes?" *New York Times*, September 19, 1961, 40.
[163] See Ford C. Frick, *Games, Asterisks, and People: Memoirs of a Lucky Fan* (New York: Crown Publishers, Inc., 1973), 158–59.
[164] "Ford Frick Reiterates Ruth Record Ruling," *Washington Post*, September 15, 1961, D1.
[165] Maris was only somewhat differential: "Babe Ruth was a big man in baseball and I don't say I'm in his caliber, but naturally I'm happy to go past Ruth's mark." See also "61st Homer Makes Roger Maris 'Happy,'" *Baltimore Sun*, October 2, 1961, 1.
[166] Unfortunately for Cobb, his biographer, Al Stump, was, as later scribes described it, an "opportunist" whose facts didn't always add up to the historical Ty Cobb. See Tripp, *Ty Cobb*, 397–404.
[167] Nathan Aleskovsky, "Among the New Books for Younger Readers," *New York Times*, April 6, 1952, BR32.

the stands and demonstrated his fistic prowess on Negro fans."[168] In these estimations, Cobb's baseball accomplishments were an afterthought, far from the most meaningful measurements of a complex career. The same pundits who gave Ruth a pass on excessive drinking and debauchery were either unwilling or felt they could not whitewash Cobb's off-the-field record during this socially turbulent period. In fact, when Cobb, as an older man, spoke up for racial integration in professional baseball, some within the African American press were astounded, describing him as a "converted southerner" and a "chastened and changed man."[169] Still, most refused to rehabilitate Cobb's image. His postwar-aligned sentiments and his charitable work through the W. H. Cobb Educational Fund did little to reignite the debate between Babe Ruth and Ty Cobb.[170]

Americans have continued to remember the 1950s with unprecedented reserves of nostalgia, even though the historical facts do not always measure up to collective memory. The same is the case for the Babe and the Roosevelts. Years later, their stars remain high in orbit without any threat of falling.[171] Their greatness had become an indispensable part of an idyllic caricature. As Claire Ruth had put it about the Ruth–Cobb debate, this was no longer an argument about baseball. America's love for Babe Ruth was bound up in their feeling that he was a "great human being," so believed his worshipers about Ruth – and perhaps they would admit in in a clearheaded moment, about themselves.

---

[168] Wendell Smith, "Cobb Isn't the Tiger He Used to Be," *Courier*, August 8, 1953, 24.
[169] Gordon Hancock, "The Great Ty Cobb," *Philadelphia Tribune*, February 16, 1952, 4.
[170] Tripp, *Ty Cobb*, 356–57.
[171] See, for example, Arthur M. Schlesinger Jr., "Rating the Presidents: Washington to Clinton," *Political Science Quarterly* 112 (Summer 1997): 179–90; Jimmy Cannon, "World's Poorer Place with Babe Ruth Gone," *Miami Herald*, July 28, 1969, 37; Mel Antonen, "Ruth Still the Greatest 60 Years After No. 60," *USA Today*, September 30, 1987, 1C; and Ralph Schoenstein, "The Modern Mount Rushmore," *Newsweek*, August 8, 1984, 9.

5

The Great Counterculture Conundrum

On February 13, 1964, Cassius Clay announced "I'm the greatest thing in all history." He was fated, said Clay to his opponent and the rest of the boxing world, to win the heavyweight championship. This was standard fare for the loquacious boxer, best remembered by his nom de guerre, Muhammad Ali. The sporting world, to acknowledge his Kentuckian roots, dubbed Clay the "Louisville Lip."[1] Others called him the "Magnificent Mouthpiece."[2] Theatre Network Television broadcasted the interview between Clay and the reigning champion, Sonny Liston. The pair were slated to fight at the Miami Beach Convention Hall in less than two weeks. The television producers had hoped that the news conference would drum up interest in the upcoming heavyweight title fight, especially since most pundits didn't believe it would be much of a contest. The oddsmakers and bookies listed Liston as a 7-1 favorite to defeat Clay, leaving the laconic champ with little reason to respond to Clay's self-congratulatory declarations of greatness.[3]

The network wanted to leverage the challenger's penchant for self-glorification. Owing to its format – just two contestants and a small ring – boxing was practically made for television.[4] The media moguls

---

[1] See, for example, Sid Ziff, "Clay the Greatest," *Los Angeles Times*, February 27, 1963, C3.
[2] Alan Goldstein, "Boxing Buffs Still Wonder How Good Is Cassius Clay," *Baltimore Sun*, March 11, 1963, S19.
[3] See Robert Lipsyte, "Clay and Liston Slug it Out in TV Battle of Barbs," *New York Times*, February 14, 1964, 21.
[4] See Randy Roberts, "The Wide World of Muhammad Ali: The Politics and Economics of Televised Boxing," in *Muhammad Ali: The People's Champ*, ed. Elliott J. Gorn (Urbana, IL: University of Illinois Press, 1995), 27.

desired to add to their profits. Capitalizing on Clay wasn't a sure thing. He was a twenty-two-year-old bombast of varying promotional success. In the months leading up to the Liston fight, Columbia Records released an LP of Cassius Clay's musings. He titled the album, *I Am the Greatest*. That collection of the boxer's monologues and poetry sold a modest 30,000 copies.[5]

Some important people took in the television program. For instance, the Beatles watched the Clay–Liston interview and were unimpressed. The group – John Lennon, Paul McCartney, George Harrison, and Ringo Starr – viewed the press conference from a room at Miami's Deauville Hotel. They had just arrived in Florida for an extended visit, mainly for a second appearance on the *Ed Sullivan Show*. The Beatles had performed a few days earlier at Sullivan's New York studio, a watershed moment witnessed by 73 million television viewers that, together with the group's arrival at Kennedy Airport two days prior, had marked the musical "British invasion" of the United States (Figure 5.1).

The Beatles found Clay's pompous speech unbecoming. The group was very self-aware – they were reluctant to risk a debut tour in the US without an American chart-topping album – and usually self-effacing, the single exception was Lennon whose temper sometimes led to self-aggrandizement, famously once declaring that he and his bandmates were "more popular than Jesus."[6] More often, the Beatles exercised self-deprecation. "We're rather crummy musicians," George Harrison once said, very flatly. "We can't sing; we can't do anything," added Paul McCartney.[7] The egocentric Clay was therefore not the Fab Four's type of champion. The Beatles took some solace that the experts on television didn't give him much of a chance against Liston.[8]

There was something ironic about the Beatles's distaste for Cassius Clay's boastfulness. The old guard of the 1950s, the so-called establishment, didn't care all that much for either. The sportswriter Jimmy Cannon complained that "Clay is part of the Beatle movement," counted among a rogues' gallery that included the Beach Boys, Andy Warhol, and a comic book hero. Clay, Wrote the crotchety Cannon:

---

[5] Brian O'Doherty, "Cassius Clay (He's the Greatest) Will Tell it all in Record Album," *New York Times*, August 1, 1963, 18.
[6] See Michael R. Frontani, *The Beatles: Image and the Media* (Jackson, MS: University Press of Mississippi, 2007), 95–105.
[7] "George, Paul, Ringo, and John," *Newsweek* 63, February 24, 1964, 54.
[8] See Bob Kealing, *Good Day Sunshine State: How the Beatles Rocked Florida* (Gainesville, FL: University Press of Florida, 2023), 32.

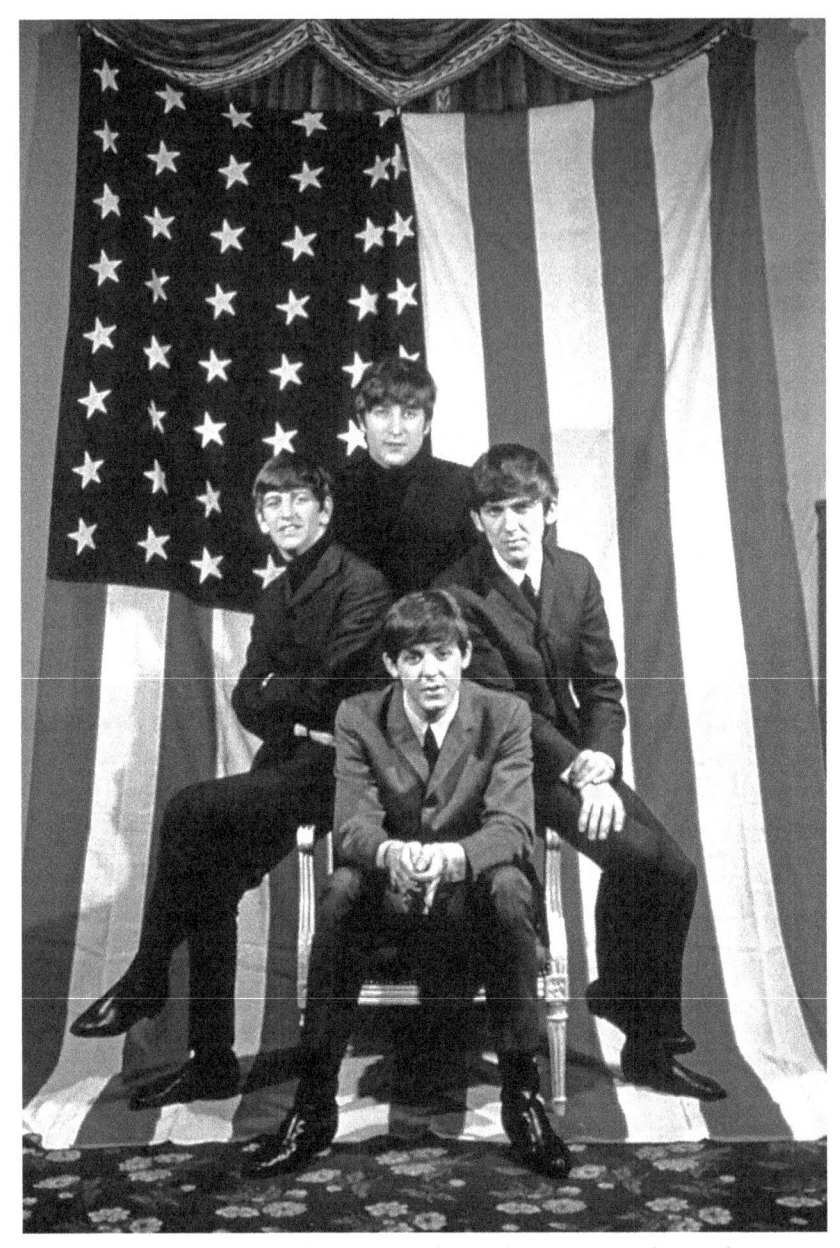

FIGURE 5.1 Upon arrival in New York in February 1964, the Beatles pose in front of an American flag, symbolic of the so-called British Invasion and the music group's fascination with US culture. Courtesy of Michael Ochs Archive/Getty Images.

fits in with the famous singers no one can hear and the punks riding motorcycles with iron crosses pinned to their leather jackets and Batman and the boys with their long dirty hair and the girls with the unwashed look at the college kids dancing naked at secret proms held in apartments and the revolt of students who get a check from dad every first of the month and the painters who copy the labels off soup cans and the surf bums who refuse to work and the whole pampered style-making cult of the bored young.[9]

That newsman's banter was not without credibility. Jimmy Cannon was regarded as boxing's very best journalist. He was resolutely committed to the craft, and even after he had "lost the use of his right arm after his stroke, he taught himself to write left-handed on yellow pads made of foolscap."[10] His peers generally agreed that Cannon possessed a rarified discernment and a wondrous way with words. But they also concurred that Cannon had a penchant for provocation, a knack for turning sports news into a melodramatic Greek tragedy. For example, he wrote about Clay's association with the Nation of Islam, a relationship made public a day after the Liston fight: "I pity Clay and abhor what he represents." The so-called Black Muslims, Cannon continued, "is a sect that deforms the beautiful purpose of religion."[11] He was convinced that the boxer was "part of the Muslim crusade of black supremacy."[12] Cannon's was a style, reportedly "no doubt refined by the wee-hours boozing for which he was famous until a stomach operation permanently disbarred him."[13] It's unknown whether that's what caused the connection for him, between Cassius Clay and the Beatles.

It wasn't so easy during the early years to discern what was so great about either the Beatles or Cassius Clay. Sure, they were relatively well-known celebrities. Pundits enjoyed writing and talking about them because they appeared as boisterous caricatures of daily life, for better or for worse.[14] Yet, they were just a handful of famous figures among a nation of celebrated people. The Fab Four were love song-playing

---

[9] See Thomas Hauser, *Muhammad Ali: His Life and Times* (New York: Simon & Schuster, 1991), 145–46.
[10] William O' Shaughnessy, *More Riffs, Rants, and Raves* (New York: Fordham University Press, 2004), 226.
[11] See Hauser, *Muhammad Ali*, 104.
[12] Jimmy Cannon, "Champions of Hate," *New York Journal American*, February 25, 1965, 22.
[13] Jonathan Yardley, "For Better and for Worse, Jimmy Cannon Influenced Sportswriting," *Sports Illustrated*, August 14, 1978, 5.
[14] Karen Sternheimer, *Celebrity Culture and the American Dream: Stardom and Social Mobility* (New York: Routledge, 2011), 5.

heartthrobs, no different, so it seemed, from Elvis Presley or Buddy Holly in the 1950s. In time, it became apparent that the group's ability to blend genres of music and conjure up clever ways to introduce vocal harmony set them apart from the past and changed the composition of modern popular music. Music experts detected their early genius in hindsight, but few recognized it in the first half of the 1960s.[15] No one anticipated Cassius Clay's rise to greatness, save for Clay. When he turned professional, Clay was a relatively small heavyweight, weighing at no more than 180 pounds, less than Floyd Patterson, and much less than Sonny Liston's 220-pound hulky build.[16] The sportswriters marveled at the agile Clay's quickness, but doubted that he could "float light a butterfly" for too long against an imposing boxer such as Liston, not without bulking up and hitting harder. Eventually, the Beatles and Clay "shook up the world," changed it, with their relative greatness.

However much their destinies overlapped, there were marked differences in the Beatles's and Cassius Clay's respective struggles for greatness. Unlike Clay, the Beatles took greatness for granted. By their time and in their counterculture, greatness was no longer a coveted commodity among young people in the 1960s. The supposedly idyllic 1950s had transitioned to a decade of civil unrest and undaunted counterculture. The women and men who had come of age in the 1950s had searched for symbolic exemplars such as Babe Ruth and Eleanor Roosevelt; individuals who purportedly represented discernable American ideals. By contrast, the flower children of the 1960s embraced a disordered counterculture that helped them come to grips with the sexual revolution and the hippie movement, assassinations of a US president and a handful of famous civil rights champions, and nuclear crises and, climactically, the Vietnam War.

The new generation held a suspicion for any sanitized model of alleged greatness. Their parents' great man was their target, the machine against which they raged. The young disestablishment rebels turned down overtures by the establishment, such as forty-four US Nobel laureates who sided with their anti-Vietnam cause; or, as the Edisonian all-knowing scientific community put it, the "rapid termination of U.S. participation in the southeast Asian war."[17] Any and all wisdom, and

---

[15] See, for example, Evan Davies, "Psychological Characteristics of Beatle Mania," *Journal of the History of Ideas* 30 (April–June 1969): 273–80.
[16] "Ingo Signs Cassius Clay," *Chicago Defender*, February 11, 1961, 24.
[17] "Dissent Spreads to Nobelists, Industrial Scientists," *Science* 168 (June 12, 1970), 1325.

certainly declarations of greatness, that stemmed from an earlier historical period reminded the counterculturists of the 1960s too much of their parents' "oversimplistic" worldviews that had, to them, enabled the myriad crises of the decade.

Clay combatted the very same disenchantment with greatness. But racism was his major hurdle. Clay was a victim of the same prejudice directed at the outspoken black athlete that devalued the merits of Jim Brown and Wilt Chamberlin. None of these men abided by the unspoken rules of the American media. His larger-than-life personality did not permit Clay to acquit himself in understated fashion, as boxer Joe Louis or Negro League standout turned Major League star Jackie Robinson had comported.

More than anyone, Clay took notice of this: "It was as though I had touched an electric switch that let loose the pent-up hatred and bitterness that a big section of White America had long wanted to unleash on me for all my cockiness and boasting, for declaring myself "the Greatest' without waiting for their kind approval."[18] He didn't do things their way, but Clay still wanted White America's respect.

Clay became hell-bent on proving the likes of Jimmy Cannon wrong about his boxing prospects and the journalist's anticipation of the Liston fight would be akin to a "sanctioned mugging."[19] The young boxer detected racism in Cannon's coverage of him, disappointment that the rising challenger did not behave like Joe Louis.[20] The up-and-coming sportswriter Bob Lipsyte, one of Clay's few defenders in the newspapers, backed up Clay's observations about Cannon and the old guard of sports journalism:

> The blacks he liked were the blacks of the thirties and the forties. They knew their place. Joe Louis called Jimmy Cannon "Mr. Cannon" for a long time. He was a humble kid. Now here comes Cassius Clay propping off and abrasive and loud, and it was a jolt for a lot of sportswriters, like Cannon. That was a transition period. What Clay did was make guys stand up and decide which side of the fence they were on.[21]

---

[18] Muhammad Ali and Richard Durham, *The Greatest: My Own Story* (New York: Random House, 1975), 144.
[19] Jimmy Cannon, "The Fight: Is Sonny Liston that Dumb?" *New York Journal American*, February 21, 1964, 1.
[20] "How the Ringside Experts Pick It," *New York Journal American*, February 24, 1964, 22. See also Jimmy Cannon, "Fast Hustle," *New York Journal American*, February 25, 1964, 27.
[21] See David Remnick, *King of the World: Muhammad Ali and the Rise of an American Hero* (New York: Random House, 1998), 157.

Among black athletes, Clay probably had it the worst. His conversion to Islam and transformation into Muhammad Ali further exacerbated his situation. On top of everything else, then, he was a "religious fanatic," according to Jimmy Cannon and other writers assigned to the sports beat.[22] For one reason or another, it was tough – ultimately, unfair – to become a great person in the United States after the crash of the idyllic 1950s. People were unmoored and unsure of whom to look toward for direction. It was a jarring experience since the 1950s had generated so much self-confidence in the many who had flourished during that period. In its wake, the aspirations for – and expectation of – American greatness were agonizingly contested. The painful fissures of the turbulent 1960s were most pronounced when traced along generational and racial lines.

Forevermore, it would be impossible for Americans to pinpoint just one or select a small handful of symbolic exemplars that captured the gist of indigenous values. If we can speak about the disenchantment of the "Long 1960s" that includes the disgrace of Richard Nixon's White House resignation, American mores, to those who once coveted them, were no longer all that discernable.[23] Life in the US had become just too fragmented, too diverse, for anyone to agree on who ought to be the greatest of all time.

***

Cassius Clay's self-confidence wasn't always absolute. In 1960, Clay won the gold medal in the light heavyweight division at the Rome Olympics. He had a presence from the start. "If anyone had held an election for mayor of the Olympic Village," wrote reporters about the gregarious boxer, "Cassius Clay would have been a prime candidate. He roamed from team to team, pausing long enough to use up dozens of rolls of film."[24] He returned to the United States with more fame and even more flamboyance. Still, his initial talking points, chanted in verse, held an altruistic tone: "To make America the greatest is my goal/So I beat the Russian, and I beat the Pole."[25]

Then Clay's rhetoric morphed from aspirational to affirmational. "Man, it's gonna be great to be great," said Clay to Dick Schapp for a

---

[22] Jimmy Cannon, *Nobody Asked Me, But: The World of Jimmy Cannon*, eds. Jack Cannon and Tom Cannon (New York: Holt, Reinhart and Winston, 1978), 152.
[23] Kathryn Schumaker, *Troublemakers: Students' Rights and Racial Justice in the Long 1960s* (New York: New York University Press, 2019), 1–10.
[24] "Cassius Lives it Up," *Newsweek*, September 19, 1960, 75.
[25] Ali and Durham, *The Greatest*, 69.

newspaper story that did much to introduce the Olympic gold medalist to a wider American readership.[26] The hyperbole took over and the superlatives multiplied as Clay joined the professional ranks and worked his way through the heavyweight challenger circuit. "I'm the boldest, the prettiest, the most superior, most scientific, most skillfullest [sic] fighter in the ring today."[27] The golden-toned, handsome, chiseled Clay gained more credence with every knockout punch. Sometimes he described himself, if it were possible, as the "double greatest;" all turns of phrase he learned from observing the eccentric performer Little Richard.[28]

Clay's initial intention was to undermine the confidence of boxers, Archie Moore and later, Sonny Liston.[29] He repeated his self-adulations so many times that he came to believe it. All the while, few had any confidence in Clay's prospects to ascend the challenger circuit and dethrone Liston, an ex-convict who had learned to box while serving time at the Missouri State Penitentiary. The press resolutely sacked Clay's boasts, the kindest dismissals simply stated that this was a "distinction most of the world isn't prepared to give him at this time."[30] Jimmy Cannon was so irritated by Clay's presumptuousness, so out of keeping with his expectation of black athletes, that the writer much preferred the company of the "thug" Liston over the younger boxer.[31] Clay's brags irked his trainers, as well.[32]

The trouble for Clay's detractors was that he always won. Then he overthrew the champ. On March 25, 1964, Clay bruised Liston's shoulder so badly that the reigning champion had to surrender after the sixth round. It was a thrilling heavyweight upset. Clay had delivered on his promise to vanquish that "big, ugly bear." After toppling Liston, Clay shouted at ringside, "I am the greatest! I am the greatest! I am king of the world." The precocious and then little-known reporter, Howard Cosell, was the first to catch Clay's attention. "Was there any single point where you knew you had him?" Again, Clay's answer had to do

---

[26] Dick Schapp, "The Happiest Heavyweight," *Saturday Evening Post*, March 25, 1961, 102.
[27] Howard M. Tuckner, "'Man, It's Great to Be Great,'" *New York Times*, December 9, 1962, 134.
[28] Ibid.
[29] See Dave Brady, "Cassius Clay, in Doggerel, Now Talking the Greatest," *Washington Post*, October 14, 1962, C5; and "Clay is 2-1 Choice Over Moore in 12-Rounder on Coast Tonight," *New York Times*, November 15, 1962, 66.
[30] Marshall Reed, "Does Cassius Clay Deserve a Crack at Liston's Title?" *National Police Gazette* 168 (March 1963): 15.
[31] Jimmy Cannon, "Just What Did Happen?" *New York Journal American*, February 26, 1964, 32.
[32] "Cassius Clay's Claim of 'Greatest' Irks Handler," *Chicago Defender*, June 12, 1963, 22.

with greatness. "I knew I had him in the first round. Almighty God was with me. I want everybody to bear witness. I am the greatest! I shook up the world! I'm the greatest thing that ever lived."[33] Later in his dressing room, Clay shouted to reporters, Jimmy Cannon included, "I'm the greatest. I told the world, I'd do it."[34] The next day, Cannon's newspaper, unapologetic but unable to make sense of it, printed a headline that asked: "Was the Fight Fixed?"[35] It wasn't. One day after that, Clay confirmed rumors that he had converted to the Nation of Islam and then announced that he had changed his name, temporarily to Cassius X, and then permanently to Muhammad Ali.

Ali was a sensation. Television networks no longer needed to strategize how to best promote the new heavyweight champion. Columbia Records reported that shortly after the Miami fight, Ali's *I Am the Greatest* album topped 500,000 sales.[36]

But Ali's victory did not validate him to the most important members of the establishment. Most reporters stuck with "Clay," refusing to refer to him by the name given to him by the controversial Nation of Islam leader, Elijah Muhammad. They loathed his friendship with Muhammad's top minister, Malcolm X. Many regarded them as a dangerous, "un-American" hate group, a symbol of what would soon be termed Black Power. Cannon compared the Nation of Islam's use of Ali with how the Nazis had leveraged heavyweight Max Schmeling in the 1930s for their fascist propaganda.[37] Political moderates worried that Muhammad and Malcolm X threatened to undermine the progress of the Civil Rights Movement. The Nation of Islam countered American racism with a belief that, as Malcolm X put it, white women and men were "inferior to Black people."[38]

The Nation of Islam divided African Americans. Contra Martin Luther King's integrationist campaign, Elijah Muhammad stridently preached separatism. He called African Americans the "original" humans and cast whites as an "evil" derivative of the more authentic

---

[33] See Dave Kindred, *Sound and Fury: Two Powerful Lives, One Fateful Friendship* (New York: Free Press, 2006), 58.
[34] "Clay Tells Everyone: 'I am the Greatest,'" *Los Angeles Times*, February 26, 1964, B1.
[35] "Was the Fight Fixed: Florida Starts Probe," *New York Journal-American*, February 26, 1964, 1.
[36] Mike Gross, "Clay Wins: Columbia Swings," *Billboard*, March 7, 1964, 4.
[37] Jimmy Cannon, "Schmeling and Clay," *New York Journal American*, February 24, 1965, 36.
[38] See Alan F. Westin, *Freedom Now!: The Civil-rights Struggle in America* (New York: Basic Books, 1964), 55.

"darker" breed. The newspapers had initially assumed that Ali had been duped. The writers frequently described him as "naïve, misguided, and uninformed, overbearing and at least slightly flaky."[39] Others allowed their disappointment for Ali's political positions to inform their opinion of his boxing achievements. They called his triumph over Liston a "fluke."[40] The "village elder," Jimmy Cannon, continued wondered aloud whether the fight had been rigged. A year later, when Ali defended his title in a very speedy rematch with Liston, Cannon questioned how a "looping tap of a right hand" could level a championship-level prizefighter such as Liston.[41] Cannon alleged that Ali's title was illegitimate through-and-through.

Jackie Robinson came to Muhammad Ali's defense. Baseball's pioneer integrationist called for Cannon and others to drop their suspicions of foul play and then dismissed African Americans' fear that Ali's affiliation with the Nation of Islam would somehow convince "Negroes en masse [to] embrace Black Muslimism."[42] Sure, admitted Robinson, Ali was "loud" and "crude," but he also carried with him an important message. Ali was not a supremacist, as Cannon and other sportswriters had suggested. "I am not advocating that Negroes think they are greater than anyone else," wrote Robinson about Ali's intentions. "But I want them to know that they are just as great as other human beings."[43]

Robinson was a lonely voice in the African American press. A Los Angeles black paper editorialized that "boxing is sport, not politics." The newspaper's publishers begged Ali to stay in his lane. They feared that Robinson was wrong, that "negroes are being divided" by Ali's allegiance to the militant Malcolm X rather than more peaceful Civil Rights leaders such as Martin Luther King Jr.[44] King agreed with that sentiment. Said King about Ali's decision: "When Cassius Clay joined the Black Muslims and started calling himself Cassius X he became a champion of racial segregation and that is what we are fighting against." Major League Baseball had recently inducted Jackie Robinson

---

[39] Jack Mann, "Greatest? How Terribly Young Is This Boy Clay," *Boston Globe*, March 9, 1964, 13.
[40] Doc Young, "Loudmouth Champ Not the Greatest," *Los Angeles Sentinel*, February 27, 1964, A11.
[41] Cannon, *Nobody Asked Me, But*, 159.
[42] Jackie Robinson, "Clay Explodes Liston Myth," *Chicago Defender*, March 14, 1964, 8.
[43] Ibid.
[44] Doc Young, "Cassius Clay Upsets Non-Sports World," *Los Angeles Sentinel*, March 12, 1964, D3A.

into the Hall of Fame, a sign of the better way, suggested King, to go about things. Then King concluded that "I think perhaps Cassius should spend more time proving his boxing skill and do less talking," a suggestion that the fighter had more work to do to achieve greatness in and out of the ring.[45] Malcolm X told King and other black leaders that they had their priorities mixed up. The baseball integrationist, Jackie Robinson, was, in Malcolm's opinion, the "white man's hero."[46] Anything less than a full embrace of Clay would, in essence, communicate to young black children that they had very little hope to grow up to become the "greatest" at anything.[47]

* * *

The Beatles regretted that they were due back to England before the Clay–Liston fight. They wanted to observe it live at the Miami Beach Convention Hall. "Boxing is about the only sport we watch," said Ringo Starr about the group's interest in the upcoming match.[48] In lieu of attending the tilt, the Fab Four tried to schedule a get-together with Sonny Liston. They were entitled, so they thought, to visit with the very greatest fighter. Liston, however, turned down the invitation to greet them, explaining to the group's publicist that he required total focus in the short time before the title fight. Others recorded that Liston had heard them perform at the Deauville Hotel (Clay was there, too) and was unimpressed. "My dog can play better drums," said Liston about Ringo Starr.[49] Liston was content to train before an entourage that included Joe Louis and Jimmy Cannon, who characteristically expressed his dim view of the Beatles and their unwelcome counterculture music.[50]

Instead, the Beatles's handler brought them to Cassius Clay's ramshackle Fifth Street Gym. The British musicians were furious, led to believe they were on their way for a gathering with Liston, not, as Lennon had put it, "that loudmouth who's going to lose."[51] Clay was

---

[45] See Remnick, *King of the World*, 211.
[46] See Gerald J. DeGroot, *The Sixties Unplugged: A Kaleidoscopic History of a Disorderly Decade* (Cambridge: Harvard University Press, 2008), 127.
[47] Ibid.
[48] See Sid Ziff, "Beatles, Clay Gag it Up at Workout," *Los Angeles Times*, February 19, 1964, 5.
[49] See Bob Mee, *Ali and Liston: The Boy Who Would Be King and the Ugly Bear* (New York: Skyhorse Publishing, 2010), 176. On Liston's and Clay's attendance at the performance, see "That Miami Sun Captures the Beatles," *Disc*, February 22, 1964, 309.
[50] Jimmy Cannon, "Million-Dollar Baby," *New York Journal American*, February 19, 1964, 34.
[51] See Robert Lipsyte, "Winner by a Decision," *Smithsonian* 34 (February 2004): 21.

unworthy of their time and even worse, late for the meeting. The Beatles remained alone in a smoke-filled sweat-reeking room. "Let's get the hell out of here," directed Lennon. But as they motioned to the gym's exit, two brawny men halted the Beatles's forward progress. The guards directed them to Clay's dressing room. They were trapped.[52]

Clay arrived ten minutes later. To make the most of it, the five young showmen (Ringo Starr was the eldest, aged twenty-three) posed in the ring, permitting photographers to snap pictures of them clowning around. Clay feigned jabs and punches. The much smaller musicians pretended to wince and collapse in the ring, playful victims of the half-dressed prizefighter, a strange juxtaposition in the printed photos that show the Beatles in stylish pants and terrycloth jackets (Figures 5.2 and 5.3). Clay declared he had much in common with the famous band: "The Beatles are the greatest and I am the greatest," he announced to the small crowd assembled in his gym.[53] Clay's boast was the worst of it, but John Lennon found the whole ordeal rather undignified, hardly in agreement with the

FIGURE 5.2 With certain unease, the Beatles pose for a playful photoshoot in Miami with heavyweight contender Cassius Clay (later Muhammad Ali). Courtesy of Bettmann/Getty Images.

[52] Ibid.
[53] Ziff, "Beatles, Clay Gag it Up at Workout," 5.

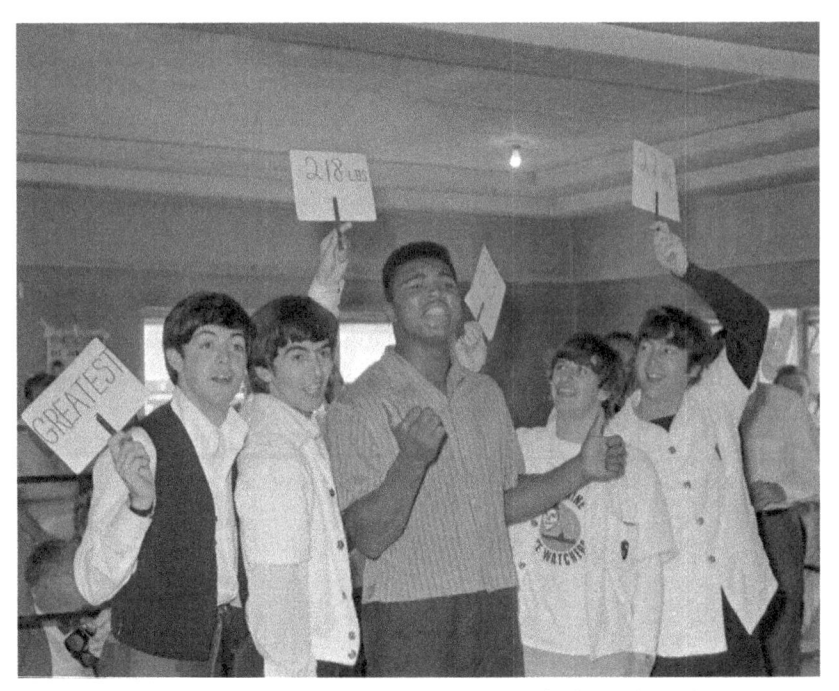

FIGURE 5.3 The Beatles were eager to conclude their photoshoot at heavyweight contender Cassius Clay's gym. Tellingly, Paul McCartney is compelled to hold a placard that declared Clay the "greatest." Courtesy of Mark and Colleen Hayward/Getty Images.

newspaper columns that claimed all parties, Lennon included, "danced and laughed and cavorted like co-conspirators in a gigantic hoax."[54]

Lennon and the other Beatles bristled at Clay's ostentatiousness. It wasn't just that they disagreed, based on the consensus predictions of sportswriters, with Clay's self-assessment. That was an afterthought. Foremost in their consideration was the association of greatness with the stodginess of the prior generation that refused to accept the musical up-and-comers with much else other than "condescension."[55] As a result, they did not put much stock into the sincere accolades, like when the music and ballet critic, Richard Buckle, described Lennon and McCartney as the "greatest composers since Beethoven."[56]

[54] Robert Lipsyte, "The Beatles and Clay Spar a Fast Roundelay," *New York Times*, February 19, 1964, 46.
[55] See Jonathan Gould, *Can't Buy Me Love: The Beatles, Britain, and America* (New York: Harmony Books, 2007), 1–11.
[56] See Hunter Davies, *The Beatles* (New York: W. W. Norton, 1996), 188.

The Beatles understood the rhythm of American life and the widely apparent cultural chasms of the 1960s. Growing up in Liverpool, the four young men were raised in a veritable way station of modern American music. During World War II, the port of Liverpool was a strategic naval site for American ships to access the European combat theater. US servicemen brought with them the American Forces Network, a government radio broadcast service that introduced the local Brits to jazz, R&B, and pop sounds from across the Atlantic.[57] The influences were evident in their earliest years, when the Beatles were more-or-less an American cover band. Their repertoire of a hundred songs included hits by Elvis Presley, Little Richard, Buddy Holly, and Chuck Berry.[58] Said McCartney, with his usual humility, "We just copied what they did."[59] No wonder, then, that Lennon had once supposedly said "I've been half-American ever since I first heard Elvis on the radio and me head turned."[60] Presley, of course, was widely described, at least by the dawn of the 1960s, as the "greatest teen idol of all time."[61]

Yet, the Beatles were also aware that their youthful irreverence and pop style was an affront to the establishment. They were duly cautioned that they shouldn't set high expectations for their upcoming visit to the United States. The trade papers agreed that "recordings made by the Beatles should find favor among indigenous teen-agers," but predicted that their notes would bottom out among other demographics. "It would not seem quite so likely that the accompanying fever known as Beatlemania will also be successfully exported. On this side of the Atlantic it is dated stuff."[62] Wrote another Beatle nonbeliever:

Visually they are a nightmare; tight, dandified, Edwardian-Beatnik suits and great pudding bowls of hair. Musically they are a near-disaster; guitars and drums slamming out a merciless beat that does away with secondary rhythms, harmony, and melody. Their lyrics (punctuated by nutty shouts of "yeah, yeah, yeah!") are a catastrophe, a preposterous farrago of Valentine-card romantic sentiments.[63]

---

[57] See Simon Philo, *British Invasion: The Crosscurrents of Musical Influence* (Lanham, MD: Rowman & Littlefield, 2015), xxviii–xxx, 25; and Jack Hamilton, *Just Around Midnight: Rock and Roll and the Racial Imagination* (Cambridge: Harvard University Press, 2016), 121–68.
[58] See Gould, *Can't Buy Me Love*, 100.
[59] See Peter Wicke, *Rock Music: Culture, Aesthetics and Sociology*, trans. Rachel Fogg (Cambridge: Cambridge University Press, 1990), 64.
[60] See Hugo Williams, *No Particular Place to Go* (London: Picador, 1982), 24.
[61] See William Leonard, "Did Presley Invent the Twist?" *Chicago Tribune*, March 4, 1962, 33.
[62] Jack Gould, "TV: It's the Beatles (Yeah, Yeah, Yeah)," *New York Times*, January 4, 1964, 47.
[63] "George, Paul, Ringo, and John," 54.

Fortunately, about 40 percent of all Americans were under twenty years old, and seventeen was the largest age cohort in the United States.[64] The Beatles and Capitol Records counted on that teenage, baby-boom market to sell albums. They needed parents to provide the allowance money to purchase the LP, not to like the music. It wasn't a secret. Their detractors – the very ones who described their outfits as "nightmarish" and their musical talents as "disastrous" – also intuited that the Beatles "give kids a chance to let off steam and adults a chance to let off disapproval."[65] The lads from Liverpool were particularly "hypnotic" to young ladies, provoking "madness." Shortly after the group's touchdown in New York and performances at Carnagie Hall and Washington, DC's Coliseum, an observer described the "violent and spectacular diversions of the young [which] are taking place in a moral vacuum caused by the abdication of their elders." Heaping the blame for the widespread teenage infatuation with the British musicians on their parents, this writer figured that "if this vacuum is filled within tin gods, it is largely because the adult world has not offered them a valid religion."[66]

The Beatles held no compunction about placating the "adult world" that had remained closed to their music as well as the attendant counterculture of that epoch. The 1960s generation didn't want to be like their parents, nor the great people whom their forebears had so saccharinely idealized. It appeared contrived, associated with, in young people's estimations, shallow platitudes and aphorisms. "I feel guilty when people say I'm the greatest guitarist on the scene," once explained Jimi Hendrix. "What's good or bad doesn't matter to me; what does matter is feeling and not feeling."[67] The Beatles, especially John Lennon, might have privately considered themselves the very best musical group in the "god-damned world."[68] Ratings did matter to them. They were alarmed when, just before departing the United Kingdom in January 1964, that the Dave Clark Five's "Glad All Over" displaced the Beatles's "I Want to Hold Your Hand" as

---

[64] See André Millard, *Beatlemania: Technology, Business, and Teen Culture in Cold War America* (Baltimore: Johns Hopkins University Press, 2012), 138.
[65] "George, Paul, Ringo, and John," 54.
[66] David Dempsey, "Why the Girls Scream, Weep, Flip," *New York Times*, February 23, 1964, SM71.
[67] Ritchie Yorke, "'I'm Into Different Things,' Says Jimi Hendrix," *Los Angeles Times*, September 7, 1969, Q20.
[68] See Barry Miles, *John Lennon in His Own Words* (London: Omnibus Press, 1994), 87.

the number one hit on the UK charts. By contrast, they were gratified that shortly after they departed New York on that initial visit the "charts crawl[ed] with Beatles," meaning twelve songs ranking in the Billboard Hot 100.[69] The group also liked to needle Mick Jagger that the Beatles's records also seemed to sell better than the Rolling Stones'.[70] But to the public the Beatles were usually careful to project a humble disposition and rigorously pushed back against designations of "greatness." They feared that such a label would place them outside of the prevailing and popular counterculture.[71]

***

The Beatles departed Fifth Street Gym and Clay stopped talking. He exited the ring and got himself ready for a post-workout rubdown. To a sportswriter who had been present at the earlier gathering, Clay privately admitted, in a hushed tone, that he had detected the group's dismal feelings about him. Upon some reflection, he confessed to Bob Lipsyte that he hadn't much fondness for those "sissy" Beatles.[72]

Despite not getting along, at least at first, the Beatles and Clay remained irrevocably linked to one another.[73] The latter joined the "Beatle movement," that is the 1960s counterculture, upon his transformation into Muhammad Ali and his conversion to the Nation of Islam. In fact, Ali dropped, at least for a short period, the grandiose greatness-talk. He no longer needed to rank with the establishment. "Most of my campaigning was not really me," he told a reporter before vanquishing Sonny Liston a second time. "Now, I don't have to talk like that."[74] His conversion to Islam also chastened him, to a degree. "Allah, the Supreme Being, is the greatest," said Ali of his faith in God. "I'm the greatest boxer, but I must be humble and can't say I'm the greatest anything anymore."[75] The press noticed that Ali stopped reciting poetry

---

[69] Jack Maher and Tom Noonan, "Chart Crawls with Beatles," *Billboard*, April 4, 1964, 1.
[70] See John McMillian, *Beatles vs. Stones* (New York: Simon & Schuster, 2013), 121–22.
[71] See David J. Atkin, "From Counterculture to Over-the-Counter Culture: An Analysis of Rolling Stones's Coverage of the New Left in the United States from 1967–1975," in *Studies in Newspaper and Periodical History*, eds. Michael Harris and Tom O'Malley (Westport, CT: Greenwood Press, 1995), 185–98.
[72] Kealing, *Good Day Sunshine State*, 78–85.
[73] In 2016, the Beatles's Paul McCartney shared some memories of friendship between he and Muhammad Ali (Cassius Clay). See David Smith, "Muhammad Ali Tributes Led by Barack Obama," *Observer*, June 5, 2016, 2.
[74] Robert Lipsyte, "Cassius Clay, Cassius X, Muhammad Ali," *New York Times*, October 25, 1964, SM29.
[75] "Words of the Week," *Jet*, January 19, 1967, 30.

about his personal greatness, replacing that with "insistent parables and tenets of the separatist group known as Black Muslims."[76]

Humility did not assuage his opponents' concerns. Jimmy Cannon warned that the Nation of Islam had remade the boxer "into an instrument of mass hate," a veritable "weapon of wickedness."[77] In November 1965, Ali fought Floyd Patterson. The self-styled "Gentleman of Boxing," Patterson was dubbed by others the "Black White Hope" who could defeat the "Black Muslim," so prayed sportswriters and boxing legends such as Jack Dempsey, Joe Louis, and Rocky Marciano.[78] These past fighters were "considered the model heavyweight champions: accommodating and controllable men."[79]

For Joe Louis, this was by design. To prepare Louis for the spotlight, his managers arranged for lessons in "table manners and elocution." If he toppled a white fighter, Louis, his trainers had preached to him, should never smile too much after vanquishing his opponent. The rule held even in 1938 when Louis crushed Max Schmeling, the so-called Nazis' champion, at Yankee Stadium. The fight lasted just two minutes and four seconds, deflated as "one of the greatest dramas of make-believe ever witnessed in America."[80] In victory, Louis was hailed as America's champion, a symbol of the anticipated triumph over German fascism.[81] For his achievement and comportment, Jimmy Cannon called Louis "perfection" and the "greatest fighter who ever lived."[82] Ali was not cut from the same cloth. Howard Cosell said that most of his fellow journalists "wanted [Muhammad Ali] to be another Joe Louis, a white man's black man."[83] That wasn't the image the '60s champ desired, however.

After Ali defeated Patterson, Jimmy Cannon had to admit that "Clay is the best around." However, he refused to elevate him above Louis, or any of the earlier heavyweight champions. Ali was the greatest,

---

[76] Robert Lipsyte, "The Champion Looks Down at His Title," *New York Times*, March 24, 1964, 41.

[77] See Hauser, *Muhammad Ali*, 104.

[78] See Remnick, *King of the World*, 275.

[79] Robert Lipsyte, "'I Don't Have to Be What You Want Me to Be,' Says Muhammad Ali," *New York Times*, March 7, 1971, SM24.

[80] See Theresa E. Runstedtler, "In Sports the Best Man Wins: How Joe Louis Whupped Jim Crow," in *In the Game: Race, Identity, and Sports in the Twentieth Century*, ed. Amy Bass (New York: Palgrave Macmillan, 2005), 48.

[81] See Mike Marqusee, *Redemption Song: Muhammad Ali and the Spirit of the Sixties* (London: Verso, 1999), 24–26.

[82] See Michael Alexander Banks, "Black Athletes in the Media" (PhD diss., City College of New York, 1993), 241.

[83] Howard Cosell, *Cosell* (Chicago: Playboy Press, 1973), 176.

relatively speaking, assessed Cannon, because no one in his generation was all that good. "Don't let anyone tell you," stated Cannon with derision, that "this great clown would get by Louis and Marciano."[84] Cannon downgraded Ali because of his out-of-the-ring work. Ali was a self-professed "race man" who freely admitted that, when push came to shove, "boxing is nothing."[85] "He did things that Joe Louis chose not to do," recalled actor James Earl Jones about Muhammad Ali.[86] Louis tried to change the world inside the ring. Ali hadn't any patience for that method since "we're still catching hell."[87]

It angered him that others did not recognize that race was the biggest factor that limited Ali's quest for greatness. He intimated similar frustration after his friend, singer Sam Cooke, was killed by a female motel manager in Los Angeles. Ali regarded Cooke as the "greatest singer in the world" and was vexed that the police were quick to accept the manager's argument of self-defense and judged the incident a justifiable homicide. Had Cooke looked more like Frank Sinatra or the Beatles, vowed Ali, "the FBI would be investigating yet and that woman would have been sent to prison."[88]

At first, Muhammad Ali had a lot of time to agitate for change. He defended his title just twice in his first two years as the champ. Then things got busier. In his third year, Ali was challenged on seven occasions and vanquished each opponent, sometimes with ungenerous quantities of brutality. Against Ernie Terrell at Houston's Astrodome in February 1967, Ali was merciless. In interviews leading up to the fight, Terrell called the champ, "Clay," refusing to use Ali's chosen Muslim name. Ali punished Terrell in the lopsided contest. "What's my name?" Ali taunted Terrell in the final rounds, as he hurled torturous jabs instead of delivering a compassionate knockout punch. "It was a bad fight, nasty with the evil of religious fanaticism," dutifully decried Jimmy Cannon. "This wasn't an athletic contest," judged Ali's most caustic critic. Then, with an ironic flourish, wrote the white journalist about the black boxer: "It was a kind of lynching."[89]

---

[84] Jimmy Cannon, "The Great Clown," *New York Journal American*, March 31, 1966, 21.
[85] Robert Lipsyte, "Children Bring Joy to World-Weary Champion," *New York Times*, February 20, 1966, S3.
[86] See Muhammad Ali, *Through the Eyes of the World* (New York: Skyhorse Publishing, 2007), 202.
[87] See Hauser, *Muhammad Ali*, 103.
[88] See Marqusee, *Redemption Song*, 100.
[89] See Hauser, *Muhammad Ali*, 165.

"Nationalism," posited a historian, "always attached itself easily to the ring." Ali's ultimate transgression was his opposition to the Vietnam War. He called it unjust. It struck his white critics odd that an athlete such as Ali whose fame came from pummeling other men would object to war on religious grounds. On the other hand, an increasing number of African Americans started to better understand Ali's perspective. Blacks were conscripted at a higher clip than whites. A greater proportion of African Americans died in Vietnam, compared to white soldiers-in-arms. The black community also found America's interest overseas very incongruous, to put it mildly. They did not comprehend, in John Lewis's words, "why President [Lyndon] Johnson can send troops to Vietnam, troops to Africa, and to the Dominican Republic, and cannot send troops to protect people in Selma, Alabama, who just want to vote."[90] Martin Luther King Jr. also came around to Ali's thinking, just as Jackie Robinson, a supporter of the Vietnam War, turned away from Ali's camp.[91] Jimmy Cannon was one of the first to note the emerging white–black divide on Muhammad Ali's actions: "There are some reporters who stress how unpopular Clay is. They mean with white people. He is the most admired fighter among Negroes since Joe Louis. He plays to them."[92]

Cannon's appreciation for the split on Ali didn't change his feelings about the boxer. "It embarrasses me," wrote Cannon, "to mention Clay in the same column as soldiers in combat in Viet Nam."[93] He called Ali a hypocrite with a "strain of evil in him."[94] To fix the problem and encourage blacks to back away from Ali, Cannon highlighted Jackie Robinson's criticisms of the boxer and support of Vietnam, as well as the news that the Hall of Fame baseball player's own son had served and was injured in battle.[95]

Then America drafted Ali. The military changed his draft status – prior to this, he was excused based on low aptitude scores – and summoned him to duty. In April 1967, Ali and twenty-five other young men appeared in an induction center in Houston. Ali was the only man who did not step forward when his name was called to join the US armed forces. The white-dominant sportswriters united in condemnation. Opined the *Washington Post*: "It is too bad he went wrong. He had the

---

[90] See Marqusee, *Redemption Song*, 171–72.
[91] Ibid., 222.
[92] Jimmy Cannon, "Clay a Paderewski Without Piano for Concert," *New York World Journal Tribune*, March 20, 1967, 25.
[93] Jimmy Cannon, "Big Mouth," *New York Journal American*, February 22, 1966, 19.
[94] Jimmy Cannon, "The Pacifist," *New York Journal American*, February 21, 1966, 32.
[95] Jimmy Cannon, "On the Lam," *New York Journal American*, March 18, 1966, 20.

makings of a national hero."[96] Stated the *Atlanta Constitution*: "You either serve or face the consequences."[97] The *World Journal Tribune* agreed: "There is no way to condone this act of unpatriotism by the champion. He has turned his back on his country and that is shameful."

The establishment's response to Ali's refusal to enlist was swift. The New York State Athletic Commission immediately suspended Ali's boxing license. The World Boxing Association stripped him of his title. Then a federal grand jury in Houston indicted him. All but one of the jurors was white.

But Ali remained resolute. He professed to his detractors that "I don't have to be what you want me to be."[98] This from a boxer who had, just three years earlier, so much desired to conform to America's highest standards of greatness. Pressed to square his patriotism as America's champ with his outright refusal to combat the Communist regime in charge of North Vietnam, Ali was clear: "I got no quarrel with them Vietcong."[99] Three weeks later, an all-white jury convicted Muhammad Ali of violating Selective Service laws. Ali appealed to the higher courts, arguing that he wasn't a draft dodger. He was a conscientious objector, a devout Muslim exercising legitimate pacifist beliefs. All told, Ali lost four years of his prime boxing career. The establishment refused him and his politics, undercutting his quest for greatness. The boxer understood this. In his own assessment, Muhammad Ali was the "greatest," the most "unpopular, undefeated heavyweight monster-in-exile."[100]

***

"The athlete of the decade," surmised Jimmy Cannon, "has to be Cassius Clay." It wasn't a compliment. Cannon detested the 1960s, eager to move on from the "trouble and the wildness and the hysterical gladness and the nonsense and the rebellion and the conflicts of race and the yearning for bizarre religions." Muhammad Ali was "all that the '60s were." In other words, good riddance to all that. Cannon especially resented the "changed values that altered the world and the feeling about Vietnam in the generation that ridiculed what their parents cherish."[101] Ali was

---

[96] Harold Kaese, "Writers Vary on Clay Action," *Boston Globe*, May 7, 1967, 61.
[97] Ibid.
[98] Robert Lipsyte, "'I'm Free to Be Who I Want,'" *New York Times*, May 28, 1967, SM15.
[99] Ibid., SM57.
[100] Ali and Durham, *The Greatest*, 248.
[101] Jimmy Cannon, "Athlete of the 60s Has to Be Cassius," *Miami Herald*, January 12, 1970, 39.

the catalyst and ruined all that Cannon had held dear; the 1950s-style mystique that had surrounded Babe Ruth and Joe Louis. He blamed Ali for Mickey Mantle's alcoholism and wished aloud that more people had looked to the gentler and quieter baseball slugger Henry Aaron as a model black sports star.[102]

Ali was the worst but certainly not the only "problem" for those looking to curb the influence of African American sports players. And, of course, boxing was not the only sport that managed expectations for black athletes. Football and basketball also held standards for its premier players and realigned power rankings to ensure that its greatest men conformed to them. In the early 1960s, for example, running back Jim Brown was professional football's greatest. After his rookie campaign, pundits deemed Brown of the Cleveland Browns (the team was named after coach Paul Brown, not the running back) the "best pro back of all time."[103] In nine seasons, Brown led the National Football League (NFL) in rushing yards eight times. The Associated Press recognized him as the NFL's Most Valuable Player three times. Brown led Cleveland to a national championship in 1964. Two years later, Governor James Rhodes of Ohio called him the "greatest of all time."[104] A few months later, still in his prime, Brown retired as the NFL's top running back based on any statistical evaluation: most rushing attempts, total yards gained, yards per game, and total touchdowns.

Brown retired with nothing left to prove and considerable ambition beyond the football gridiron. He reinvented himself as a movie star and became a vocal civil rights activist, the founder of the Negro Industrial Economic Union. Brown also convened the so-called Ali Summit in Cleveland, a press conference that featured prominent black athletes and, after some debate, lent public support to Muhammad Ali's fight against conscription (Figure 5.4).[105]

With that, the retired running back had crossed a redline. The press was determined to drop Brown and find a new greatest-ever football star. The unofficial search ended with the fleetfooted halfback, O. J. Simpson. In 1968, Simpson won the coveted Heisman Trophy for his stellar rushing

[102] See Jimmy Cannon, "Who You Are," *New York Journal American*, March 27, 1966, 40.
[103] "Jim Brown Termed 'Best of All Time,'" *Austin Statesmen*, October 28, 1958, 21. Brown took that station away from Jim Thorpe, who had been deemed football's absolute greatest. See, for example, H. G. Salsinger, "Thorpe Grid's No. 1, But Coach Dissents," *Sporting News*, February 8, 1950, 1.
[104] Jim Brown "'Greatest of All Time,' – Ohio Governor," *Afro-American*, January 29, 1966, 9.
[105] See Dave Zirin, *Jim Brown: Last Man Standing* (New York: Blue Rider Press, 2018), 146–51.

FIGURE 5.4 The Ali Summit featured some of the greatest African American athletes, such as those seated (from left to right): Bill Russell, Cassius Clay, Jim Brown, and Lew Alcindor. Courtesy of Bettmann/Getty Images.

for the University of Southern California (USC). The Buffalo Bills selected him first in the subsequent NFL draft, after Simpson's USC coach had gushed that the young star was the "finest player I've ever coached." He didn't stop there. Simpson was, attested USC Coach John McKay, "the finest human being."[106] Disturbing, perhaps, by what we now know about Simpson's personal life, the sports scribes back then liked that Simpson was, at the time, married to his high school sweetheart.[107] That contrasted with Brown, whose divorce from Sue Brown in the late 1960s spilled into the pages of the tabloids, involved infidelity and domestic violence that, for prejudiced journalists, confirmed certain racist stereotypes.[108]

O. J. Simpson helped paper over Brown's fallen star. In 1973, Simpson broke Brown's single-season rushing record, the first back to

[106] See William N. Wallace, "Simpson Needs 1,051 Yards in 9 Games to Snap Jim Brown's Mark," *New York Times*, October 21, 1973, 249.
[107] See Peter Wood, "What Makes Simpson Run?" *New York Times*, December 14, 1975, SM10.
[108] See "Trouble Plagues Jim Brown," *Call and Post*, August 16, 1969, 1A. See also A. S. "Doc" Young, "Jim Brown to Marry Student, 18," *Los Angeles Sentinel*, January 10, 1974, A1.

ever surpass 2,000 yards in a campaign. The mark convinced many sportswriters that Simpson had eclipsed Brown as football's all-time greatest.[109] Some had been waiting for a measurable excuse to move on from Brown. The prideful Brown refused to concede his top station; he even challenged Simpson, eleven years his junior, to a televised one-on-one athletic skills competition to settle the dispute, an offer that Simpson declined.[110]

From Simpson's vantage point, he had nothing to gain from a competition with Brown. By the mid 1970s, Simpson held a more promising acting career than Brown. *Ladies' Home Journal* published two polls of hundreds of school-age children that placed Simpson atop a list of American heroes. By this time, Leo Löwenthal's leisure-aligned "idols of consumption" had overtaken the statesmen and scientists who achieved tangible accomplishments as "idols of production." It's ironic, since it was a credit to the nameless and faceless "producers" at IBM and AT&T who advanced satellite technology, improved the typewriter, and invented the personal computer to enable the increased and overpowering attention paid to athletes and entertainers. For boys, Simpson ranked ahead of Elton John, John Wayne, Chris Evert, and Neil Armstrong. For girls, Simpson polled better than Billie Jean King, Mary Tyler Moore, and Katherine Hepburn. Just ten years removed from unimpeachable stardom, Jim Brown didn't crack the poll's top fifty candidates for greatest child hero.[111]

There were off-the-court standards in professional basketball, as well. Sportswriters in the 1960s tended to prefer the mild-mannered Oscar Robertson over more controversial stars such as Wilt Chamberlain and Bill Russell.[112] The preference for Robertson was informed by that 1950s standard of greatness that searched for symbolic exemplars that positively redounded to American ideals rather than those who propelled change. The press liked the shorter (although he was still 6 foot 5 inches), more approachable Robertson. Fans could relate to his

[109] Skim Myslenski, "O. J.'s the Greatest—2,003 Yards," *Los Angeles Times*, December 17, 1973, C1.
[110] Joan Ryan, "Simpson Chases Brown, Specter Chases Simpson," *Washington Post*, September 18, 1977, D8. On Brown's insistence that he was better than Simpson, see "Jim Brown, Ex-Bruiser, Defends Nudity, Affairs," *Afro-American*, November 13, 1976, 9.
[111] "Who Are the Kids' Heroes & Heroines?" *Ladies' Home Journal* 93 (August 1976): 108–109.
[112] The "greatest-of-all-time" enthusiasm around Robertson began when he played college basketball for Cincinnati, before suiting up in the professional ranks. See Lou Smith, "Postman Rings Twice," *Cincinnati Enquirer*, February 11, 1960, 43.

abilities to shoot and pass a basketball, even though they couldn't do it as well as the Cincinnati Royals' and Milwaukee Bucks' point guard. By contrast, very few could connect to the close-to-the-rim domination of relative giants, Chamberlain and Russell (Figure 5.5).[113]

Robertson's pristine personal life also factored into his greatness. Americans approved of Mazell Robertson's testimony about her son's God-fearing disposition, that he was a Christian equipped with a "great respect for the Lord." According to Mrs. Robertson, the devout basketballer's "faith has carried him as far as he has gone."[114] The sports journals appreciated that Robertson was a family man with a "pretty wife" and liked to snap photographs of him, dressed in dapper attire, beside his small children outside his redbrick home.[115]

FIGURE 5.5 The Celtics' Bill Russell guards his rival Wilt Chamberlain (#13) of the Philadelphia 76ers in 1966. Courtesy of Underwood Archives/ Getty Images.

[113] Les Skinner, "Amazed N. Y. with 56-Point Record Show," *Sporting News*, January 22, 1958, 6.
[114] Ibid., 5.
[115] See Earl Lawson, "A Writer Probes for Real Big O," *Sporting News*, March 15, 1969, 29.

Popular opinion discounted Russell, even as the Celtics dominated the NBA, winning eight consecutive championships from 1959 to 1966.[116] Part of the problem was that pundits recognized Russell as Boston's best player on near-unbeatable teams that included Hall of Famers Bob Cousy, John Havlicek, Tom Heinsohn, Bill Sharman, K. C. Jones, Sam Jones, and Frank Ramsey. But there was more to it. Like Jim Brown, Russell did not ingratiate himself to the press by his support of Muhammad Ali. Russell's politics also disqualified him as basketball's greatest athlete. The undaunted Russell leveraged his basketball platform – as player and later as coach – to question the course of the Civil Rights Movement, sometimes in support of Black Power and in opposition to the amenable integrationist strategies of Martin Luther King Jr.[117]

Wilt Chamberlain fared better than Bill Russell. The press endowed more individual greatness to Chamberlain even though his squads managed to defeat Russell's Boston teams just once (1967) during the Celtics' reign throughout most of the 1960s.[118] Chamberlain received his fair share of votes as the "greatest ever," especially from opponents who couldn't figure out how to stop the big man from scoring against them.[119]

Both Robertson and Chamberlain fit the American criteria for greatness as changemakers. Before Robertson, no one had excelled on the hardwood court in so many areas: scoring, passing, rebounding, and defense. At 7 foot 1 and almost 300 pounds, Chamberlain was bigger and stronger than every other player in the league, and it wasn't even

---

[116] See Furman Bisher, "Chuck Hyatt—Still a Champ," *Sporting News*, February 24, 1960, 1; and "Alex Rates Robertson as Greatest, But Chamberlain as Most Valuable," *Sporting News*, March 14, 1964, 34. Among the few articles I found that called Russell the greatest, most were authored during his college career at the University of Kansas, not in the NBA. See, for example, John Barrington, "Bill Russell Said to Be 'Greatest,'" *New Journal and Guide*, March 31, 1956, 21.

[117] See Aram Goudsouzian, "Bill Russell and the Basketball Revolution," *American Studies* 47 (Fall/Winter 2006): 61–85.

[118] Chamberlain once explained the difference between his and Russell's championship success this way. See Pete Axthelm, "Wilt Chamberlin, Victory in Our Time," *Los Angeles Times*, October 27, 1968, A43. Notwithstanding, some Chamberlain detractors faulted him for being a "born loser." When the Milwaukee Bucks drafted Lew Alcindor, a local writer hoped the tall man was "cut from the same pattern as Bill Russell," a "born winner" rather than Chamberlain, a "born loser." Importantly, the writer did not miss the opportunity to elevate Russell over Chamberlain as a "greater" player. See Glenn Miller, "The Celtics, of Course," *Wisconsin State Journal*, May 8, 1969, 25.

[119] Jimmy Cannon, "Rivals Unstinting in Salute to Stilt," *Sporting News*, November 4, 1959, 1.

close. He had a Babe Ruth-like effect. To curb Chamberlain's physical advantage, the NBA changed rules to make it easier to defend him.[120]

But Robertson absorbed more of the greatest-of-all-time discussion, partly because of his more "agreeable" personal life. Chamberlain was a lifelong bachelor and something of a womanizer. He preferred the company of white women who, in his estimation, shared with him "common interests and aptitudes."[121] His penchant for Caucasian companions upset White America that still looked down on interracial relationships. That Chamberlain made public his belief that black women were unsophisticated also caused considerable consternation for the African American community.[122]

Chamberlain betrayed expectations of black athletes in the political sphere, as well. In 1968, Chamberlain joined Richard Nixon's presidential campaign as an "Aide for Community Relations."[123] Nixon hoped to parlay Chamberlain's star power into African American votes. "We see things the same way," said Chamberlain about his relationship with Nixon, "and I'm going to be working with him during and after the campaign. I gave a lot of thought to this decision."[124] But the black community didn't agree. Some 90 percent of African American voters casted a ballot for Nixon's Democrat opponent, Hubert Humphrey. Nixon dropped Chamberlain from his fold after winning the election. In 1972, Nixon gave up on the African American vote and did not invite Chamberlain back to his campaign. The basketball star admitted that the US president had used him, albeit very unsuccessfully.[125]

***

The Beatles took a different path than Ali and other outspoken black athletes who refused to align with others' expectations. The once-contrarian music group made peace with the establishment. The rise of the so-called concept album pressed the Beatles and America to come to terms with the Fab Four's greatness. Before then, sales of the 45 rpm 7-inch double-sided single were the primary product that earned successful musicians and their labels sizable fortunes. To generate collateral income, the top

---

[120] Jim Heffernan, "Attendance Soars as Young Giant Revolutionizes Game," *Sporting News*, November 18, 1959, 7.
[121] Chamberlain and Shaw, *Wilt*, 261.
[122] Lynn Sharpe, "Wilt: A Personal Foul," *Encore* 3 (December 1973): 26–27.
[123] "Wilt Chamberlain for Nixon," *New York Times*, June 29, 1968, 30.
[124] "Wilt Chamberlain in Nixon's Camp," *New York Amsterdam News*, July 13, 1968, 30.
[125] Wilt Chamberlain and David Shaw, *Wilt: Just Like Any Other 7-Foot Black Millionaire Who Lives Next Door* (New York: Macmillan Publishing Co., 1973), 206.

musicians collected those singles and other tracks into a 12-inch LP (i.e., "long playing") record. The single, however, "provided the main share of the vinyl market."[126] Then the Beatles released *Rubber Soul* and changed the economics of the American music industry.

The impact was immediate. In January 1966, Brian Wilson of the Beach Boys gathered with friends at his dining room table to listen to the new Beatles album. "Under a cloud of pot smoke," recalled Wilson, "it was a ceremonial event." No one present felt worthy enough to venture an opinion on the Beatles's LP until the virtuoso Wilson weighed in. "I'm flipped by it," he exclaimed. "I can't believe it."

"John and Paul, those guys are geniuses," remarked another person present, now free to offer an assessment.

Wilson concurred. "That album is just blowing my mind. They put only great stuff on the album. That's what I want to do."[127] The recently released Beatles record, the tenth overall, was their first to consist entirely of original songs. The group's earlier LPs included cover songs, "filler" tracks that stretched the material to, well, "fill" both sides of the vinyl record. But *Rubber Soul* was complete with original songs.

And they were good songs. The critics praised each track as parts of a whole album that was evidence of an "evolving style that is related to but distinctly different from its earlier disks." Their music wasn't aimed at teenagers. Another reviewer marveled how "the Beatles are still finding different ways to make us enjoy listening to them."[128]

The Beatles were proud of their new sound, probably relieved that the risk of placing so much stock in a full album had paid off. In interviews, the Fab Four explained that their fame and fortune had freed them to experiment, to "begin" an "adult life," even as "people have always wanted us to stay the same," said Paul McCartney. But "adult," he likely didn't realize was a word best associated with the establishment. John Lennon agreed with McCartney, though he didn't associate the Beatles's development with adulthood. To him, the new album represented a new era for the group. "You don't know us if you don't know *Rubber Soul*. All our ideas are different now."[129] It was much more than George Harrison's use of an Indian sitar on "Norwegian Wood." To be sure, they drew those ideas from a wide host of music. In hindsight,

---

[126] Roy Shuker, *Popular Music Culture: The Key Concepts* (London: Routledge, 2022), 369.
[127] Brian Wilson and Todd Gold, *Wouldn't It Be Nice: My Own Story* (New York: HarperCollins, 1991), 129.
[128] Hamilton, *Just Around Midnight*, 145.
[129] Ibid.

The Great Counterculture Conundrum 187

music historians have dissected each song in the album – for instance, "Michelle," "Drive My Car," and "Nowhere Man" – to detect the influences of jazz, country, gospel, psychedelia, folk, and Motown on the Beatles's so-called transitional record.[130] The creativity, ultimately, was in how the Beatles mixed those sounds together. "Our best influences now are ourselves," boasted McCartney. It was a very different stance than his earlier comments claiming to be a copycat cover band. "We are so well established that we can bring fans along with us and stretch the limits of pop."[131]

The reception among the American establishment changed them, just as the Fab Four remade the establishment. The more grown-up Beatles were no longer all that timid about their greatness. That they had captured all this in a single album lent credence to the pop music craft and provided a new method to measure musical greatness, even if they still publicly eschewed most attempts to describe them by such superlatives. The Beatles had set off a musical competition to push the limits of musical ingenuity and package the new concoction in a "thematic" LP. "Thus began," wrote music historian Steve Turner, "the pop equivalent of an arms race where, inspired by the advances of those they considered to be their most worthy opposition, singers and groups tried to maintain or advance their position by developing challenging new sounds."[132] Turner provided a list of the collegial competitors:

> The hard core of this movement included the Beatles, the Beach Boys, the [Rolling] Stones, the Byrds, the Who, the Animals, the Yardbirds, the Kinks, Bob Dylan, the Impressions, Smokey Robinson, and the Motown writing, arranging, and producing team Holland-Dozier-Holland. There was no resentment between the participants, but they all kept a close watch on each other and tried to come up with new material that would top everyone else's achievements.[133]

Popular culture has papered over just how close public opinion was about these groups, particularly the Beach Boys and the Rolling Stones. In the 1960s, some experts had determined that Wilson's Beach Boys were "musically more significant probably than either Lennon/McCartney or Bob Dylan."[134] When Mick Jagger's Rolling Stones arrived in the United States, the second wave of the British invasion,

---

[130] See, for example, Andrew Grant Jackson, *1965: The Most Revolutionary Year in Music* (New York: St. Martin's Press, 2015), 218–30.
[131] See "Bards of Pop," *Newsweek*, March 21, 1966, 102.
[132] Steve Turner, *Beatles '66: The Revolutionary Year* (New York: HarperCollins, 2016), 44.
[133] Ibid., 44–45.
[134] Michael Wood, "The Beach Boys: Energetic Requiem," *New Society*, January 2, 1969, 880.

the newspapers reported about the Stones that "in some places they're more popular than the Beatles."[135] They remained, in many people's estimation, the Beatles's "chief rival."[136]

But in his mind, Brian Wilson was the Beatles's main competition (Figure 5.6). Staying apace with the Beatles became Wilson's mantra. "My chief concern," admitted Wilson, "was to stay atop the field of artists, like the Beatles and Bob Dylan."[137] His Beach Boys bandmate, Mike Love, recalled that "when the Beatles did something that surpassed anything we had done, it made us all the more determined."[138] To the public, Wilson, like McCartney, exercised self-deprecation and an aloofness to any manner of greatness rankings.[139] To his friends, however, Wilson confessed a desire to leap above the Beatles after

FIGURE 5.6 In 1966, the Beach Boys examine *Hit Parade* magazine, one of many music tabloids that printed cover stories on the rivalry between the Beach Boys and the Beatles. Courtesy of Michael Ochs Archive/Getty Images.

[135] Eddy Gilmore, "'Rolling Stones' Arriving in U.S.," *San Bernadino County Sun*, June 1, 1964, 12.
[136] Jack Kroll, "Beatles vs. Stones," *Newsweek*, January 1, 1968, 62.
[137] Wilson and Gold, *Wouldn't It Be Nice*, 121.
[138] Mike Love and James S. Hirsch, *Good Vibrations: My Life as a Beach Boy* (New York: Blue Rider Press, 2016), 125.
[139] See, for example, "The New Pop Giants," *London*, February 4, 1967, 44.

their latest record. "I'm going to make the greatest album! The greatest rock album ever made!"[140] The next morning Wilson got to work on "God Only Knows."

Brian Wilson, concerned about his mental health, had already stopped touring with the Beach Boys. He had time and had become obsessed by the proposition of producing a concept album that could top *Rubber Soul*, his only self-determined path to greatness. He spent four months experimenting with jazz, doo-wop, choral, and classical music. Wilson required four music studios to record his opus. He hired musicians to play twenty-seven different instruments, including unconventional ones like the glockenspiel, Theremin, ukulele, harpsichord, and the accordion. Wilson used computers to layer harmonies that no live iteration of the Beach Boys could replicate. The album's lyrics departed from earlier Beach Boys tunes that had centered on "teenage themes," namely, surfing and girls. The new tracks were more adult, focused on complicated, soul-searching notions such as loneliness and faith.

The Beach Boys' *Pet Sounds* appeared in May 1966. The LP reached the tenth spot on Billboard's list, a failing mark by Beach Boys standards. Wilson was deflated by the American reception. Capitol Records had desired an album with a more "bankable old-style," but Wilson insisted on a thematic album that parted ways with that earlier incarnation of Beach Boys musical success.[141]

But the Beatles liked it a lot, as did the music aficionados in England who were convinced that the "Beach Boys are the best group in the USA."[142] Wilson's work motivated the Beatles to further push the envelope. The group's producer, George Martin, remembered it as the culmination of a "curious transatlantic slugging match."[143] It was likely far more civil than that, however. Paul McCartney told friends that *Pet Sounds* "blew me out of the water."[144] In search of inspiration to compose the final tracks of an upcoming Beatles concept album, McCartney, moved by the Baroque-style of Wilson's "God Only Knows," composed "Here, There, and Everywhere." The track was one of fourteen songs released on *Revolver*. Despite the indignant outcries against John

---

[140] Wilson and Gold, *Wouldn't It Be Nice*, 130.
[141] See Keith Badman, *The Beach Boys: The Definitive Diary of America's Greatest Band: On Stage and in the Studio* (San Francisco: Backbeat Books, 2004), 134.
[142] Rick Dane, "The Beach Boys—Good Vibrations," *London Life*, November 5, 1966, 53.
[143] George Martin and William Pearson, *Summer of Love: The Making of Sgt. Pepper* (New York: Macmillan, 1994), 49.
[144] Badman, *The Beach Boys*, 135.

Lennon's blasphemous boasts about beating Jesus in a theoretical popularity contest, the group's newest record climbed to the top of all reputable music charts, much to the envy of Brian Wilson.

In June 1967, Brian Wilson stopped competing. The Beatles's newest concept album, *Sgt. Pepper's Lonely Hearts Club Band* "broke his heart."[145] Musicologists debate whether *Sgt. Pepper* "grew naturally" from the Beatles's earlier work, part of a changemaking movement that "helped revolutionize the life style of young people" or whether the group had "moved on to a higher artistic plateau," previously unreachable by popular music.[146]

There was no doubt about its historical reception, however. The Beatles, claiming the persona of a fictional Sgt. Pepper band, "shook up the world," to borrow from Cassius Clay, with an album that, by the 1970s, was recalled as the very greatest record of all time on the grounds that there wasn't a "rock fan" who could "forget their feelings upon first hearing this monumental album."[147]

The critics hailed it. They fawned over the technical aspects of "Strawberry Fields Forever" and the sound engineering of "Lucy in the Sky with Diamonds." They marveled about the thoughtful lyrics of "When I'm Sixty-Four" and the instrumentals of "A Day in the Life." Withal, it was, according to critical judgment, a "musical *event*, comparable to a notable new opera of symphonic work."[148] "Music," suggested a second commentator, "may never be the same again."[149] Yet another reviewer was further dumbfounded, convinced that "this is like no sound I have ever heard."[150] The press made much ado over the album's cover art, a tableau of famous people that included, likely a reaction to his earlier snub, the felled heavyweight boxing champion, Sonny Liston.[151] In toto, the album was "equal to any song that Schubert ever wrote."[152] As lyricists, McCartney and Lennon were

---

[145] See Jade Wright, "SMILE: Brian Wilson's in Town," *Liverpool Echo*, August 21, 2009, 27.
[146] Christopher Porterfield and Jesse Birnbaum, "The Messengers," *Time*, September 22, 1967, 60. See also Allan F. Moore, *The Beatles: Sgt. Pepper's Lonely Hearts Club Band* (Cambridge: Cambridge University Press, 1997), 19–25.
[147] Paul Gambaccini, *Rock Critics' Choice: The Top 200 Albums* (London: Omnibus Press, 1978), 8.
[148] "Sgt. Pepper," *New Yorker*, June 24, 1967, 23.
[149] Jim Hoagland, "Pop Goes on a Trip," *Washington Post*, June 18, 1967, L1.
[150] Ernie Santosuosso, "Sgt Pepper's Hot LP," *Boston Globe*, June 18, 1967, 18A.
[151] Frontani, *The Beatles*, 145.
[152] See Michael R. Frontani, "The End of Fantasy: The Beatles, Magical Mystery Tour, and the Counterculture," in *The Beatles, Sgt. Pepper, and the Summer of Love*, eds. Kenneth Womack and Kathryn B. Cox (Lanham, MD: Lexington Books, 2017), 202.

proclaimed Britian's "Poet Laureates," rated beside their hallowed English-forebears Charles Dickens and Lewis Carroll.[153]

The acclaim surrounding the new, adult-sounding Beatles album fully transitioned the group into the mainstream. The most astute observers might have detected the change in the months before the album's debut. On a CBS news special "Inside Pop," the composer Leonard Bernstein of the New York Philharmonic made a case for why more grown-ups should drop their grievances and embrace the Beatles's "real inventions" and innovations in the world of music. The catalyst for Bernstein's program was the release of a double A-side single featuring "Penny Lane" and "Strawberry Fields Forever," before the songs were incorporated into *Sgt. Pepper*. Bernstein dissected the musical genius behind "Penny Lane," lending credence, by virtue of the composer's own highbrow station, to the pop band.[154]

After *Sgt. Pepper* the sea change was apparent. "Suddenly," observed George Harrison, "we find that all the people who thought they were beyond the Beatles are fans."[155] Likewise, an English professor from Rutgers University penned a long essay, purporting to represent "literary and academic grown-ups," that declared *Sgt. Pepper* an "astounding accomplishment for which no one could have been wholly prepared."[156]

The mainstreaming of the Beatles held consequences. It authenticated their greatness but also marked the "beginning of the end" for the Beatles's role as counterculture standard-bearers. Instead, the Beatles were branded "middle-of-the-road."[157] To a certain extent, they had restored American young people's belief in the great changemaker. *Sgt. Pepper* resonated. "The lyrics," offered one teenager to a Chicago journalist,

---

[153] See Jack Kroll, "It's Getting Better," *Newsweek*, June 26, 1967, 70; and Herbert A. Kenny, "The Sgt Pepper Band," *Boston Globe*, August 13, 1967, A21. The one exception was Richard Goldstein, who opined in the *New York Times* that the new album was "nothing beautiful." Others "almost lynched" Goldstein – they figured he was "old" even though Goldstein was twenty-three – for his musical apostasy. See Richard Goldstein, "We Still Need the Beatles, But ...," *New York Times* June 18, 1967, 104; and Robert Christgau, "Secular Music," *Esquire* 68 (December 1967): 283. For the reviewer's rebuttal, see Richard Goldstein, "Are They Waning?" *New York Times*, December 31, 1967, 62.

[154] Frontani, *The Beatles*, 153–54.

[155] See Porterfield and Birnbaum, "The Messengers," 61.

[156] Richard Poirier, "Learning from the Beatles," *Partisan Review* 35 (Fall 1867): 526–27.

[157] See Ralph Brauer, "Iconic Modes: The Beatles," in *American Popular Music: Readings from the Popular Press*, vol. II, ed. Timothy E. Scheurer (Bowling Green, OH: Bowling Green State Popular Press, 1990), 153.

"fit in with our search for meaning in a pretty complex world."[158] Yet, a growing contingent faulted the Beatles for their muted opposition to the Vietnam War. John Lennon once rambled on an admission that "If you can say that war is no good, and a few people believe you, then it might be good. I don't know. I can't say too much, though. That's the trouble."[159] The most antiwar people condemned the group's "Revolution" song in 1968 as too little, too late.[160] The New Left charged that the Beatles's decision to halt live performances and to masquerade as a fictional Sgt. Pepper band was because they were "afraid of confronting reality."[161] By contrast, Mick Jagger and the Rolling Stones engaged "real life and how to deal with it."[162] Of course, the real standard bearer in the cause, by then, was Muhammad Ali.

To everyone else beyond those counterculture holdouts, the Beatles were the very greatest. Fans debated which Beatles album was the greatest, but they were certain that no one else had produced an LP – the metric, used ubiquitously by now, to evaluate musical greatness – that approached their genius. In 1970, when the Beatles broke up, adults and young people grieved together. They mourned the fall of the "greatest pop-rock phenomenon of the '60s," the "world's greatest group."[163] The establishment that had not too long before then feared the implications of the Beatles, memorialized them as the uncontested "philosopher-kings of pop."[164]

***

Muhammad Ali was also deemed a philosopher. But in his exile, Ali had no truck for the establishment. Instead, he became an inextricable

---

[158] Mary Merryfield, "Our Teens Get the Message from Song Lyrics," *Chicago Tribune*, September 17, 1967, F4. At least one school leader in the Chicago suburbs concurred, remarking that "if you want to know what youths are thinking and feeling you cannot find anyone who speaks for them or to them more clearly than the Beatles." See John Leo, "Educators Urged to Heed Beatles," *New York Times*, July 25, 1967, 29.

[159] See Turner, *Beatles '66*, 86.

[160] See Frontani, *The Beatles*, 193.

[161] See Jeffrey Roessner, "We All Want to Change the World: Postmodern Politics and the Beatles's White Album," in *Reading the Beatles: Cultural Studies, Literary Criticism, and the Fab Four*, eds. Kenneth Womack and Todd F. Davis (Albany, NY: State University of New York Press, 2006), 149.

[162] See McMillian, *Beatles vs. Stones*, 189.

[163] See Derek Taylor, "The Beatles Split: Report from a Front-Row Seat," *Chicago Tribune*, July 26, 1970, G58.

[164] Richard Goldstein, "The Beatles: Inspired Groovers," *New York Times*, December 8, 1968, 181.

part of the antiwar and Civil Rights movements, an "urbanized philosopher" – very different, of course, from the Beatles's style – with a penchant for humming Bob Dylan's protest song "Blowin' in the Wind."[165] Barred from the ring, Ali made good use of his time, speaking to young people on college campuses. He was an antiwar evangelist. In 1968, for example, the peripatetic pugilist delivered speeches at more than 200 universities.[166]

Bill Russell had anticipated Ali's impact after departing Jim Brown's Ali Summit. "I'm not worried about Muhammad Ali," said the basketball star. "He is better equipped than anyone I know to withstand the trials in store for him. What I'm worried about is the rest of us."[167] Some, like sprinters Tommie Smith and John Carlos, drew from Ali's courage, defiantly protesting the boxer's predicament as they received their gold and bronze medals, respectively, at the 1968 Olympics in Mexico City.[168]

Then Muhammad Ali got his second chance at greatness. On June 28, 1971, the United States Supreme Court overturned the lower court's conviction. By then, public opinion had flipped on the Vietnam War. Off-the-record sources informed journalists Bob Woodward and Scott Armstrong that the justices were desperate to release Ali. Clever, face-saving judicial options didn't surface. As a last resort, the high court relied on a technical error. The government had failed to specify its reasons for rejecting Ali's application for draft exemption. It was therefore impossible for the Supreme Court to test the grounds for the Justice Department's decision to deny Ali and so the conviction had to be reversed.[169] The Supreme Court mandated the New York State Boxing Commission to reinstate Ali, eager to retake his title as an "incomparable hero of almost mythological dimension."[170]

Ali's ascent was near-mythical. It was also a struggle. He lost his first opportunity to reclaim his title against Joe Frazier. It was Ali's

---

[165] See Larry Neal, "Uncle Rufus Raps on the Squared Circle," *Partisan Review* 39 (Spring/Summer 1972): 51; and Marqusee, *Redemption Song*, 175.
[166] See Simon Hall, *Rethinking the American Anti-War Movement* (New York: Routledge, 2012), 78.
[167] Bill Russell and Tex Maule, "I Am Not Worried about Ali," *Sports Illustrated*, June 19, 1967, 18.
[168] See Douglas Hartmann, *Race, Culture, and the Revolt of the Black Athlete: The 1968 Olympic Protests and Their Aftermath* (Chicago: University of Chicago Press, 2003).
[169] Bob Woodward and Scott Armstrong, *The Brethren: Inside the Supreme Court* (New York: Simon & Schuster, 1979), 157.
[170] Mark Kram, "At the Bell," *Sports Illustrated*, March 8, 1971, 20.

first defeat in the professional ranks. Ali worked his way, Sisyphus-like, back up the challenger circuit. He ran into trouble against Ken Norton, losing once but defeating him on the second try. By the time Ali was scheduled for a rematch with Frazier, the latter had lost the championship mantle to George Foreman.[171]

Foreman was a bruising boxer and a gold medalist at the Mexico City Olympics. After he defeated a Russian boxer in the heavyweight finals, Foreman made meaning of the triumph by waving an American flag, a symbolic act of Cold War patriotism and satisfaction with the United States that contrasted with the Smith's and Carlos's public antiwar opposition and solidarity with Muhammad Ali.

In October 1974, Ali fought Foreman.[172] One billion people watched the "Rumble in the Jungle" in Zaire, better known today as the Congo. Oddsmakers assessed Ali a 3-1 underdog against the powerful Foreman. The wise sports scribes – sans Jimmy Cannon who had died months before the bout – doubted the older Ali's spryness to avoid Foreman's assault.[173] But that wasn't Ali's plan. Instead, he leaned back on the ring's ropes so that his head was beyond Foreman's reach. His friend Jim Brown and rival Joe Frazier colored announcer David Frost's otherwise evenhanded television broadcast with biased cheering for the challenger's novel strategy. Both figured Ali fared better in the taxing humidity of the African night. Ali capably absorbed extended punches and exhausted the mighty Foreman. By the eighth round, Foreman was spent, unable to exercise his strength. A series of punches and a strong left hook by Ali in the closing seconds of that round felled the champ.

Muhammad Ali reclaimed the heavyweight championship and for the first time obtained the consensus agreement that he was the greatest.[174] "Am I the greatest of all time?" Ali asked the ring commentator. "You've proved it," responded David Frost (Figure 5.7).[175]

---

[171] See Lewis Erenberg, *The Rumble in the Jungle: Muhammad Ali & George Foreman on the Global Stage* (Chicago: University of Chicago Press, 2019), 37–61.
[172] Prior to the fight, Foreman had taken issue with Ali's greatness talk: "When you begin thinking 'I'm the greatest,' you're in real trouble." See 'Think You're 'Greatest' and You're in Trouble," *Afro-American*, February 3, 1973, 7.
[173] Dave Anderson, "Foreman 3-1 Over Ali in Zaire Tonight," *New York Times*, October 29, 1974, 47.
[174] "Is Ali Really 'the Greatest'?—Experts Look Again," *Afro-American*, November 9, 1974, 1–2.
[175] Erenberg, *The Rumble in the Jungle*, 161.

FIGURE 5.7 Muhammad Ali was so convinced he was the "greatest" that he made the phrase the title of his autobiography, published in 1975. Courtesy of Evening Standard, Hulton Archive/Getty Images.

The press agreed. "Of course he's the greatest," judged a sportswriter.[176] "Anyone who doubts that he is the greatest of all time," warned an Ali fan to any potential detractor, "should climb into the ring with him."[177]

Ali mostly permitted others to coronate him. In the shadow of Richard Nixon's Watergate scandal and the United States' retreat from Vietnam, the flag-waving Foreman was a "Great White Hope," like Floyd Patterson before him, that by this time Americans had little use for. They no longer lionized the establishment. The pleasantness of the 1950s, the feting of US presidents and the search for reassurance from their decisions, was at an end. Instead, they recalibrated their cultural sensibilities and realigned their sights on changemakers. "People of every nationality, color, religious persuasion celebrated the victory of Ali."[178]

Muhammad Ali was an "authentic American," not just the darling of the counterculture and a subset of African Americans. "American

[176] Ibid., 171.
[177] Seku S. Wattara, "Muhammad Ali's Victory," *Jet*, November 28, 1974, 4.
[178] Quincy Troupe, "The Spiritual Victory of Muhammad Ali," *Black World* 24 (January 1975): 34.

white people (especially the young) greet the victory with such unrestrained joy," observed the writer Quincy Troupe, "There were rumors of some young whites doing cart-wheels down Broadway in New York City."[179] His case was further bolstered by the reports on Elijah Muhammad's failing health and Ali's refusal to support Muhammad's disciple, Louis Farrakhan.[180] Troupe prayed that Ali's victory proved that the "old ways are not the ways anymore to do things," a symbol of "those new and spiritual forces that will not give way in the face of tremendous adversity."[181]

Muhammad Ali had remade the establishment. The Associated Press polled the sports writers and dubbed the boxer "the greatest" and *Sports Illustrated* made him Sportsman of the Year in 1974. President Gerald Ford invited Ali to visit with him at the White House.[182] The White House had lost luster, but it gained some back with the champ's arrival. New York held a "Muhammad Ali Day," at which everyone but the suddenly humble Ali reflected on his greatness.[183] Muhammad Ali went the distance against the ignominy of greatness in the 1960s and knocked out his racist opposition. Just in case, Ali incorporated G.O.A.T. Inc. The acronym stood for "Greatest of All Time." The agency managed the boxer's intellectual property and his protect his hard-earned legacy.[184] Perhaps Ali feared that after so much hard work to acquire greatness and spending so much time with the disenfranchised and the disenchanted, the term was bound to lose its all-important worth. He was right.

---

[179] Ibid., 35.
[180] See David K. Wiggins, "Victory for Allah: Muhammad Ali, the Nation of Islam, and American Society," in *Muhammad Ali: The People's Champ*, ed. Elliott J. Gorn (Urbana, IL: University of Illinois Press, 1995), 112.
[181] Troupe, "The Spiritual Victory of Muhammad Ali," 36–37.
[182] See "Ali 'Greatest' of '74, A.P.'s Poll Testifies," *New York Times*, January 17, 1975, 28.
[183] Frank J. Prial, "Ali, the Greatest, is Given the City's Mostest," *New York Times*, December 10, 1974, 35. For young Shelly Sykes' poem mentioned in Prial's report, see "Ali is the Greatest," *New York Amsterdam News*, December 28, 1974, B1. See also See David Condon, "There's Uncertainty about Ali Future," *Chicago Tribune*, November 5, 1974, C3; and Charles Maher, "The Art of Promoting: That's Where Ali's the Greatest," *Los Angeles Times*, August 11, 1974, C1.
[184] See Ben Zimmer, "Word on the Street: The GOAT Gets the Gold," *Wall Street Journal*, August 20, 2016, C4.

Conclusion

Michael Jordan in the "Age of Lists"

In 1984, Bob Knight telephoned his friend Stu Inman about the upcoming NBA draft. Knight had a unique perspective to share with the Portland Trail Blazers' general manager. The Indiana University basketball coach was moonlighting as head man of the US Olympic basketball team. The squad was full of All-American collegians, some destined for professional basketball stardom. Portland had lost a coin flip to the Houston Rockets and was relegated to second position in the upcoming June draft. Houston, everyone expected, had its sights on Akeem (later, "Hakeem") Olajuwon, the local standout from the University of Houston. Rumor had it that Inman intended to select the 7 foot 1 Sam Bowie from the University of Kentucky. A year earlier, the Trail Blazers had drafted promising guard, Clyde Drexler, and Inman believed the team required a tall center to complement Drexler's game.[1]

Knight begged Inman to reconsider. In the preceding Olympic tryouts, just a handful of players had avoided Knight's famously fiery wrath. The brightest light at the Olympic trials was Michael Jordan of the University of North Carolina.[2] The humble shooting guard had won a national championship in Chapel Hill and was the reigning college player of the year according to nearly every magazine and poll. "You have to pick Jordan," Knight implored Inman. "He's unbelievable."

However, Jordan did not fit the championship blueprint. The best NBA teams held a height advantage to prevail over other squads. A year

---

[1] See Filip Bondy, *Tip-Off: How the 1984 NBA Draft Changed Basketball Forever* (Cambridge, MA: Da Capo Press, 2007), 109–20.
[2] See John Feinstein, "Knight's Olympians Glow with Discipline," *Washington Post*, June 30, 1984, D4.

earlier, the Philadelphia 76ers had helped the fleet swingman Julius Erving win a championship by acquiring the big man, Moses Malone. As sensational as he was, Oscar Robertson did not win the NBA Finals until the Milwaukee Bucks drafted the 7 foot 2 center, Lew Alcinder. Concomitant to Knight's and Inman's conversation, the towering Alcinder, by then known as Kareem Abdul-Jabbar, was embattled in a championship duel against a roster of Boston Celtics giants: Robert Parush at 7 foot 1, Kevin McHale at 6 foot 10, and Larry Bird at 6 foot 9.

Inman's resistance to Knight's recommendation was therefore most understandable. "We already have a shooting guard," replied Inman, referring to Drexler. The Portland top executive then rehearsed the conventional wisdom that informed the need to draft a center.

Knight was insistent. "Pick Jordan and play him at center."[3]

Inman didn't change his mind. Houston, as expected, used the first pick on Olajuwon and paired him with another 7-footer, Ralph Simpson. With the second selection, the Portland Trail Blazers tapped Bowie, whose career and considerable height was undermined by a series of leg injuries.

The Chicago Bulls "settled" on Jordan, after the team's front office failed to trade the pick for a veteran center. The local newspapers slammed Chicago's decision, convinced that the 6 foot 6 shooting guard had peaked in college and could never become the woeful franchise's vaunted "savior."[4]

The critics were right and wrong. Jordan hadn't peaked in college. In his inaugural campaign, Jordan placed third overall in scoring and was voted the league's Rookie of the Year. He was "gravity-defying," nicknamed, as was his best-selling Nike sneaker, "Air Jordan," for his acrobatic slam dunks.[5] Jordan became a "cult hero, a player who puts people in the seats and then makes them stand up in appreciation of his spectacular play."[6] In 1988, Jordan won his first MVP award and was also voted Defensive Player of the Year. He was a financial boon for the NBA and, by virtue of unprecedented popularity, Jordan, by his third season in the pros, earned, through endorsements, three times his annual Bulls salary.[7]

---

[3] See L. Jon Werheim, *Glory Days: The Summer of 1984 and the 90 Days that Changed Sports and Culture Forever* (Boston: Houghton Mifflin Harcourt, 2021), 107.
[4] See Bob Logan, "Bulls Hope Jordan's a Savior," *Chicago Tribune*, June 17, 1984, C1.
[5] See "Air Jordan Takes Off," *Newsweek*, June 17, 1985, 79.
[6] "Jordan's Glamour Fills League Arenas," *Chicago Tribune*, December 16, 1986, C10.
[7] Phil Patton, "The Selling of Michael Jordan," *New York Times*, November 9, 1986, SM48.

Conclusion: Michael Jordan in the "Age of Lists"

On the other hand, the Chicago Bulls did not rank among the NBA's best teams. In his stellar 1988 campaign, Jordan won his first playoff series. After that, though, the Bulls were eliminated in the subsequent round by the Detroit Pistons' infamous "Bad Boys." When experts indulged in that parlor game of rating the NBA's elite, they rarely placed Jordan in their highest class, certainly not as basketball's greatest player ever.[8] The most demeaning assessments suggested that Jordan was much more of a "circus act" than a truly great basketball player.[9]

Working against Jordan was the pervasive disinterest in winnowing decision making to just one great individual. The Beatles and Muhammad Ali notwithstanding, America had not fully recovered from the devaluation of greatness in the turbulent 1960s. The "cult of veneration" had been strained, perhaps broken.[10] Sure, Watergate had muted conversations about great US presidents. But Americans were no longer satisfied with a sole great American changemaker. Life was much more complicated, it seemed, after the 1960s and a one-size-fits-all greatest-of-all-time hero did not resonate the same as it had several decades prior. In the sporting world, people in the 1970s and 1980s talked a lot about "great" athletes – O. J. Simpson in football; Jack Nicklaus in golf; Billie Jean King in tennis – but did not see much of a need to single out the very greatest.[11]

Take professional basketball, for example. It was no longer a narrow debate between Wilt Chamberlain and Oscar Robertson. Americans wanted more options. The same anti-Vietnam and Civil Rights forces that had aided Muhammad Ali, resurfaced Bill Russell's case among the basketball titans.[12] A new generation of fans nominated more recent stars such as Kareem Abdul-Jabbar, Julius Erving, Magic Johnson, and Larry Bird.[13] Each held qualities and appearances that suited a multiplicity of American images and points of view. Jabbar was countercultural.

---

[8] See Gerry Greene, "Great Debate: Naming Best Players of All Time," *Orlando Sentinel*, May 11, 1990, C1.
[9] Thomas Boswell, "What Jordan Needs Is a Complement," *Washington Post*, March 18, 1988, F4.
[10] Robert Michels, *Political Parties: A Sociological Study of the Oligarchical Tendencies of Modern Democracy*, trans. Eden and Cedar Paul (New York: Hearst's International Library, Co., 1915), 63–68.
[11] See, for example, Parton Keese, *The Measure of Greatness: An Inquiry into the Unique Traits and Talents that Set Certain Athletes Apart from the Rest of the Field* (Englewood Cliffs, NJ: Prentice-Hall, Inc., 1981).
[12] Mark Heisler, "12 Years Later, Another View," *Los Angeles Times*, February 26, 1981, B1.
[13] Bill Reynolds, "The Best?" *St. Louis Dispatch*, May 21, 1989, F1.

Erving, "Dr. J," operated with utmost precision. Magic was a leader and supremely cool. The most talked about, by the 1980s, was Bird, "the slow white kid from French Lick, Indiana." Bird, according to a goodly number, was the "best who ever played this silly game."[14]

People, NBA legends included, seemed to enjoy playing the parlor game rather than decide on a single great player.[15] That search for the "chosen one," the American ideal had all but vanished. Back in the 1970s, Wilt Chamberlain had predicted that "some kid who's in junior high school now may be better than any of us one day."[16] At that time, Michael Jordan was about to matriculate to Trask Middle School in Wilmington, North Carolina. But no one was inclined to suggest that Jordan was the fulfilment of Chamberlain's prophecy.

People replaced the greatest-of-all-time debate with list-making (a fad that made British writers Norris and Ross McWhirter, founders of *The Guinness Book of Records* in 1955, very popular in the United States). Americans furnished lists to further discussion, not to end it. The trend frustrated Jim Brown, for example, who had taken much pride in his football status and could not understand the motivation to reconsider his station with O. J. Simpson, let alone Franco Harris, Walter Payton and then, owing to the increased prominence of the quarterback, Joe Montana.[17]

List-making signaled a final change in greatness discussions in the twentieth century. It also emphasizes the uniqueness of Michael Jordan's rise to the top of American popular culture. He was the exception that proved the rule. Jordan's case helps summarize and clarify the themes that anchor this book's chapters.

* * *

[14] "Magic and Wilt are Tops in Bird's Book," *Los Angeles Times*, February 3, 1986, C2. See also Ray Didinger, "Best of All Time?" *Philadelphia Daily News*, May 14, 1985, 100.

[15] See Sam Smith, "The Greats All Agree: Jordan One of Greatest," *Chicago Tribune*, June 4, 1989, D13. For his part, Wilt Chamberlain did much to self-promote his cause. See Mike Lupica, "Time Hasn't Shrunk Wilt's Ego," *New York Daily News*, February 25, 1982, 119. Interestingly, Bill Russell claimed in his memoir that he and Chamberlain avoided these conversations during their playing days. See Bill Russell and Taylor Branch, *Second Wind: The Memoirs of an Opinionated Man* (New York: Random House, 1979), 158.

[16] Chamberlain and Shaw, *Wilt*, 302.

[17] See Dave Anderson, "Jim Brown's Bad Dream," *New York Times*, November 21, 1983, C4; and "Who's the Greatest?" *USA Today*, November 20, 1987, 1C. A few went back in time and argued for Gale Sayers. See George Puscas, "Halas Admired Clark, but Sayers the Best," *Detroit Free Press*, September 2, 1988, 48.

Conclusion: Michael Jordan in the "Age of Lists" 201

The writer David Wallechinsky called the moment an "Age of Lists." Why did lists proliferate and captivate Americans? The sense among many was that lists helped sort through the massive social upheaval of the 1960s. The ensuing Watergate scandal and Richard Nixon's subsequent White House resignation seemed to confirm the nation's distrust of decision makers. Lists, conversely, provided a feeling of careful curation; or a presentation of options that empowered individuals to make up their own minds.

That was the experts' take. The social scientist Amitai Etzioni offered at the dawn of the Age of Lists that the circumstance was "part of a desperate effort to find fixed points of reference."[18] Etzioni pointed to the decentralization of American life, wrought by Watergate and the Civil Rights Movement.[19] Wallechinsky had a similar inkling about America's newfound fascination with lists. "In a busy, troubled time, a simple list is easy to read and digest and remember," he wrote. "A simple list diverts and relaxes."[20] The sociologist Joel Best thought about the situation in terms of "choices." All observers agreed that without hope for achievable consensus and in an American society posed with more contingencies, the production of lists helped make sense of seemingly endless options.[21]

Wallechinsky knew all this firsthand. He had gained some renown for producing a hefty (in hardcover, sandwiching 1,400 pages of paper, it weighed five pounds) almanac of miscellanea. The first edition of the *People's Almanac* climbed to the very peak of the *New York Times'* trade paperback bestseller list.[22] Book reviewers and radio interviewers focused on chapter 24, a slim twenty-five-page section with an unimaginative title, "LISTS—1 TO 10 (OR MORE)."[23] Readers were entranced, reflected, Wallechinsky, about odd compilations of "Celebrities Who've Been Psychoanalyzed," "Dogs that Bite the Most," and companion lists of the "Most Loved Person in History" and "Most Hated Person in History," based on an annual poll conducted by the Madame Tussauds

---

[18] See Kenneth Turan, "Hall of Famers," *Washington Post*, June 27, 1977, B1.
[19] See similar remarks by Etzioni in Michael Kernan, "Keepers of the Fame," *Washington Post*, May 6, 1986, C4.
[20] Ibid.; David Wallechinsky, Irving Wallace, and Amy Wallace, *The Book of Lists* (New York: William Morrow and Company, Inc., 1977), xix–xx.
[21] See Joel Best, *Everyone's a Winner: Life in Our Congratulatory Culture* (Berkeley, CA: University of California Press, 2011), 117–21.
[22] "Book Ends," *New York Times*, May 16, 1976, 219.
[23] David Wallechinsky and Irving Wallace, *The People's Almanac* (Garden City, NY: Doubleday & Company, Inc., 1975), 1224–48.

Wax Museum. He further fed readers' interest a bit more in a second edition of the almanac, collecting a new chapter, this time thirty-two pages in length, of strange lists such as "15 Famous Epileptics," and the "25 Most Written-About People of All Time."[24]

People wanted more. They desired more Halls of Fame, things like: the Car Collectors' Hall of Fame, National Business Hall of Fame, National Cowgirl Hall of Fame, National Fresh Water Fishing Hall of Fame, Plastics Hall of Fame, Recreational Vehicle/Mobile Home Hall of Fame, and the Quilters Hall of Fame. These comprise a small sample of the forty Halls of Fame consecrated during the 1970s.[25] In fact, two-thirds of all Halls of Fame built in the United States during the twentieth century were founded in the final three decades. Victor Danilov counted about 250 Halls of Fame worldwide. All but thirty (twelve erected in Canada) were established in the United States.[26]

Wallechinsky satisfied the legions of "listomaniacs" by compiling three huge volumes aptly titled *The Book of Lists*. The first installment sold 18 million copies in about two dozen countries.[27] Owing to Wallechinsky's penchant for the weird, the book included the "12 Greatest Jews of All Time," "10 Best Forgers of All Time," "10 Most Beautiful Words in the English Language," and "20 Members of President Nixon's Original Enemies List." Wallechinsky also solicited Charles Schultz to rank the "Greatest Cartoon Characters of All Time." Schultz self-indulgently rated Charlie Brown and Snoopy above Dagwood and Superman. None of Walt Disney's creations appeared in Schultz's list.[28]

The composition of greatness lists was a decidedly different project than the earlier efforts to single out a changemaking symbolic exemplar. Lists, invariably, start a conversation rather than end a discussion with a definitive decision. Lists proffer choices. Choice was a feature of modern life that, as the sociologist Peter Berger taught long ago, signaled the end of straightlaced thinking about a myriad of

---

[24] David Wallechinsky and Irving Wallace, *The People's Almanac*, #2 (New York: William Morrow and Company, Inc., 1978), 1100–32.
[25] Victor J. Danilov, *Hall of Fame Museums: A Reference Guide* (Westport, CT: Greenwood Press, 1997), 22–23.
[26] Ibid., 4.
[27] Publishing information was shared in Irving Wallace, David Wallechinsky, Amy Wallace, and Sylvia Wallace, *The Book of Lists*, #2 (New York: William Morrow and Company, Inc., 1980), xvii.
[28] David Wallechinsky, Irving Wallace, and Amy Wallace, *The Book of Lists* (New York: William Morrow and Company, Inc., 1977), 232–33.

Conclusion: *Michael Jordan in the "Age of Lists"* 203

subjects – from religion to retail.[29] To be sure, I don't mean to suggest that the list, as an institution, was invented at this late date. In 1909, Norman Hapgood and William Patten of *Collier's* commissioned Harvard's Charles Eliot to assemble a "Five-Foot Shelf" of classic books.[30] Two decades later, The Pulitzer Prize nonfiction writer Will Durant composed a number of lists on the greatest thinkers, poets, and events in world history.[31]

These inventories, however, tended to be pithier, meant to reach consensus. Even Arthur Schlesinger's exhaustive lists of presidents were segmented into subcategories to narrow the field of "greats." The more recent incarnation of list production is not at all interested in great symbolic exemplars. On the contrary, they seek to provide a menu of options for readers to consider, perhaps mix and match attributes, and to find in the many complex personalities something unique, even great, about themselves.

Besides Wallechinsky, another major contributor to the growing industry of list-making was Michael Hart. His involvement was inspired by a career change. Hart had practiced law in New York for eight years but the "lure of the scientific world was stronger."[32] In 1969, he enrolled in Princeton University, determined to earn a doctorate in astronomy. Hart was an introverted person but, after getting to know him, friends and acquaintances learned much about his variegated interests. For instance, Hart was a chess master and, much more darkly, as he would write about much later in his career, was something of a white nationalist.[33]

Hart nurtured an odd curiosity at the Princeton dining hall. There, he sat with other astronomers-in-training, marveling about the advances made by their professional forebears. "One day, while I was having lunch with some of my fellow graduate students," recalled Hart, "the question arose: Who were the greatest astronomers who ever lived?"

---

[29] See Peter L. Berger, *The Heretical Imperative: Contemporary Possibilities of Religious Affirmation* (Garden City, NY: Anchor Press, 1979), 1–29.
[30] See Henry James, *Charles W. Eliot: President of Harvard University, 1869–1909*, vol. 2 (Boston: Houghton Mifflin Company, 1930), 293–301.
[31] These list-minded essays are collected in Will Durant, *The Greatest Minds and Ideas of All Time*, ed. John Little (New York: Simon & Schuster, 2002).
[32] The quote is derived from an undated clipping, Mark Finston, "One Hundred 'Bigs' Who Changed the World," *Newark Star-Ledger*.
[33] See Russell K. Nieli, "Michael H. Hart," in *Contemporary Voices of White Nationalism in America*, eds. Carol M. Swain and Russ Nieli (Cambridge: Cambridge University Press, 2003), 184–202.

Hart led the historical discussion that centered on the merits of the Italian heliocentrist scientist Galileo Galilei. "We batted the idea around for a while, and eventually reached a consensus."[34] Hart cared for the conversation much more than the conclusion.

The discussion animated Hart. His wide knowledge offered him a competitive advantage. Hart eagerly entertained similar debates. He enjoined others to consider who might be the greatest physicist of all time (Albert Einstein). Then the greatest chemist (Antoine Lavoisier). He didn't even require the dining hall. The exercise, he recognized, could be done alone, accomplished without peer review. "Eventually," remembered Hart, "this led me to make a list of the 100 greatest people in history."[35] He spent three years researching and rewriting his list and then published a book.

Hart intuited the new role of lists in American life. He had no designs on settling any debates. He was a self-described provocateur and wanted to provide his readers with something to talk about. "My book doesn't finish any arguments," he admitted. "It starts arguments rather than finishes them."[36] He likewise confessed that "not one friend or relative agrees with my selections. I will be astonished if anyone agrees with them."[37]

The first draft of Hart's list was informed by some calculation of "Importance" and "Admirability."[38] The criteria privileged scientists and faith founders. Hart's preliminary ranking began with Jesus, Newton, Muhammad, Buddha, and then Confucius.

Then Hart introduced "Influence" and shook up his rankings. Hart's great people, as others had already discovered, ought to be changemakers. He read hundreds of history books to reevaluate his earlier lists, breaking them down by place of origin, profession, and epoch. He used these facts to separate a "person who is almost exclusively responsible for a significant event or movement" from "one who played a less dominant role in a more important movement."[39] By November 1974, Hart merged his list with a graduate school friend (J. Richard Gott,

---

[34] Michael H. Hart to G. Birch Ripley, July 10, 1993, personal papers of Michael H. Hart. A copy is in the possession of the author.
[35] Ibid.
[36] "100 Top Humans," *Baltimore Sun*, November 2, 1978, 27.
[37] See Sidney Fields, "The 100 Who Molded the World," *Daily News*, May 25, 1978, 93.
[38] Michael H. Hart Notes, undated, in the possession of the author.
[39] Michael H. Hart, *The 100: A Ranking of the Most Influential Persons in History* (New York: Hart Publishing Company, Inc., 1978), 28.

Conclusion: Michael Jordan in the "Age of Lists"

who eventually became a well-known expert on time travel). Their latest thinking moved Adolf Hitler down to twenty-six and Abraham Lincoln up to forty-eight. Hart kept on tinkering.

Hart's self-published book appeared in 1978 and caused a sensation. The first 5,000 copies of the heavy tome of 572 pages sold out after a few months. His long list was reproduced in *Newsweek* and republished in newspaper columns in Baltimore, Cincinnati, Miami, Pittsburgh, Washington, DC, and San Antonio, where Hart served, by then, as an astronomy professor at Trinity University. His final list kept Isaac Newton as the runner-up but flipped first and third place: Jesus and Muhammad. He switched the two religion founders "in large part because of my belief that Muhammad had a much greater personal influence on the formulation of the Moslem religion than Jesus had on the formulation of the Christian religion."[40]

Hardly anyone, very likely, purchased Hart's book to be convinced about a rigid formulation of American greatness. "There is very little chance you will agree with his list," cautioned a journalist. "In fact, unless you are a historian, there is very little chance you will recognize all the names."[41] Another reviewer anticipated that the book would become good "fodder for feuds and maybe a duel or two."[42] Some pious women and men wrote to the local newspapers, devoutly determined to "take a stand for Christ our savior."[43] Others were upset that Hart, after thinking it over some more, relegated Lincoln to "honorable mention" because, predicted Hart, the United States would have had to eventually free its slaves no matter who was president. Critics censored him for ignoring Muhammad Ali.[44] Hart also received flak for omitting Winston Churchill and Mahatma Gandhi, and inserting just two women (Queen Elizabeth I, ranked 65; and Queen Isabella, ranked 94). Hart didn't mind. He was glad that his list had inspired a lot of debate.

* * *

Michael Jordan was an exception to the list fad. Basketball provided Jordan with a worldwide stage and influence that far surpassed other athletes and cultural icons. This included the peerless Hockey star,

---

[40] Ibid.
[41] "A Most Exclusive List (Jesus Finished Third)," *Detroit Free Press*, March 19, 1978, 1C.
[42] Michael Gartner, "100 Reasons to Feud with Your Friends," *Wall Street Journal*, July 19, 1978, 12.
[43] Annie Beavers, "Ranking Christ Third Is Pure Absurdity," *Detroit Free Press*, March 30, 1978, 8.
[44] Jack Smith, "A New 'Greatest of All Time,'" *Los Angeles Times*, August 13, 1978, G1.

Wayne Gretzky (nicknamed the "Great One").[45] No one ascended in other areas of American life. No one upended the Beatles in music, Lincoln in politics, or Eleanor Roosevelt as the world's greatest ever woman, however that could be properly measured. In the boxing ring, Floyd Mayweather retired with a 50–0 record, including twenty-six consecutive wins with world titles on the line. Yet, when Mayweather proclaimed himself greater than Muhammad Ali, much of the sports world turned him down. Ali's defenders claimed he had faced more talented fighters and had done much more for people outside of the ring.[46] Few appeared enthusiastic to relegislate greatness.

At the close of the 1980s, just a few questioned where Michael Jordan stood among professional basketball's greatest. "I would never have called him the greatest player I'd ever seen if I didn't mean it," said Larry Bird. "It's just God disguised as Michael Jordan."[47] Just a handful agreed with Thomas Boswell that the oversized "national worship" of Jordan was "idolatrous." Boswell claimed Jordan's soaring feats had "been done before, and better," by hoopsters who had accomplished much more in the postseason than "his Airness."[48] The Chicago press published Boswell's opinion as a foil, a counterpoint to the prevailing position that Jordan was "not merely one of the greatest, as Boswell would like you to believe, but The Greatest. Period. Paragraph. End of argument."[49]

By the 1990s, Jordan ended all debate by the sheer force of his basketball output. In 1991, the Chicago Bulls rampaged through the playoffs. Jordan, the league MVP for a second occasion, avenged earlier, demoralizing defeats by sweeping the Detroit Pistons in the conference finals and toppled Magic Johnson's Los Angeles Lakers to claim his first championship.[50] He climbed to the top with running mate Scottie Pippen, not

---

[45] On Gretzky and his personal feelings on "greatness," see Wayne Gretzky and Rick Reilly, *Gretzky: An Autobiography* (Toronto: HarperCollins, 1990), 104–20. See also Steven J. Jackson, "Gretzky, Crisis, and Canadian Identity in 1988: Rearticulating the Americanization of Culture Debate," *Sociology of Sport Journal* 11, no. 4 (1994): 428–46.

[46] See, for example, Marc Rasbury, "Floyd Mayweather Needs a Boxing Lesson," *New York Beacon*, April 30, 2015, 24.

[47] John Powers, "Air Jordan Sails, but Bulls Crash," *Boston Globe*, June 10, 1986, A16.

[48] Thomas Boswell, "Jordan Not on Par with Best of All Time," *Chicago Sun-Times*, June 2, 1989, 94. Originally published as Thomas Boswell, "Statistics Leave Jordan's Greatness Up in the Air," *Washington Post*, May 26, 1989, D1.

[49] Terry Boers, "Stats Inaccurate Gauge of Airness' Greatness," *Chicago Sun-Times*, June 2, 1989, 94.

[50] See, for example, Jan Hubbard, "Jordan Proves He's World's Best Player," *Sporting News*, June 24, 1991, 44.

some juggernaut center, the kind coveted by the Houston and Portland teams that passed on him in the 1984 draft. He was a changemaker. Jordan won the next two NBA championships (and another MVP award) and was the best player on the inaugural "Dream Team" that swept through international competition at the 1992 Olympics in Barcelona, a global event that proved the value of Jordan's "brand" throughout the world.[51] Then again, no one doubted Jordan's immense fame. He ranked just behind Pope John Paul II as the "world's most admired man."[52] When he appeared on her television show, Oprah Winfrey correctly introduced Jordan as the "most famous man on the planet."[53]

Jordan's fame merely approximated his greatness. On its own, as Winfrey no doubt knew, fame had long since been devalued as a form of cultural currency. The prediction made in 1968 for an Andy Warhol exhibit, that "in the future, everyone will be world-famous for fifteen minutes," had come to fruition – to an extent. A presently outdated technology, television, decades ago, was he "most potent medium."[54] American households watched an average of fifty hours of television per week, observing people and places previously unknown to them. Through TV, individuals with an otherwise limited reach circumscribed to local climes could become known to thousands and millions of viewers.[55] The NBA evolved with Michael Jordan. In the early 1980s, the NBA playoffs were often unceremoniously broadcast by CBS on tape delay. Larry Bird and Magic Johnson skyrocketed national interest in the sport. Their contests were shown live as must-see TV. In turn, Michael Jordan sent the NBA's popularity over the moon, typically showcasing a triple-header on the Sunday *NBA on NBC* program.[56]

It was Jordan's elevation measured by standards of greatness that defied the crushing force of the list-makers. Foremost, he was a

[51] See Jack McCallum, *Dream Team: How Michael, Magic, Larry, Charles, and the Greatest Team of All Time Conquered the World and Changed the Game of Basketball Forever* (New York: Ballantine Books, 2012), 184–91, 266–71; and Larry Bird, Earvin Magic Johnson and Jackie MacMullan, *When the Game Was Ours* (Boston: Mariner Books, 2010), 256–59.
[52] See James Naughton, "Despair Jordan," *Washington Post*, October 10, 1993, C1.
[53] See Vicki Abt and Leonard Mustazza, *Coming after Oprah: Cultural Fallout in the Age of the Talk Show* (Bowling Green, OH: Bowling Green State University Popular Press, 1997), 80.
[54] Joshua Meyrowitz, *No Sense of Place: The Impact of Electronic Media on Social Behavior* (New York: Oxford University Press, 1985), 127.
[55] Ibid., 131–32.
[56] See Pete Croatto, *From Hang Time to Prime Time* (New York: Atria Books, 2020), 303–12.

changemaker who broke the blueprint followed almost unconditionally by NBA teams. That, however, would not have been sufficient. Jordan seemed to intuit the benchmarks and avoid the stumbling blocks of American greatness. Off the hardwood floors, the handsome and well-spoken Jordan curated an impeccable image. In August 1991, Gatorade launched a "Be Like Mike" advertising campaign built on the proposition that children of all types dreamed to "move" and "groove" like Jordan. His friend and rival Charles Barkley warned that neither he nor Jordan were worthy role models. Regular people, cautioned Barkley, couldn't aspire to "fly like Mike."[57] Jordan, however, indulged in his relatability, as did his business partners. He was, to draw from an earlier historical example, no unreachable Babe Ruthian figure of the 1920s. Jordan's corporate sponsors such as Nike and Hanes took great pains – like concealing that Michael and Juanita Vanoy had their first child out of wedlock – to project Jordan in commercials as a family man and role model.[58] America was invested in Jordan and worked hard to ensure, unlike the case with Edgar Allen Poe much earlier, that Jordan's reputation and fame enhanced his greatness rather than detracted from it.

But was Michael Jordan really all that relatable? Charles Barkley had a point and Jordan enthusiasts needed to reckon with that. Most Americans could not move or groove like him when they dribbled and shot baskets in their backyards. He was more like Ruth and less like Cobb. The solution was to downplay Jordan's acrobatics in favor of a more applicable skill. "One aspect of his greatness," opined a writer about Jordan, "is that he thinks faster than his opponents." He wasn't just a talented "showman," an unfair stereotype of the black athlete. The measure of Jordan's greatness had been limited by earlier critics who had judged that the Bulls' shooting guard was "somehow less an all-around player than the workmanlike, meticulous Bird."[59] Of course, Larry Bird was white and therefore looked (although much taller) than many Americans (Figure C.1). His working-class Midwestern background seemed to match accolades heaped on the cerebral Southerner, Ty Cobb. Jordan

---

[57] See David Gelman, Karen Springen, and Sunadsan Raghavan, "I'm Not a Role Model," *Newsweek*, June 28, 1993, 56–57.
[58] See Mary G. McDonald, "Michael Jordan's Family Values: Marketing, Meaning, and Post-Reagan America," in *From Jack Johnson to LeBron James: Sports, Media, and the Color Line*, ed. Chris Lamb (Lincoln, NE: University of Nebraska Press, 2016), 468–500.
[59] David Breskin, "Michael Jordan, in His Own Orbit," *Gentleman's Quarterly* 59 (March 1989): 322.

Conclusion: Michael Jordan in the "Age of Lists" 209

FIGURE C.1 Michael Jordan "flying" past Larry Bird in a playoff game in 1987. Back then, though, more pundits preferred Bird's "greatness" over Jordan's. Courtesy of Bettmann/Getty Images.

leveraged this newfound reputation as a scholar athlete and demurred attempts by people such as the novelist John Edgar Wideman to describe his style as a return to "African-American roots on the playground."[60]

[60] John Edgar Wideman, "Michael Jordan Leaps the Great Divide," *Esquire* 114 (November 1990): 145. Wideman understood that Jordan, who grew up "middle-class" and maintained an "apolitical" stance, "broke down nearly all racial

A lot of money depended on Jordan's responses to magazine interviews. The basketball hero was astute about this and exercised caution, not wanting to narrow his scope of influence. He wasn't the first. In the 1980s, the NBA had capitalized on the Larry Bird–Magic Johnson dyad that purported racial harmony and a commercial reach that pacified Ronald Reagan's New Right that had previously dismissed professional basketball as "drug infested" and "too black." Bird and Johnson "played basketball the right way." Johnson, as a black man, emerged as a promotional darling, amenable to all.[61]

Jordan established a professional persona that elevated that image even further than his basketball predecessors. In 1989, NBA Entertainment produced a documentary, *Come Fly With Me*, that told Jordan's story and raised him to an all-knowing-answer-man, a fount of American culture and values.[62] His agent David Falk described the Jordan brand this way: "Spectacular talent, midsized, well-spoken, attractive, accessible, old-time values, wholesome, clean, natural, not too Goody Two-shoes, with a bit of devilry in him."[63] It therefore did not strike many as odd when, asked about Jordan's racial identity, Chicago Bulls owner Jerry Reinsdorf said that "Michael has no color."[64] Of course, Michael Jordan was a black man. His boss, Reinsdorf, however, meant that Jordan's impact could not be plotted along racial lines. On the other hand, reports that Jordan liked to gamble in Atlantic City surprised and, not in a positive way, "humanized" him for many observers.[65] Ever careful to maintain his image, Jordan and his team refused to indulge questions about it. His categorical response to reporters on a casino trip during a playoff series against the New York Knicks was "no comment."[66]

boundaries." On Jordan's middle-class upbringing, see David Scott, "Moving On," *Charlotte Observer*, May 6, 1984, 40.
[61] See Cheryl L. Cole and David L. Andrews, "'Look—It's NBA Showtime!' Visions of Race in the Popular Imaginary," *Cultural Studies* 1 (1996): 141–81.
[62] See Douglas Kellner, "The Sports Spectacle, Michael Jordan, and Nike: Unholy Alliance?" in *Michael Jordan, Inc.: Corporate Sport, Media Culture, and Late Modern America*, ed. David L. Andrews (Albany, NY: State University of New York Press, 2001), 45.
[63] See Curry Kirpatrick, "In an Orbit All His Own," *Sports Illustrated*, November 9, 1987, 93.
[64] See David L. Andrews, "The Fact(s) of Michael Jordan's Blackness: Excavating a Floating Racial Signifier," *Sociology of Sport Journal* 13, no. 2 (1996): 125–58.
[65] See Bob Verdi, "Jordan Rules Reveals No Surprises; High Highness Is Human after All," *Sporting News*, December 2, 1991, 6; and Dave Anderson, "Jordan's Atlantic City Caper," *New York Times*, May 27, 1993, B11.
[66] Melissa Isaacson, "Jordan Leaves Gambling Story Up in Air," *Chicago Tribune*, October 17, 1992, 1.

Conclusion: Michael Jordan in the "Age of Lists" 211

The Jordan image was also unconditionally apolitical. In 1990, the North Carolina native refused to endorse African American candidate Harvey Gantt. Gantt challenged the incumbent "white racist" Jesse Helms for a Senate seat in the Tar Heel State. Helms won a very narrow election; Jordan's support would have likely flipped the decision. To a friend, Jordan explained his reluctance on economic grounds: "Republicans buy shoes, too."[67] Jordan's stance reminded some of decades ago when Muhammad Ali and other "athletes were more courageous."[68] His biggest skeptics charged that "Ali didn't want to 'carry a sign'; Jordan only wants to carry the signs he gets paid for carrying."[69] However, Jordan recognized that for sustainable greatness, political points of view were a liability. Just ask Charlie Chaplin or Charles Lindbergh.

* * *

Most dramatically, Jordan was the great American figure that people recalled and hoped would return and restore cultural order. In 1993, Jordan retired from the NBA, having, in his words, "nothing more to prove in basketball."[70] It was a Jim Brown-like decision. Some figured that Jordan would recede into the background of basketball conversations, just another name to recall in the Age of Lists. "They said football would never be the same when Jim Brown retired in his prime," said Kevin McHale, formerly of the Boston Celtics. "It goes on. I mean, I can guarantee you people, in five years, people will be saying, 'Michael who?' The names on the backs of the jerseys change; the league just keeps rolling on."[71] Yet, Jordan defied the opaqueness of the era. He remained in most people's minds the greatest of all time.

Jordan didn't fade. To the contrary, the news provided a renewed opportunity to solidify Jordan's stature and make meaning of his American greatness. The sport scribes announced the departure of the

---

[67] See Sam Smith, *Second Coming: The Strange Odyssey of Michael Jordan – from Courtside to Home Plate and Back Again* (New York: HarperCollins, 1995), xix. Subsequent retellings of this exchange replaced "shoes" with "sneakers."
[68] Kevin Merida, "Just Do It!" *Washington Post*, June 16, 1996, C4.
[69] See Marqusee, *Redemption Song*, 296.
[70] Ira Berkow, "Suddenly, Michael Doesn't Play Here Anymore," *New York Times*, October 7, 1993, B17. Part of Jordan's decision making to retire (the first time) was to preserve his professional legacy and persona. He feared public display of a decline in his skills. He told a reporter, "There would be a long line of articles saying so-and-so killed Jordan tonight. I'll step away before I subject myself to that." See Mark Vancil, "Enjoy Him While You Can," *Sporting News*, June 14, 1993, 37.
[71] Peter May, "Changing of the Guard in Order," *Boston Globe*, October 7, 1993, 55.

"greatest ever" and more long-windedly the "greatest basketball player yet to grace this particular planet."[72] It was a Babe Ruth moment, paralleling the demise of the slugger just as the United States headed into the Cold War. *Newsweek* produced a special issue titled "The Greatest Ever," and its editor memorialized the career of a changemaker whose impact went far beyond the basketball court: "Suspended in air, he reshaped his sweat and sinew into a work of art, a metaphor for the limitlessness of human potential. That he might finish with a thunderous dunk was lagniappe."[73] NBA Commissioner David Stern made Jordan's resignation and towering station official: "You don't replace somebody like Michael Jordan or Babe Ruth."[74]

The nostalgia for Jordan was even more acute than the longing for Ruth in the 1950s. Just a few, such as that erstwhile Jordan-doubter, Thomas Boswell, thought that the rising generation of NBA stars could ably replace him. Boswell counted on Shaquille O'Neill, Latrell Sprewell, and Mitch Richmond to provide star power to the league.[75] Others recognized that it was no simple matter to replace a "Basketball Deity."[76] Those concerned worried that the NBA's "image was dribbling away." Like in the pre-Jordan era, there was wide suspicion of drug use among players. The ratings of the 1994 NBA Finals between the Houston Rockets and the New York Knicks were paltry, some 30 percent below the marks achieved by the championship series played a year before by Michael Jordan's Chicago Bulls and Charles Barkley's Pheonix Suns.[77] The league was desperate. It instituted rule changes to drive up offensive statistics to help players artificially reach Jordan's scoring plateau.[78]

---

[72] See Erik Brady, "Michael Jordan: Greatest Ever?" *USA Today*, May 17, 1993, 1A; and Bob Ryan, "10 Years of Jordan Courting Greatness," *Sport* (December 1993): 26. See also Greg Boeck, "Fans Insist Jordan is NBA's Best," *USA Today*, May 24, 1993, 3C. See Dan Shaughnessy, "Best of Best? Some Votes for Jordan," *Boston Globe*, June 18, 1993, 29. Some incorrigible "homers" in Boston still rooted for their very greatest. See "A Sample of What You Had to Say," *Boston Globe*, June 20, 1993, 58. See also Bob Ryan, "Great Revelation: Russell Is the Legend of Them All," *Boston Globe*, April 22, 1995, 81.

[73] John Leland, "Farewell Michael and Thanks for the Memories," *Newsweek: Collector's Issue* (October/November 1993): 9.

[74] Greg Boeck, *USA Today*, October 7, 1993, 8C.

[75] Thomas Boswell, "Just Fine, Thank You," *Washington Post*, January 19, 1994, B8.

[76] Bryan Burwell, "Time is Right for an Air Apparent to Emerge," *USA Today*, November 4, 1994, 2C.

[77] John Dempsey, "NBA's Image Dribbles Away," *Variety*, June 27, 1994, 27.

[78] Erik Brady, "Michael Jordan: New Heights in Sight?" *USA Today*, March 15, 1995, 1A.

Conclusion: Michael Jordan in the "Age of Lists"

A handful placed their hope in the young Grant Hill of the Detroit Pistons. Hill was the son of a famous former NFL running back and, like Jordan, a collegiate champion – at North Carolina's rival, Duke – with a highlight reel of sensational plays. He was very well-spoken. Rumor had it that he was very respectful toward his mother. As a rookie, the handsome Hill played the piano on David Letterman's late-night talk show. In that inaugural season, the hardworking forward led the NBA All-Star Game fan ballot, more "by virtue of his own virtue" than because he was the NBA's very best player.[79]

Grant Hill could save the NBA (Figure C.2). He emerged as the marketing solution to the void created by Michael Jordan's exit: "The whole world is praying Grant Hill is the prototype of the next generation of sports star: intelligent, appealing, immensely talented. Why

FIGURE C.2 The media had hoped Detroit's Grant Hill would emerge as the NBA's next great pitchman after Michael Jordan's 1993 retirement. But in short order, Jordan returned to basketball and (literally) wrestled the mantle away from Hill. Courtesy of Matt Campbell/AFP/Getty Images.

[79] Tom Junod, "The Savior," *Genteman's Quarterly* 65 (April 1995): 172.

he even plays the piano."[80] The face of a franchise that once billed itself the "Bad Boys," Hill allayed all concerns, describing he and his Piston teammates as "nice boys."[81] Promoters viewed Hill, like Jordan before him, as a "good Negro," the "anti-Shaq," a reference to the then-Orlando Magic big man who "cuts rap records" and "isn't as appealing to Madison Avenue."[82] That Hill was not as talented as Jordan was beside the point.

Then the NBA was no longer in need of a savior. Grant Hill and any other potential heir apparent was summarily dismissed as duplicative to the real McCoy. Michael Jordan's agent faxed a two-word official statement on behalf of his client: "I'm back." With intentional religious symbolism, Jordan's return to the Chicago Bulls was hailed as a "Second Coming."[83] Basketball magazines wrote that Jordan's comeback was "more like Jesus or Dr. King returning to save our souls."[84]

Jordan's Bulls won three straight NBA championships. Now the incredulous Thomas Boswell was convinced that Jordan was the greatest of all time.[85] Privately, the prideful Wilt Chamberlain told Jordan that he, not the Bulls guard, had the better career of the pair. Publicly, however, Chamberlain gracefully allowed that "this is Michael's time."[86] At Jordan's second retirement press conference (he made a brief, less heroic second comeback), NBA Commissioner David Stern reiterated what he had said the prior time, but with perhaps fuller conviction: "It's a great day because the greatest basketball player in the history of the game is getting an opportunity to retire with the grace that described his play."[87]

---

[80] Ibid., 171.
[81] Sam Smith, "Heir Jordan? No, but Pistons' Hill May Come Close," *Chicago Tribune*, October 27, 1994, 3. See also David DuPree, "This Piston's Firing," *USA Today*, December 6, 1994, 1C.
[82] John Feinstein, "Grant the Good," *Inside Sports* 18 (May 1995): 59.
[83] David DuPree, "The Verdict on Jordan: 'Simply the Best,'" *USA Today*, April 22, 1996, 10E.
[84] Scoop Jackson, "The New Testament," *Slam* 2 (July 1995): 43.
[85] See Thomas Boswell, "The Greatest of Our Time," *Washington Post*, November 10, 1999, D1; and Thomas Boswell, "For Our Heroes, Time Keeps on Passing," *Washington Post*, March 15, 2000, D1.
[86] Greg Boeck, "Best of the Best," *USA Today*, February 10, 1997, 4C. For an account of Chamberlain's and Jordan's debate about each other see, "Q&A: Bill Walton," *Sporting News*, April 22, 2005, 78. Other older stars also maintained their high status. See Roscoe Nance, "NBA Names 50 Best Players in Its History," *USA Today*, October 30, 1996, 1C; See Geoff Hobson, "Big O Rates Jordan among Game's Best," *Cincinnati Enquirer*, October 7, 1993, 42; and Oscar Robertson, *The Big O: My Life, My Times, My Game* (Lincoln, NE: University of Nebraska Press, 2010), 204.
[87] Malcolm Moran, "The Greatest of All-Time," *Chicago Tribune*, January 14, 1999, 14.

Conclusion: Michael Jordan in the "Age of Lists"

Polls placed Jordan alongside Muhammad Ali as the greatest athlete of the century. Babe Ruth, Wilt Chamberlain, and Jim Brown were rated below them on lists not meant for much debate.[88]

***

Michael Jordan was the last greatest of all time measured by the variables outlined in this book. After him, the value of American greatness plummeted. Even during Jordan's reign, the philosopher and social critic Allan Bloom wrote that America by and large "denies greatness and wants everyone to feel comfortable in his skin without having to suffer unpleasant comparisons."[89] Television had created an incalculable roster of famous people. The notion of "celebrity," it seemed to Bloom, was all but worthless. One step above that designation, greatness had been spread far too thin and lost its luster, as well.

The Digital Age of the twenty-first century solidified this sentiment and "created a culture of self-celebrification."[90] With the rise of on-demand YouTube video clips and social media, "new stars were popping up and grabbing the spotlight."[91] This era has witnessed the emergence of Kim Kardashian and other social media stars who are "famous for being famous."[92] They represent the worst fears of Leo Löwenthal's warnings about the rise of the "idols of consumption" – celebrities whose fame is attributed for their wide influence rather than meaningful achievement. These women and men have used new technologies and media for personal gain and in fulfillment of an American Dream that afforded them that self-indulgent opportunity.

As a cultural commodity, greatness surfaced as fame started to lose value at the start of the twentieth century. A hundred years later, greatness had by and large replaced famousness, as the latter, from a social perspective, was all but bankrupt. Hence, the recent run on "greatness." Much had changed since Henry MacCracken furnished a Hall

---

[88] See Dave Kindred, "The Last Fight in Them," *Sporting News*, January 25, 1999, 71; Mart Reihart, "No Comparison," *Sporting News*, February 8, 1999, 7; and John Rawlings, "So Long, Michael," *Sporting News*, January 25, 1999, 223.

[89] Allan Bloom, *The Closing of the American Mind: How Higher Education Has Failed Democracy and Impoverished the Souls of Today's Students* (New York: Simon & Schuster, 1987), 66.

[90] Douglas and McDonell, *Celebrity*, 240.

[91] Ibid., 230.

[92] See "Kim Kardashian: Social Capital: Twitter: @FTLex," *Financial Times*, September 9, 2022, 26.

of Fame in the Bronx to protect greatness's high value. But just as in past iterations, greatness still suggested something illuminating about the American rank and file:

What changes the dynamic, of course, is that stars aren't the only ones tweeting, or blogging, or chatting, or otherwise engaging in the public cybersphere that for many now constitutes the waking world. We all are, and in the doing of it we are taking part in a profound conceptual cultural shift—the large-scale broadcasting and fictionalization of the self. If the counterculture years saw the rise of mass bohemianism (everyone wanting to be different from the grown-ups) and the Gen-X years the codification of alt (everyone wanting to be different from everyone else), the Internet era has provided the tools to finally realize the urge to be different—and, most important, to be seen and recognized while being different.[93]

Greatness was no longer a scarce resource. It appeared to happen in a flash. In September 2000, the performer L.L. Cool J released a song (and album) titled "G.O.A.T." Inspired by the acronym coined by Muhammad Ali, the popular rapper announced that he was the "greatest rapper of all time." The song was well-received, even though it didn't "make anyone believe L.L.'s the greatest rapper ever."[94] Many others became overeager to lay claim for themselves or others to the mantle of the greatest of all time – in something. Popular and more studious-minded literature is chock-full of unscientific declarations of greatness for outstanding architects, and video game characters (most often, Super Mario and Pacman), and even sociology teachers.[95] Lately, Sterling Children's Books produced a series on "Making the Case for the Greatest of All Time," featuring the likes of basketball star LeBron James, football legend Tom Brady, tennis champion Serena Williams, and Olympic gold medalist Simone Biles. Suddenly, an increasing number of people could call themselves the "greatest" without much pushback from critics who wished to limit the word's use to aspire and inspire change.

In isolation, each of these greatness debates offers some insight into what Americans wish to see in their great people: namely, options.

---

[93] Ty Burr, *Gods Like Us: On Movie Stardom and Modern Fame* (New York: Pantheon Books, 2012), 330.
[94] Ronin Ro, "L.L. Cool J," *Vibe*, September 1, 2000, 240.
[95] See Paul Volponi, *The Great G.O.A.T. Debate: The Best of the Best in Everything from Sports to Science* (London: Rowman & Littlefield, 2022); and Joy Pierce, "Fishing with the GOAT: Honoring Norman K. Denzin," in *Festschrift in Honor of Norman K. Denzin: He Knew His Song Well*, ed. Shing-Ling S. Chen (Bingley, UK: Emerald Publishing Group, 2022), 157–63.

Conclusion: Michael Jordan in the "Age of Lists" 217

The group that now prefers LeBron James over Michael Jordan may be in search of a black basketball superstar who takes political risks during the renewed and unsettling rise of racial tensions in the United States.[96] Tom Brady's climb to the top of professional football rankings says much about his Super Bowl heroics but perhaps even more about our desire to look past cheating and sportsmanship for the sake of preserving a great, handsome, well-spoken NFL champion.[97] The same is the case after Brady's longtime coach, Bill Belichick left the New England Patriots. In early 2024, the reports tended to valorize Belichick's Boston coaching tenure. Why did journalists pass on tearing into Belichick, a much less likable figure than his great quarterback? I suspect that if they had, it would have called into question Tom Brady's legacy. There are values pertaining to gender stereotypes and mental health in the greatness discussions that center on Serena Williams and Simone Biles.[98] From a perfunctory Internet search, one can pluck designations of greatness in a host of fields and without much trouble discern something very keen about the writer or speaker who had uttered that superlative declaration. What the statements suggest about the subjects under discussion is, and always has been, far less clear.

Collectively these inflated and unchecked conversations about greatness betoken a desire for Americans to detect, by any means possible, greatness within themselves. "We live in a time and place characterized by status affluence," surmised Joel Best about the present abundance of self-congratulatory culture.[99] He registered a change from a more traditional thinking about greatness and other status-laden terms such as honor. These used to be "scarce commodities, for which there is still competition that results in a few winners and lots of losers."[100] The inflation of awards and superlatives, as well as the promotion of rankings of all types, suggests that contemporary Americans judge everyone and everything by a rigged scale of "good," "great," and "greatest." But

---

[96] See Joshua Wright, "Be Like Mike? The Black Athlete's Dilemma," *Spectrum* 4 (Spring 2016): 1–19.
[97] See Chuck Klosterman, "Tom Brady Is," *Gentlemen's Quarterly*, December 1, 2015, 249–50.
[98] See Andy Bull, "The Greatest: Serena Williams—An Icon Who Broke Barriers and Shattered Records," *Guardian*, July 1, 2020, 38; and "Ms. Biles Sticks the Landing," *Washington Post*, August 29, 2023, A16.
[99] Best, *Everyone's a Winner*, 142.
[100] Ibid.

the simple truth is that greatness was a commodity in flux from the start. Its terminological malleability was at times an asset and in less auspicious historical circumstances a liability – or worse, a rather meaningless word. The Age of Lists proved that a single greatest figure was less useful than an inventory of options. It foretold of a later period, our time when change is rapid, and everyone is great.

Index

Abdul-Jabbar, Kareem, 198, 199
Addams, Jane, 2, 151, 152, 153
Age of Lists, 201, 218
Aked, Charles, 55, 56, 57, 118, 128, 163, 198
Ali, Muhammad, 4, 5, 120, 161, 166, 168, 169, 175, 176, 177, 178, 179, 180, 184, 192, 193, 194, 195, 196, 199, 205, 206, 211, 215, 216
American dream, 82, 84, 86, 130, 215
antisemitism, 2, 74, 109
Aryanism, 35, 108

Barkley, Charles, 208
baseball, 97, 122, 123, 124, 125, 126, 127, 128, 129, 130, 131, 132, 133, 134, 135, 136, 137, 138, 139, 140, 157, 158, 159, 169, 170, 178, 180
basketball, 5, 180, 182, 183, 184, 185, 193, 197, 199, 205, 206, 210, 211, 212, 214, 216, 217
Beach Boys, 161, 186, 187, 189
Beatles, the, 2, 4, 161, 163, 164, 170, 171, 172, 173, 174, 175, 177, 185, 186, 187, 188, 189, 190, 191, 192, 193, 199, 206
Bent, Silas, 97, 132
Berger, Peter, 202
Best, Joel, 201, 217
Biles, Simone, 217
Bird, Larry, 206
Black Muslims, 163, 169, 176
Boone, Daniel, 96

Boorstin, Daniel, 144
Borglum, Gutzon, 143
Boswell, Thomas, 212
boxing, 86, 161, 163, 165, 169, 170, 176, 177, 179, 180, 190, 193, 206
Brady, Tom, 216, 217
Brokaw, Tom, 124, 141, 147
Brown, Jim, 165, 180, 182, 184, 193, 194, 200, 211, 215
Bryan, William Jennings, 36, 46, 49, 143
Butler, Nicholas Murray, 33
Byrnes, James, 108

Cannon, Jimmy, 4, 161, 163, 165, 166, 167, 168, 169, 170, 176, 177, 178, 179, 194
Carnegie, Andrew, 18, 32
cartoons, 202
Carver, Raymond, 2
Chamberlain, Wilt, 182, 184, 199, 200, 214, 215
Chaplin, Charlie, 4, 81, 82, 83, 84, 85, 86, 87, 88, 89, 90, 92, 100, 102, 103, 104, 105, 106, 111, 113, 114, 115, 116, 117, 118, 119, 120, 121, 125, 211
   Communism and, 113, 117
   Hollywood Walk of Fame and, 117
Chaplin, Charlie Jr., 118
Chesterton, G. K., 47, 48, 49, 71
Civil Rights Movement, 158, 168, 184, 193, 201
Clay, Cassius, 161, 163, 164, 165, 166, 169, 170, 179, 190

Index

Cobb, Ty, 122, 123, 124, 125, 126, 127, 128, 129, 130, 132, 133, 134, 135, 136, 137, 138, 140, 141, 156, 158, 159, 208
Comiskey, Charles, 125, 126, 127
Communism, 113, 117
Coolidge, Calvin, 60, 94, 95, 96, 148
counterculture, 161, 164, 170, 174, 175, 191, 192, 195, 216
Crockett, Davy, 96

Daniel, Dan, 133, 137, 138, 140
Danilov, Victor, 202
Dean, James, 124
DiMaggio, Joe, 8, 140, 158
Disney, Walt, 81, 82, 87, 88, 98, 99, 100, 101, 102, 103, 110, 111, 112, 113, 202
Donald Duck, 110, 111, 112, 113, 125
Durant, Will, 203
Dylan, Bob, 187, 188, 193

Edison, Thomas, 2, 47, 48, 51, 52, 53, 54, 55, 56, 57, 58, 59, 60, 61, 68, 71, 82, 122, 149, 164
Einstein, Albert, 5, 47, 48, 49, 71, 72, 73, 74, 75, 76, 77, 78, 79, 80, 204
Eisler, Hanns, 114
Eliot, Charles, 203
Emerson, Ralph Waldo, 10, 24, 26, 31, 37, 77, 106
Erskine, John, 95
Erving, Julius, 198
Etzioni, Amitai, 201
eugenics, 3, 28, 29, 31, 33, 35, 108

feminism, 5, 154
Fireside Poets, 26, 27, 30, 35, 36, 39, 42, 43, 44
Flynn, John, 146
football, 9, 100, 180, 182, 199, 200, 211, 216, 217
Ford, Gerald, 196
Ford, Henry, 2, 7, 10, 14, 35, 41, 47, 48, 51, 55, 56, 59, 60, 61, 62, 63, 64, 65, 66, 67, 68, 69, 70, 71, 76, 82, 83, 118, 127, 130, 141, 142, 152, 158, 215
Foreman, George, 194, 195
Fosdick, Henry Emerson, 77, 78, 79, 80
Frankfurt School, 6, 8
Frazier, Joe, 193, 194

Freehof, Solomon, 79
Freud, Sigmund, 73, 75, 86, 103

Galton, Francis, 3, 28, 29, 30, 31, 32, 33, 35, 38, 108
Gantt, Harvey, 211
Gibbons, James, 57
Gould, Helen, 13, 14, 15, 16, 17, 19, 20, 24, 28
Gould, Jay, 13, 14, 15, 17, 18, 19, 21, 24, 28, 60, 105
Great Depression, 103, 104, 105, 106, 110, 124, 141, 145
Great Man Theory, 31
Greatest Generation, 124, 141, 145
greatness
  1950's mythology of, 2, 124, 125, 141, 147, 157, 164, 166, 180, 182, 195
  American conceptions of, 4, 19, 106
  cartoons and, 98, 100, 101, 105
  celebrity culture and, 6
  change and, 19
  changemakers and, 2, 18, 25, 28, 36, 46, 61, 68, 81, 126, 142, 146, 147, 151, 152, 184, 191, 195, 199, 204, 207, 208, 212
  Christian faith and, 13, 61, 71, 72, 73, 74, 77, 78, 79, 97, 116, 183, 205
  European conceptions of, 3, 20
  feminists and, 3, 149, 150, 151, 153, 154
  history of discourse on, 1, 217
  lists and, 8, 12, 23, 26, 48, 57, 60, 67, 130, 148, 150, 176, 181, 193, 197, 200, 201, 202, 203, 204, 211, 215, 217, 218
  measurement of, 18
  social needs and, 106
  sports and, 5, 14, 16, 60, 69, 91, 93, 96, 105, 122, 123, 126, 127, 128, 129, 130, 132, 133, 136, 137, 138, 140, 158, 161, 163, 164, 165, 166, 169, 170, 172, 175, 176, 178, 180, 181, 182, 183, 194, 195, 196, 199, 206, 207, 211, 213, 217
  subjective, 83
Griswold, Rufus, 40, 41, 42, 43

Hadley, Arthur, 44
Hall of Fame of Great Americans, 10, 11, 12, 13, 16, 18, 20, 22, 27, 34, 35, 44, 46, 60

Index

Hapgood, Norman, 203
Harrison, George, 161, 186, 191
Hart, Michael, 203, 204
Henderson, Ricky, 128
Hereditary Genius, 29, 30
Herrick, Myron, 94
Hill, James J., 32
Hollywood Walk of Fame, 117, 120, 121
Hoover, J. Edgar, 115
House Un-American Activities Committee, 114, 115, 116, 118

Ickes, Harold, 107
Inman, Stu, 197, 198
Intellectual Egalitarianism, 33

Jagger, Mick, 175, 187, 192
James, LeBron, 216
James, William, 31, 33, 34, 35, 54
Jefferson, Thomas, 9, 106, 143, 146
Jesus, 205
Jordan, Michael, 2, 5, 197, 200, 205, 206, 207, 208, 210, 212, 213, 214, 215, 217
  apolitical image of, 211
  awards won by, 198
  considered greates player in basketball, 206
  fame of, 207
  greatness of, 215
  at the Olympic trials, 197

Karno, Fred, 83, 84, 85, 86
King, Martin Luther Jr., 169, 178, 184
Knight, Bob, 197

L.L. Cool J, 216
Lee, Robert E., 12, 23, 24, 25, 36, 45, 51, 106
Lenard, Phillipp, 73
Lennon, John, 161, 170, 171, 172, 173, 174, 186, 187, 189, 190, 192
Lincoln, Abraham, 2, 23, 119, 120, 143, 144, 145, 146, 148, 149, 205, 206
Lindbergh, Anne Morrow, 107
Lindbergh, Charles, 4, 82, 83, 90, 91, 92, 93, 94, 95, 96, 97, 98, 99, 100, 102, 106, 107, 108, 109, 110, 132, 211
Liston, Sonny, 161, 163, 164, 165, 167, 169, 170, 175, 190
Lodge, Henry Cabot, 143

Longfellow, Henry Wadsworth, 10, 24, 26, 27, 30, 36, 37, 41, 42
Löwenthal, Leo, 6, 7, 8, 81, 82, 123, 182, 215

MacCracken, Henry Mitchell, 10, 11, 12, 13, 14, 15, 16, 18, 20, 21, 22, 23, 24, 27, 30, 34, 35, 36, 37, 44, 45, 46, 215
Mack, Connie, 127, 137, 138
Malamud, Bernard, 123
Malcolm X, 168, 169, 170
Malone, Moses, 198
Maris, Roger, 157
Marshall, Edward, 53, 54
Mayweather, Floyd, 206
McCartney, Paul, 161, 172, 173, 186, 187, 188, 189, 190
McCormick, Robert Rutherford, 57, 62, 63, 64, 67
McHale, Kevin, 211
Meany, Tom, 138
Mickey Mouse, 2, 4, 81, 82, 83, 98, 99, 100, 101, 102, 103, 104, 105, 106, 110, 111, 112, 113, 125
Montana, Joe, 200
motion pictures, 85, 90, 92, 99, 101, 103, 117, 118, 119, 120

Nation of Islam, 163, 168, 169, 175, 176
Nazi Germany, 6, 29, 107, 108, 109, 113, 168, 176
Nixon, Richard, 1, 166, 185, 195, 201, 202

O'Connell, William Henry, 72, 73, 74, 75, 76, 77
Orteig, Raymond, 91, 92, 93, 95

Pasteur, Louis, 52, 78
Patten, William, 203
Patterson, Joseph Medill, 62
Pelé, 1
Philipson, David, 68, 79
Plane Crazy, 98, 99
Poe, Edgar Allan, 6, 12, 35, 36, 37, 38, 39, 40, 41, 42, 43, 44, 45, 46, 51, 67, 103, 106, 118, 208
Poets and Poetry of America, 40
Pope, Alexander, 68
Presley, Elvis, 124, 164, 173
Progressive Era, 82, 86, 93
propaganda, 69, 76, 112, 146, 168

racism, 73, 109, 138, 165, 168
Reagan, Ronald, 9, 210
Reuterdahl, Arvid, 75, 76
Rice, Grantland, 127, 129, 132, 135, 140
Richmond, Mitch, 212
Rickenbacker, Eddie, 91
Robertson, Oscar, 182, 183, 198, 199
Robinson, Jackie, 165, 169, 170, 178
Rockefeller, John D., 18, 32, 77
Rojek, Chris, 8, 82
Rolling Stones, 175, 187, 192
Roosevelt, Eleanor, 2, 5, 101, 125, 142, 148, 149, 150, 151, 153, 154, 155, 156, 164, 206
Roosevelt, Franklin, 2, 8, 9, 23, 26, 31, 52, 69, 107, 119, 125, 142, 143, 145, 146
Roosevelt, Theodore, 53, 60, 96, 119, 143, 151
Rose, Pete, 128
Russell, Bill, 182, 184, 193, 199
Ruth, Babe, 4, 8, 60, 97, 122, 123, 124, 125, 127, 130, 132, 133, 134, 135, 136, 138, 139, 140, 141, 157, 158, 159, 164, 180, 185, 208, 212, 215

Schlesinger, Arthur, 145, 146, 147, 148, 203
Schultz, Charles, 202
Shaw, George Bernard, 29, 52
Sheen, Fulton, 48
Sherwood, Robert, 108
Simpson, O. J., 180, 181, 182, 199, 200
Simpson, Ralph, 198
Social Darwinism, 32, 34
Spencer, Herbert, 31, 32
Steamboat Willie, 99
Stedman, Clarence, 44
Steinmetz, Charles, 52
Sugarman, Harry, 117
Sumner, WIlliam Graham, 33, 34

Temperance Movement, 44
Thorndike, Edward, 33
transatlantic flight, 82, 92, 95, 107

Vietnam War, 120, 164, 178, 192, 193

Wallechinsky, David, 201, 202, 203
Warhol, Andy, 161, 207
Warner Brothers, 113
Washburn, George, 44
Washington, George, 2, 18, 19, 23, 69, 106, 143, 144, 145
Weyland, Paul, 73
Whittier, John Greenleaf, 36, 43
Williams, Serena, 217
Wilson, Brian, 186, 188, 189, 190
Winfrey, Oprah, 207
Woods, Frederick Adams, 33
World War II, 4, 6, 106, 107, 110, 113, 115, 123, 141, 145, 149, 173